Laying Down the Rails
A Charlotte Mason Habits Handbook

by
Sonya Shafer

Cover Photo: John Shafer
Cover Design: Ruth Shafer

Published by
Simply Charlotte Mason, LLC
P. O. Box 892
Grayson, Georgia 30017-0892

ISBN: 978-1-61634-021-6

SimplyCharlotteMason.com

Contents

Laying Down the Rails 5
Introduction 7

Part 1: The Importance of Rails

Chapter 1: About Habits 11

Part 2: Laying Down the Rails

Chapter 2: How to Cultivate Good Habits 21
Chapter 3: Decency and Propriety Habits 27
    Cleanliness 28
    Courtesy 30
    Kindness 31
    Manners 34
    Modesty and Purity 35
    Neatness 38
    Order 39
    Regularity 41
    Other Habits of Decency and Propriety 42

Chapter 4: Mental Habits 49
    Attention 50
    Imagining 61
    Meditation 63
    Memorizing 65
    Mental Effort 67
    Observation 70
    Perfect Execution 74
    Reading for Instruction 77
    Remembering 81
    Thinking 84
    Other Mental Habits 86

Chapter 5: Moral Habits 91
    Integrity 92
    Obedience 96
    Personal Initiative 101
    Reverence 103
    Self-Control 105
    Sweet, Even Temper 108

    Truthfulness 110

    Usefulness 117

Chapter 6: Physical Habits 121

    Alertness to Seize Opportunities 122

    Fortitude 123

    Health 127

    Managing One's Own Body 129

    Music 133

    Outdoor Life 135

    Quick Perception of Senses 137

    Self-Control in Emergencies 139

    Self-Discipline in Habits 142

    Self-Restraint in Indulgences 144

    Training the Ear and Voice 145

Chapter 7: Religious Habits 147

    Regularity in Devotions 148

    Reverent Attitude 153

    Sunday-Keeping 155

    Thanksgiving 157

    Thought of God 159

Chapter 8: A Family Habit of Reading Aloud 163

Part 3: Repairing the Rails

Chapter 9: Breaking a Bad Habit 167

Chapter 10: Dealing with Lying 171

Chapter 11: Dealing with Dawdling 181

Chapter 12: Dealing with Malicious, Mean Behavior 193

Chapter 13: Dealing with Temper Tantrums 195

Chapter 14: Dealing with a Sullen, Moody Child 207

Appendix

Laying Down the Rails Checklist 223

Habits Index 237

Personal Help 239

Laying Down the Rails

"Just as it is on the whole easier for the locomotive to pursue its way on the rails than to take a disastrous run off them, so it is easier for the child to follow lines of habit carefully laid down than to run off these lines at his peril. It follows that this business of laying down lines towards the unexplored country of the child's future is a very serious and responsible one for the parent. It rests with him to consider well the tracks over which the child should travel with profit and pleasure; and, along these tracks, to lay down lines so invitingly smooth and easy that the little traveller is going upon them at full speed without stopping to consider whether or no he chooses to go that way" (Vol. 1, p. 109).

Introduction

In the years that I've been using a Charlotte Mason-style education with my children, I have frequently heard people refer to the importance Charlotte placed on habits, frequently read portions in her writings about habits, and just as frequently wished there were someplace I could find all of her comments on habits compiled. "A complete list of all the habits she mentioned would be nice," I would think, "and a collection of her thoughts and suggestions arranged with each habit would be even better!"

I never found one. So I created one. In this book I have tried to compile and organize all the habits Charlotte referred to in her writings, along with her thoughts and practical suggestions for each. I have also added some modern examples that illustrate the importance of those habits and a few practical tips of my own. Excerpts from Charlotte Mason's books are surrounded by quotation marks and accompanied by references as to which books in the series they came from.

Vol. 1: Home Education
Vol. 2: Parents and Children
Vol. 3: School Education
Vol. 4: Ourselves
Vol. 5: Formation of Character
Vol. 6: A Philosophy of Education

Comments or suggestions that have been added by the author of this book are not in quotation marks and have no reference.

I hope this collection may be of help to you as you seek to lay down the rails of habit "on which the life of the child may run henceforth with little jolting" (Vol. 1, p. 107).

Part 1

The Importance of Rails

Chapter 1
About Habits

Habits are an important part of a Charlotte Mason education and, more than that, of parenting in general. Charlotte did us all a great service when she emphasized just how important and useful these habits are. Yes, cultivating good habits in your child requires intentional effort; but oh, how wonderful are the results! Habits can overcome your child's natural tendencies. The habits you build into your child's life now will have many years to strengthen and will eventually make up his character as an adult.

As you read Charlotte's thoughts on habits, may you be encouraged and motivated anew to lay down the rails of good habits upon which your child can run well into the future!

1. Forming habits intentionally and thoughtfully is an important part of education.

"Therefore we are limited to three educational instruments—the atmosphere of environment, the discipline of habit, and the presentation of living ideas" (Vol. 1, Preface).

"By EDUCATION IS A DISCIPLINE, is meant the discipline of habits formed definitely and thoughtfully, whether habits of mind or body" (Vol. 1, Preface).

"Education is a discipline—that is, the discipline of the good habits in which the child is trained. Education is a life, nourished upon ideas; and education is an atmosphere—that is, the child breathes the atmosphere emanating from his parents; that of the ideas which rule their own lives" (Vol. 2, p. 247).

"Education is a Discipline—By this formula we mean the discipline of habits formed definitely and thoughtfully whether habits of mind or of body" (Vol. 6, p. 99).

" 'Habit is TEN natures!' If I could but make others see with my eyes how much this saying should mean to the educator! How habit, in the hands of the mother, is as his wheel to the potter, his knife to the carver—the instrument by means of which she turns out the design she has already conceived in her brain. Observe, the material is there to begin with; his wheel will not enable the potter to produce a porcelain cup out of coarse clay; but the instrument is as necessary as the material or the design. It is unpleasant to speak of one's self, but if the reader will allow me, I should like to run over the steps by which I have been brought to look upon habit as the means whereby the parent may make almost anything he chooses of his child. That which has become the dominant idea of one person's life, if it be launched suddenly at another, conveys no very great depth or weight of meaning to the second person—he wants to get at it by degrees, to see the

> "Habit, in the hands of the mother, is as his wheel to the potter."

steps by which the other has travelled. Therefore, I shall venture to show how I arrived at my present position, which is, from *one* of the three possible points of view—The formation of habits *is* education, and *Education is the formation of habits"* (Vol. 1, p. 97).

"The call for strenuousness comes with the necessity of forming habits; but here again we are relieved. The intellectual habits of the good life form themselves in the following out of the due curriculum in the right way. As we have already urged, there is but one right way, that is, children must do the work for themselves. They must read the given pages and tell what they have read, they must perform, that is, what we may call the *act of knowing*. We are all aware, alas, what a monstrous quantity of printed matter has gone into the dustbin of our memories, because we have failed to perform that quite natural and spontaneous 'act of knowing,' as easy to a child as breathing and, if we would believe it, comparatively easy to ourselves. The reward is two-fold: no intellectual habit is so valuable as that of attention; it is a mere habit but it is also the hall-mark of an educated person. Use is second nature, we are told; it is not too much to say that 'habit is ten natures,' and we can all imagine how our work would be eased if our subordinates listened to instructions with the full attention which implies recollection. Attention is not the only habit that follows due self-education. The habits of fitting and ready expression, of obedience, of good-will, and of an impersonal outlook are spontaneous bye-products of education in this sort. So, too, are the habits of right thinking and right judging; while physical habits of neatness and order attend upon the self-respect which follows an education which respects the personality of children" (Vol. 6, pp. 99, 100).

2. Habit can be more powerful than natural tendencies.

" 'Habit is *ten* natures.' If that be true, strong as nature is, habit is not only as strong, but *tenfold* as strong. Here, then, have we a stronger than he, able to overcome this strong man armed.

"But habit runs on the lines of nature: the cowardly child *habitually* lies that he may escape blame; the loving child has a hundred endearing *habits*; the good-natured child has a *habit* of giving; the selfish child, a *habit* of keeping. Habit, working thus according to nature, is simply nature in action, growing strong by exercise.

"But habit, to be the lever to lift the child, must work contrary to nature, or at any rate, independently of her" (Vol. 1, p. 105).

"The extraordinary power of habit in forcing nature into new channels hardly requires illustration; we have only to see a small boy at a circus riding two barebacked ponies with a foot on the back of each, or a pantomime fairy dancing on air, or a clown behaving like an indiarubber ball, or any of the thousand feats of skill and dexterity which we pay our shillings to see—mental feats as well as bodily, though, happily, these are the rarer—to be convinced that exactly anything may be accomplished by training, that is, the cultivation of persistent habits" (Vol. 1, p. 106).

3. *The longer a habit is performed without lapses, the stronger it becomes.*

"But,—supposing that the doing of a certain action a score or two of times

"Education is the formation of habits."

in unbroken sequence forms a habit which it is as easy to follow as not; that, persist still further in the habit *without lapses*, and it becomes second nature, quite difficult to shake off; continue it further, through a course of years, and the habit has the strength of *ten* natures, you cannot break through it without doing real violence to yourself;—grant all this, and also that it is possible to form in the child *the habit* of doing and saying, even of thinking and feeling, all that it is desirable he should do or say, think or feel,—and do you not take away the child's free-will, make a mere automaton of him by this excessive culture?" (Vol. 1, p. 110).

"The fact is, that the things we do a good many times over leave some sort of impression in the very substance of our brain; and this impression, the more often it is repeated, makes it the easier for us to do the thing the next time. We know this well enough as it applies to skating, hockey, and the like. We say we want practice, or, are out of practice, and must get some practice; but we do not realise that, in all the affairs of our life, the same thing holds good. What we have practice in doing we can do with ease, while we bungle over that in which we have little practice.

"This is the *law of habit*, which holds good as much in doing kindnesses as in playing the piano. Both habits come by practice; and that is why it is so important not to miss a chance of doing the thing we mean to do well. We must not amuse ourselves with the notion that we have done something when we have only formed a good resolution. Power comes by *doing* and not by *resolving*, and it is habit that serves us, whether it be the habit of Latin verse or of carving. Also, and this is a delightful thing to remember, every time we do a thing helps to form the habit of doing it; and to do a thing a hundred times without missing a chance, makes the rest easy" (Vol. 4, Book 1, pp. 208, 209).

4. Habit is inevitable.

"In the first place, whether you choose or no to take any trouble about the formation of his habits, it is *habit*, all the same, which will govern ninety-nine one-hundredths of the child's life: he is the mere automaton you describe. As for the child's becoming the creature of habit, that is not left with the parent to determine. We are all mere creatures of habit. We think our accustomed thoughts, make our usual small talk, go through the trivial round, the common task, without any self-determining effort of will at all. If it were not so—if we had to think, to deliberate, about each operation of the bath or the table—life would not be worth having; the perpetually repeated effort of decision would wear us out. But, let us be thankful, life is not thus laborious. For a hundred times we act or think, it is not necessary to choose, to will, say, more than once. And the little emergencies, which compel an act of will, will fall in the children's lives just about as frequently as in our own. These we cannot save them from, nor is it desirable that we should. What we can do for them is to secure that they have habits which shall lead them in ways of order, propriety, and virtue, instead of leaving their wheel of life to make ugly ruts in miry places.

"And then, even in emergencies, in every sudden difficulty and temptation that requires an act of will, why, conduct is still apt to run on the lines of the familiar habit. The boy who has been accustomed to find both profit and pleasure in his books does not fall easily into idle ways because he is attracted by an idle

"Every time we do a thing helps to form the habit of doing it."

schoolfellow. The girl who has been carefully trained to speak the exact truth simply does not think of a lie as a ready means of getting out of a scrape, coward as she may be" (Vol. 1, pp. 110, 111).

"We have lost sight of the fact that habit is to life what rails are to transport cars. It follows that lines of habit must be laid down towards given ends and after careful survey, or the joltings and delays of life become insupportable. More, habit is inevitable. If we fail to ease life by laying down habits of right thinking and right acting, habits of wrong thinking and wrong acting fix themselves of their own accord. We avoid decision and indecision brings its own delays, 'and days are lost lamenting o'er lost days.' Almost every child is brought up by his parents in certain habits of decency and order without which he would be a social outcast. Think from another point of view how the labour of life would be increased if every act of the bath, toilet, table, every lifting of the fork and use of spoon were a matter of consideration and required an effort of decision! No; habit is like fire, a bad master but an indispensable servant; and probably one reason for the nervous scrupulosity, hesitation, indecision of our day, is that life was not duly eased for us in the first place by those whose business it was to lay down lines of habit upon which our behaviour might run easily" (Vol. 6, p. 101).

"Each of us has in his possession an exceedingly good servant or a very bad master, known as Habit. The heedless, listless person is a servant of habit; the useful, alert person is the master of a valuable habit" (Vol. 4, Book 1, p. 208).

5. Habits produce character.

"How does this bear on the practical work of bringing up children? In this way: We think, *as we are accustomed to think*; ideas come and go and carry on a ceaseless traffic in the rut—let us call it—you have made for them in the very nerve substance of the brain. You do not deliberately intend to think these thoughts; you may, indeed, object strongly to the line they are taking (two 'trains' of thought going on at one and the same time!), and objecting, you may be able to barricade the way, to put up 'No Road' in big letters, and to compel the busy populace of the brain-world to take another route. But who is able for these things? Not the child, immature of will, feeble in moral power, unused to the weapons of the spiritual warfare. He depends upon his parents; it rests with them to initiate the thoughts he shall think, the desires he shall cherish, the feelings he shall allow. Only to initiate; no more is permitted to them; but from this initiation will result the habits of thought and feeling which govern the man—his *character*, that is to say. But is not this assuming too much, seeing that, to sum up roughly all we understand by heredity, a child is born with his future in his hands? The child is born, doubtless, with the tendencies which should shape his future; but every tendency has its branch roads, its good or evil outcome; and to put the child on the right track for the fulfilment of the possibilities inherent in *him*, is the vocation of the parent.

"This relation of habit to human life—as the rails on which it runs to a locomotive—is perhaps the most suggestive and helpful to the educator; for just as it is on the whole easier for the locomotive to pursue its way on the rails than to take a disastrous run off them, so it is easier for the child to follow lines of habit carefully laid down than to run off these lines at his peril. It follows that this

"The habits of the child produce the character of the man."

business of laying down lines towards the unexplored country of the child's future is a very serious and responsible one for the parent. It rests with him to consider well the tracks over which the child should travel with profit and pleasure; and, along these tracks, to lay down lines so invitingly smooth and easy that the little traveller is going upon them at full speed without stopping to consider whether or no he chooses to go that way" (Vol. 1, pp. 108, 109).

"The habits of the child produce the character of the man, because certain mental habitudes once set up, their nature is to go on for ever unless they should be displaced by other habits. Here is an end to the easy philosophy of, 'It doesn't matter,' 'Oh, he'll grow out of it,' 'He'll know better by-and-by,' 'He's so young, what can we expect?' and so on. Every day, every hour, the parents are either passively or actively forming those habits in their children upon which, more than upon anything else, future character and conduct depend" (Vol. 1, p. 118).

"You will see that it is because of the possibilities of ruin and loss which lie about every human life that I am pressing upon parents the duty of saving their children by the means put into their hands. Perhaps it is not too much to say, that ninety-nine out of a hundred lost lives lie at the door of parents who took no pains to deliver them from sloth, from sensual appetites, from willfulness, no pains to fortify them with the *habits* of a good life" (Vol. 1, p. 330).

"As has been well said, 'Sow an act, reap a habit; sow a habit, reap a character; sow a character, reap a destiny.' And a great function of the educator is to secure that acts shall be so regularly, purposefully, and methodically sown that the child shall reap the habits of the good life, in thinking and doing, with the minimum of conscious effort" (Vol. 2, p. 124).

"Educate the child in right habits and the man's life will run in them, without the constant wear and tear of the moral effort of decision. Once, twice, three times in a day, he will still, no doubt, have to choose between the highest and the less high, the best and the less good course. But all the minor moralities of life may be made habitual to him. He has been brought up to be courteous, prompt, punctual, neat, considerate; and he practises these virtues without conscious effort. It is much easier to behave in the way he is used to, than to originate a new line of conduct" (Vol. 2, p. 124).

6. *"The mother who takes pains to endow her children with good habits secures for herself smooth and easy days."*

"It is pleasant to know that, even in mature life, it is possible by a little persistent effort to acquire a desirable habit. It is good, if not pleasant, to know, also, with what fatal ease we can slip into bad habits. But the most comfortable thing in this view of habit is, that it falls in with our natural love of an easy life. We are not unwilling to make efforts in the beginning with the assurance that by-and-by things will go smoothly; and this is just what habit is, in an extraordinary degree, pledged to effect. The mother who takes pains to endow her children with good habits secures for herself smooth and easy days; while she who lets their habits take care of themselves has a weary life of endless friction with the children. All day she is crying out, 'Do this!' and they do it not; 'Do that!' and they do the

"The mother who takes pains to endow her children with good habits secures for herself smooth and easy days."

other" (Vol. 1, pp. 135, 136).

"In conclusion, let me say that the education of habit is successful in so far as it enables the mother to *let her children alone*, not teasing them with perpetual commands and directions—a running fire of *Do* and *Don't*; but letting them go their own way and *grow*, having first secured that they will go the right way, and grow to fruitful purpose. The gardener, it is true, 'digs about and dungs,' prunes and trains, his peach tree; but that occupies a small fraction of the tree's life: all the rest of the time the sweet airs and sunshine, the rains and dews, play about it and breathe upon it, get into its substance, and the result is—peaches. But let the gardener neglect *his* part, and the peaches will be no better than sloes" (Vol. 1, p. 134).

7. Children can pick up habits from the actions and attitudes of those around them.

"There are the children trained in careful habits, who never soil their clothes; those trained in reticent habits, who never speak of what is done at home, and answer indiscreet questions with 'I don't know'; there are the children brought up in courteous habits, who make way for their elders with gentle grace, and more readily for the poor woman with the basket than for the well-dressed lady; and there are children trained in grudging habits, who never offer to yield, or go, or do.

"Such habits as these, good, bad, or indifferent, are they natural to the children? No, but they are what their mothers have brought them up to; and as a matter of fact, there is *nothing* which a mother cannot bring her child up to, and there is hardly a mother anywhere who has not some two or three—crotchets sometimes, principles sometimes—which her children never violate. So that it comes to this—given, a mother with liberal views on the subject of education, and she simply cannot help working her own views into her children's habits; given, on the other hand, a mother whose final question is, 'What will people say? what will people think? how will it look?' and the children grow up with habits of seeming, and not of being; they are content to appear well-dressed, well-mannered, and well-intentioned to outsiders, with very little effort after beauty, order, and goodness at home, and in each other's eyes" (Vol. 1, p. 105, 106).

"And here comes in the consideration of outside influence. Nine times out of ten we begin to do a thing because we see some one else do it; we go on doing it, and—there is the habit! If it is so easy for ourselves to take up a new habit, it is tenfold as easy for the children; and this is the real difficulty in the matter of the education of habit. It is necessary that the mother be always on the alert to nip in the bud the bad habit her children may be in the act of picking up from servants or from other children" (Vol. 1, p. 118).

8. Training in good habits is linked to discipline of the will, developing a response to conscience, and teaching about God.

"Here, indeed, more than anywhere, 'Except the Lord build the house, they labour but in vain that build it'; but surely intelligent co-operation in this divine work is our bounden duty and service. The training of the will, the instruction

"Habit begins as a cobweb, and ends as a cable."

of the conscience, and, so far as it lies with us, the development of the divine life in the child, are carried on simultaneously with this training in the habits of a good life; and these last will carry the child safely over the season of infirm will, immature conscience, until he is able to take, under direction from above, the conduct of his life, the moulding of his character, into his own hands" (Vol. 2, p. 90).

"It is unnecessary to enumerate those habits which we should aim at forming, for everyone knows more about these than anyone practises. We admire the easy carriage of the soldier but shrink from the discipline which is able to produce it. We admire the lady who can sit upright through a long dinner, who in her old age prefers a straight chair because she has arrived at due muscular balance and has done so by a course of discipline. There is no other way of forming any good habit, though the discipline is usually that of the internal government which the person exercises upon himself; but a certain strenuousness in the formation of good habits is necessary because every such habit is the result of conflict. The bad habit of the easy life is always pleasant and persuasive and to be resisted with pain and effort, but with hope and certainty of success, because in our very structure is the preparation for forming such habits of muscle and mind as we deliberately propose to ourselves" (Vol. 6, pp. 101, 102).

9. We must train our children in habits of decency and propriety, moral habits, mental habits, physical habits, and religious habits.

"Consider how laborious life would be were its wheels not greased by habits of cleanliness, neatness, order, courtesy; had we to make the effort of decision about every detail of dressing and eating, coming and going, life would not be worth living. Every cottage mother knows that she must train her child in habits of decency, and a whole code of habits of propriety get themselves formed just because a breach in any such habit causes a shock to others which few children have courage to face. Physical fitness, morals and manners, are very largely the outcome of habit; and not only so, but the habits of the religious life also become fixed and delightful and give us due support in the effort to live a godly, righteous and sober life" (Vol. 6, p. 103).

"I need not refer again to the genesis of a habit; but perhaps most of us set ourselves more definitely to form physical and moral than we do to form intellectual habits. I will only mention a few such, which should be matters of careful training during the period of childhood" (Vol. 3, pp. 119, 120).

"A great function of the educator is to secure that acts shall be so regularly, purposefully, and methodically sown that the child shall reap the habits of the good life, in thinking and doing, with the minimum of conscious effort."

Part 2

Laying Down the Rails

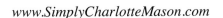

Chapter 2
How to Cultivate Good Habits

The principles given here can apply to the formation of just about any habit.

1. Be consistently diligent to deal with your child the first time and every time he offends.

"Deal with a child on his *first offence*, and a grieved look is enough to convict the little transgressor; but let him go on until a habit of wrong-doing is formed, and the cure is a slow one; then the mother has no chance until she has formed in him a contrary habit of well-doing" (Vol. 1, p. 19).

• Sometimes simply diverting the child's thoughts is enough to direct the child into a good habit and prevent the formation of a bad one.

"We all know how important this, of changing children's thoughts, diverting, is in the formation of habit" (Vol. 3, p. 23).

• Attention to the small things will reap a reward.

"Let us not despise the day of small things nor grow weary in well-doing; if we have trained our children from their earliest years to prompt mechanical obedience, well and good; we reap our reward. If we have not, we must be content to lead by slow degrees, by ever-watchful efforts, by authority never in abeyance and never aggressive, to 'the joy of self-control,' the delight of proud chivalric obedience which will hail a command as an opportunity for service" (Vol. 3, p. 23).

• Discipline is not just punishment.

"Not mere spurts of occasional punishment, but the incessant watchfulness and endeavour which go to the forming and preserving of the habits of the good life, is what we mean by discipline; and, from this point of view, never were there such disciplinarians as the parents who labour on the lines we would indicate. Every habit of courtesy, consideration, order, neatness, punctuality, truthfulness, is itself a schoolmaster, and orders life with the most unfailing diligence" (Vol. 2, p. 173).

• Remember that you are working to give your child something much more valuable than gold or silver.

"A habit is so easily formed, so strong to compel. There are few parents who would not labour diligently if for every month's labour they were able to endow one of their children with a large sum of money. But, in a month, a parent may begin to form a habit in his child of such value that money is a bagatelle by

Notes

comparison. We have often urged that the great discovery which modern science has brought to the aid of the educator is, that every habit of the life sets up, as it were, a material record in the brain tissues. We all know that we think as we are used to think and act as we are used to act. Ever since man began to notice the ways of his own mind, this law of habit has been matter of common knowledge, and has been more or less acted upon by parents and other trainers of children. The well-brought-up child has always been a child carefully trained in good habits" (Vol. 2, pp. 173, 174).

2. Devote yourself to the formation of one habit at a time, keeping watch over those habits already formed.

" 'But,' you say, 'if habit is so powerful, whether to hinder or to help the child, it is fatiguing to think of all the habits the poor mother must attend to. Is she never to be at ease with her children?'

"Here, again, is an illustration of that fable of the anxious pendulum, overwhelmed with the thought of the number of ticks it must tick. But the ticks are to be delivered tick by tick, and there will always be a second of time to tick in. The mother devotes herself to the formation of one habit at a time, doing no more than keep watch over those already formed. If she be appalled by the thought of overmuch labour, let her limit the number of good habits she will lay herself out to form. The child who starts in life with, say, twenty good habits, begins with a certain capital which he will lay out to endless profit as the years go on" (Vol. 1, p. 136).

3. Develop your own habit of watchfulness and cultivating good habits in your child.

"The mother who is distrustful of her own power of steady effort may well take comfort in two facts. In the first place, she herself acquires the *habit* of training her children in a given habit, so that by-and-by it becomes, not only no trouble, but a pleasure to her. In the second place, the child's most fixed and dominant habits are those which the mother takes no pains about, but which the child picks up for himself through his close observation of all that is said and done, felt and thought, in his home" (Vol. 1, pp. 136, 137).

"We need not add that authority is just and faithful in all matters of promise-keeping; it is also considerate, and that is why a good mother is the best home-ruler; she is in touch with the children, knows their unspoken schemes and half-formed desires, and where she cannot yield, she diverts; she does not crush with a sledge-hammer, an instrument of rule with which a child is somehow never very sympathetic" (Vol. 3, p. 23).

4. Motivate your child with an interesting and inspiring example of a person who possesses the habit you want the child to develop.

"A habit is set up by following out an initial idea with a long sequence of corresponding acts. You tell a child that the Great Duke slept in so narrow a bed that he could not turn over, because, said he, 'When you want to turn over it's time to get up.' The boy does not wish to get up in the morning, but he does wish to be like the hero of Waterloo. You stimulate him to act upon this idea day after

Charlotte put the most emphasis in her writings on three habits: obedience, attention, and truthfulness. Those habits might be a great place to start.

"The mother devotes herself to the formation of one habit at a time, doing no more than keep watch over those already formed."

day for a month or so, until the habit is formed, and it is just as easy as not to get up in good time" (Vol. 2, p. 125).

"We entertain the idea which gives birth to the act and the act repeated again and again becomes the habit; 'Sow an act,' we are told, 'reap a habit.' 'Sow a habit, reap a character.' But we must go a step further back, we must sow the idea or notion which makes the act worth while. The lazy boy who hears of the Great Duke's narrow camp bed, preferred by him because when he wanted to turn over it was time to get up, receives the idea of prompt rising. But his nurse or his mother knows how often and how ingeniously the tale must be brought to his mind before the habit of prompt rising is formed; she knows too how the idea of self-conquest must be made at home in the boy's mind until it become a chivalric impulse which he cannot resist. It is possible to sow a great idea lightly and casually and perhaps this sort of sowing should be rare and casual because if a child detect a definite purpose in his mentor he is apt to stiffen himself against it" (Vol. 6, p. 102).

5. Be careful not to excuse a lapse in a good habit.

"When parent or teacher supposes that a good habit is a matter of obedience to his authority, he relaxes a little. A boy is late who has been making evident efforts to be punctual; the teacher good-naturedly foregoes rebuke or penalty, and the boy says to himself,—'It doesn't matter,' and begins to form the unpunctual habit. The mistake the teacher makes is to suppose that to be punctual is troublesome to the boy, so he will let him off; whereas the office of the habits of an ordered life is to make such life easy and spontaneous; the effort is confined to the first half dozen or score of occasions for doing the thing" (Vol. 6, pp. 102, 103).

• Think of a good habit as a delight.

"The forming of habits in the children is no laborious task, for the reward goes hand in hand with the labour; so much so, that it is like the laying out of a penny with the certainty of the immediate return of a pound. For a habit is a delight in itself; poor human nature is conscious of the ease that it is to repeat the doing of anything without effort; and, therefore, the formation of a habit, the gradually lessening sense of effort in a given act, is pleasurable. This is one of the rocks that mothers sometimes split upon: they lose sight of the fact that a habit, *even* a good habit, becomes a real pleasure; and when the child has really formed the habit of doing a certain thing, his mother imagines that the effort is as great to him as at first, that it is virtue in him to go on making this effort, and that he deserves, by way of reward, a little relaxation—she will let him break through the new habit a few times, and then go on again. But it is not going on; it is beginning again, and beginning in the face of obstacles. The 'little relaxation' she allowed her child meant the forming of another contrary habit, which must be overcome before the child gets back to where he was before.

"As a matter of fact, this misguided sympathy on the part of mothers is the one thing that makes it a laborious undertaking to train a child in good habits; for it is the nature of the child to take to habits as kindly as the infant takes to his mother's milk" (Vol. 1, pp. 121, 122).

"Every habit has its beginning. The beginning is the *idea* which comes with a stir and takes possession of us."

Shutting the Door

In *Home Education* (pp. 122–124) Charlotte wrote a living example to help us understand how to cultivate a good habit. The story, given here in its entirety, focuses on the habit of shutting the door when entering or exiting a room (a necessary courtesy in Victorian homes of Charlotte's day). Though the habit itself is of little consequence today, the principles of cultivating the habit remain consistent.

"For example, and to choose a habit of no great consequence except as a matter of consideration for others: the mother wishes her child to acquire the habit of shutting the door after him when he enters or leaves a room. Tact, watchfulness, and persistence are the qualities she must cultivate in herself; and, with these, she will be astonished at the readiness with which the child picks up the new habit.

" 'Johnny,' she says, in a bright, friendly voice, 'I want you to remember something with all your might: never go into or out of a room in which anybody is sitting without shutting the door.'

'But if I forget, mother?'

'I will try to remind you.'

'But perhaps I shall be in a *great* hurry.'

'You must always make time to do that.'

'But why, mother?'

'Because it is not polite to the people in the room to make them uncomfortable.'

'But if I am going out again that *very* minute?'

'Still, shut the door, when you come in; you can open it again to go out. Do you think you can remember?'

'I'll try, mother.'

'Very well; I shall watch to see how few "forgets" you make.'

"For two or three times Johnny remembers; and then, he is off like a shot and half-way downstairs before his mother has time to call him back. She does not cry out, 'Johnny, come back and shut the door!' because she knows that a summons of that kind is exasperating to big or little. She goes to the door, and calls pleasantly, 'Johnny!' Johnny has forgotten all about the door; he wonders what his mother wants, and, stirred by curiosity, comes back, to find her seated and employed as before. She looks up, glances at the door, and says, 'I said I should try to remind you.' 'Oh, I forgot,' says Johnny, put upon his honour; and he shuts the door that time, and the next, and the next.

"But the little fellow has really not much power to recollect, and the mother will have to adopt various little devices to remind him; but of two things she will be careful—that he never slips off without shutting the door, and that she never lets the matter be a cause of friction between herself and the child, taking the line of his friendly ally to help him against that bad memory of his. By and by, after, say, twenty shuttings of the door with never an omission, the habit begins to be formed; Johnny shuts the door as a matter of course, and his mother watches him with delight come into a room, shut the door, take something off the table, and go out, again shutting the door.

"Now that Johnny always shuts the door, his mother's joy and triumph begin

"If we wish children to be able, when they grow up, to keep under their bodies and bring them into subjection we must do this *for* them in their earlier years."

to be mixed with unreasonable pity. 'Poor child,' she says to herself, 'it is very good of him to take so much pains about a little thing, just because he is bid!' She thinks that, all the time, the child is making an effort for her sake; losing sight of the fact that the *habit* has become easy and natural, that, in fact, Johnny shuts the door without knowing that he does so. Now comes the critical moment. Some day Johnny is so taken up with a new delight that the habit, not yet fully formed, loses its hold, and he is half-way downstairs before he thinks of the door. Then he does think of it, with a little prick of conscience, strong enough, not to send him back, but to make him pause a moment to see if his mother will call him back. She has noticed the omission, and is saying to herself, 'Poor little fellow, he has been very good about it this long time; I'll let him off this once.' He, outside, fails to hear his mother's call, says, to himself—fatal sentence!—'Oh, it doesn't matter,' and trots off.

"Next time he leaves the door open, but it is not a 'forget.' His mother calls him back in a rather feeble way. His quick ear catches the weakness of her tone, and, without coming back, he cries, 'Oh, mother, I'm in *such* a hurry,' and she says no more, but lets him off. Again he rushes in, leaving the door wide open. 'Johnny!'—in a warning voice. 'I'm going out again just in a minute, mother,' and after ten minutes' rummaging he does go out, and forgets to shut the door. The mother's mis-timed easiness has lost for her every foot of the ground she had gained" (Vol. 1, pp. 122–124).

6. Don't resort to nagging; expect (and reinforce those expectations for) prompt obedience after one quiet yet firm telling.

" 'I'm sure I am always telling her'—to keep her drawers neat, or to hold up her head and speak nicely, or to be quick and careful about an errand, says the poor mother, with tears in her eyes; and indeed this, of 'always telling' him or her is a weary process for the mother; dull, because hopeless. She goes on 'telling' to deliver her own soul, for she has long since ceased to expect any result: and we know how dreary is work without hope. But, perhaps, even his mother does not know how unutterably dreary is this 'always telling,' which produces nothing, to the child. At first he is fretful and impatient under the patter of idle words; then he puts up with the inevitable; and comes at last hardly to be aware that the thing is being said. As for any impression on his character, any habit really formed, all this labour is without result; the child does the thing when he cannot help it, and evades as often as he can. And the poor disappointed mother says, 'I'm sure I've tried as much as any mother to train my children in good habits, but I have failed' " (Vol. 2, p. 174).

"The discipline of habit is at least a third part of the great whole which we call education."

Chapter 3
Decency and Propriety Habits

Habits of Decency and Propriety refer to those habits that we should instill in a child so he will not be "a social outcast" (Vol. 6, p. 101). Charlotte believed that a child would learn most of these character traits as he lived in an atmosphere that was permeated with them. In other words, we should try to make these habits a natural part of our homes.

"The whole group of habitudes, half physical and half moral, on which the propriety and comfort of everyday life depend, are received passively by the child; that is, he does very little to form these habits himself, but his brain receives impressions from what he sees about him; and these impressions take form as his own very strongest and most lasting habits. Cleanliness, order, neatness, regularity, punctuality, are all 'branches' of infant education. They should be about the child like the air he breathes, and he will take them in as unconsciously" (Vol. 1, pp. 124, 125).

"Every look of gentleness and tone of reverence, every word of kindness and act of help, passes into the thought-environment, the very atmosphere which the child breathes; he does not think of these things, may never think of them, but all his life long they excite that 'vague appetency towards something' out of which most of his actions spring" (Vol. 2, p. 36).

In this chapter you will find Charlotte's comments on

Cleanliness	**Modesty and Purity**
Courtesy	**Neatness**
Kindness	**Order**
Manners	**Regularity**

Plus several more habits that Charlotte mentioned but didn't elaborate on.

Candor	**Meekness**
Courage	**Patience**
Diligence	**Respect for Other People**
Fortitude	**Temperance**
Generosity	**Thrift**
Gentleness	

"Cleanliness, order, neatness, regularity, punctuality, are all 'branches' of infant education. They should be about the child like the air he breathes, and he will take them in as unconsciously."

Cleanliness
Careful to keep clean

Michelle unconsciously braced herself as she unlocked the door to the condominium. They had rented this place without seeing it, and she was not quite sure what to expect. Some of the past vacation rental units had been less than stellar.

But as Michelle swung open the door, a fresh, clean smell enveloped her and seemed to invite her in. She could feel her shoulder muscles relaxing after that long drive and knew that a smile was playing on her lips as she stepped inside and looked around the sparkling clean room. Yes, this was going to be a wonderful place to call "home" for the next few days!

Isn't it amazing how much effect cleanliness has on our frame of mind? People who are used to a clean, fresh-smelling environment quickly notice when those elements are missing. Take for an example, what happens to your spirits when you open the door after the baby's nap and meet full force the odor of a dirty diaper, followed by the sight of a new "finger painting" spread around the walls and crib. Cleanliness matters!

Fortunately, cleanliness is a habit that we can cultivate in our children by example and surroundings, for the most part. We don't have to be paranoid about germs or compulsive about scrubbing, but we can intentionally create a fresh, clean environment in our homes for our children (and us) to enjoy.

Charlotte's Thoughts on Cleanliness

1. Keep your child's room clean, aired, and odor-free.

"It is hardly necessary to say a word about the necessity for delicate cleanliness in the nursery. . . . It needs much watchfulness to secure that there shall not be the faintest odour about the infant or anything belonging to him, and that the nurseries be kept sweet and thoroughly aired" (Vol. 1, p. 125).

2. Teach your child to air out any clothing or bedding that will be used again before washing.

"One or two little bits of tidiness that nurses affect are not to be commended on the score of cleanliness:—the making up of the nursery beds early in the morning, and the folding up of the children's garments when they take them off at night. It is well to stretch a line across the day nursery at night, and hang the little garments out for an airing, to get rid of the insensible perspiration with which they have been laden during the day. For the same reason, the beds and bedclothes should be turned down to air for a couple of hours before they are made up" (Vol. 1, p. 126).

3. Allow your child to get dirty, but teach him how to clean himself up.

"The children, too, should be encouraged to nice cleanliness in their own persons. We have all seen the dainty baby-hand stretched out to be washed; it has got a smudge, and the child does not like it. May they be as particular when they

> "Character is the result not merely of the great ideas which are given to us, but of the habits which we labour to form *upon those ideas.*"

are big enough to wash their own hands! Not that they should be always clean and presentable; children love to 'mess about' and should have big pinafores for the purpose. They are all like that little French prince who scorned his birthday gifts, and entreated to be allowed to make dear little mud-pies with the boy in the gutter. Let them make their mud-pies freely; but that over, they should be impatient to remove every trace of soil, and should do it *themselves*" (Vol. 1, p. 127).

4. Teach your child how to groom himself adequately and to wash his hands before meals.

"Young children may be taught to take care of their finger-nails, and to cleanse the corners of eyes and ears. As for sitting down to table with unwashed hands and unbrushed hair, that, of course, no decent child is allowed to do" (Vol. 1, p. 127).

5. By the age of five or six, your child should be able to bathe himself properly.

"Children should be early provided with their own washing materials, and accustomed to find real pleasure in the bath, and in attending to themselves. There is no reason why a child of five or six should not make himself thoroughly clean without all that torture of soap in the eyes and general pulling about and poking which children hate, and no wonder. Besides, the child is not getting the *habit* of the daily bath until he can take it for himself" (Vol. 1, p. 127).

Questions to Ask about Cleanliness

- Am I careful to air my child's room?
- Do I try to keep my child's room smelling sweet and fresh, or do I make excuse because of the child's gender, age, or hobbies?
- Am I enlisting my older child's help in keeping his own room (and the rest of the house) clean and fresh?
- Am I teaching my child to air out clothing and bedding that will be used again before washing?
- Do I allow my child to get dirty and clean himself up?
- Do I consistently require washed hands for family meals?
- Am I teaching my child to groom himself adequately, including caring for his fingernails, cleaning in the "corners," and brushing or combing his hair?
- Am I taking steps to teach my child how to attend to himself in his bath or shower?

More Quotes on Cleanliness

"Certainly this is a duty, not a sin. 'Cleanliness is indeed next to godliness.'"—John Wesley

"Cleanness of body was ever deemed to proceed from a due reverence to God, to society, and to ourselves."—Francis Bacon

"Sow an act, reap a habit; sow a habit, reap a character; sow a character, reap a destiny."

Courtesy

Behavior marked by respect for and consideration of others

"Say 'please,' " Karen prompted her little one, holding the banana piece in the baby's line of vision.

"Pees," the little one replied.

Karen smiled and handed the piece of banana to the child. The chubby little hand reached out and grasped the fruit. Karen did not let go, despite the baby-tugs she felt.

"Thank you," she prompted pleasantly, still holding on to the banana.

"Tanku," repeated the child.

"Very good!" Karen encouraged, and let go of the treat.

Courtesy seems like a small thing—until we encounter rudeness. Then we realize what a difference simple courtesy can make! The good news is that, like so many other habits of Decency and Propriety, your child can learn courtesy by living in a courteous environment and receiving some simple coaching from you.

You can also set a good example by being courteous to others, including your child. (When you tell your child to do something, do you say "please" and "thank you"?)

Charlotte's Thoughts on Courtesy

1. Do not allow your child to neglect showing courtesy just because a person is familiar to him. Familiarity should not breed disrespect.

"We English people are rather ready to think that it does not much matter how we behave, so long as our hearts are all right; and some of us miss our chance of doing the Kindness of Courtesy, and adopt a hail-fellow-well-met manner, which is a little painful and repellent, and therefore a little unkind" (Vol. 4, Book 1, p. 100).

"We owe knowledge to the ignorant, comfort to the distressed, healing to the sick, reverence, courtesy and kindness to all men, especially to those with whom we are connected by ties of family or neighbourhood; and the sense of these dues does not come by nature" (Vol. 3, p. 85).

"To listen with all one's mind is an act of delicate courtesy which draws their best out of even dull people" (Vol. 4, Book 1, p. 76).

"So of the other manifestations of love—kindness, courtesy, friendliness; these the parents must get from their children, not upon demand, but as love constrains them. Make occasions for services, efforts, offerings: let the children feel that their kindness is a power in the lives of their parents. I know of a girl upon whom it dawned for the first time, when she was far in her 'teens,' that she had any power to gratify her mother. Do not let the little common courtesies and attentions of daily life slip,—the placing of a chair, the standing aside or falling behind at proper times, the attentive eye at table, the attentive ear and ready response to

"To listen with all one's mind is an act of delicate courtesy."

question or direction. Let the young people feel that the omission of these things causes pain to loving hearts, that the doing of them is as cheering as the sunshine; and if they forget sometimes, it will only be that they forget, not that they are unwilling, or look upon the amenities of life as 'all bosh!'

"Again, let there be a continuous flow of friendliness, graciousness, the pleasantness of eye and lip, between parent and child. Let the boy perceive that a bright eye-to-eye 'Good-morning, mother,' is gladness to her, and that a cold greeting with averted face is like a cloud between his mother and the sun" (Vol. 5, pp. 202, 203).

2. Encourage your child to give and return courteous gestures, such as shaking hands and waving.

"We miss, too, the courtesies of gesture; it is good in a German or Danish town to see one errand-boy raise his hat to another, or school-boy to school-boy, or porter to laundress, without any sense of awkwardness; but in these matters we have got into a national bad habit. In this field, perhaps, the rich and the poor meet together, because there is not in either an unconscious struggle after social status which does not belong to them, and so both can afford to be simple, considerate, gracious, and courteous to all who come in their way" (Vol. 4, Book 1, p. 100).

Questions to Ask about Courtesy

- Is my child demonstrating courtesy consistently, even to familiar people like close friends and relatives?
- Is my child learning to give and return courteous gestures, like shaking hands and waving?
- Am I setting a good example by exhibiting courtesy on the telephone and in person?
- Am I trying to be courteous to my child?

More Quotes on Courtesy

"Politeness is the art of choosing among one's real thoughts."—Abel Stevens

"Life is not so short but that there is always time for courtesy."—Ralph Waldo Emerson

"If a man be gracious and courteous to strangers, it shows he is a citizen of the world."—Francis Bacon

Kindness
Friendly regard shown toward another

It had been a long week. The baby was just beginning to keep some food down after battling the flu for several days. The house was a mess: dishes, toys,

"We know that to form in his child right habits of thinking and behaving is a parent's chief duty, and that this can be done for every child definitely and within given limits of time."

Notes

laundry, and dirty bathrooms lay untouched because Susan had been attending to the baby every moment, not to mention the other two children.

I'm so glad Mrs. Len is coming over with that tea, Susan thought again. *She'll be able to tell if Baby is getting dehydrated.*

As the doorbell rang, Susan suddenly felt a little self-conscious. *The house is such a mess! I hope she won't think we live like this all the time!*

But kind Mrs. Len not only brought the promised tea and pronounced the baby "progressing nicely," but also rolled up her sleeves, put on an apron, and washed dishes, picked up toys, did laundry, and cleaned the bathrooms.

We've all experienced moments of kindness that stand out in our memories. It might have been something as dramatic as Susan's situation or something that seemed much smaller to the giver but made a huge impact on us just the same.

What a wonderful habit to build into your child's life: kindness! With this habit he will touch innumerable lives.

Charlotte's Thoughts on Kindness

1. Encourage your child to think the best of other people.

"There are always two ways of understanding other people's words, acts, and motives; and human nature is so contradictory that both ways may be equally right; the difference is in the construction we put upon other people's thoughts. If we think kindly of another's thoughts—think, for example, that an ungentle action or word may arise from a little clumsiness and not from lack of kindness of heart—we shall probably be right and be no more than fair to the person concerned. But, supposing we are wrong, our kind construction will have a double effect. It will, quicker than any reproof, convict our neighbour of his unkindness, and it will stir up in him the pleasant feelings for which we have already given him credit" (Vol. 4, Book 1, pp. 101, 102).

2. Teach your child not to assume that others will laugh at him for being kind.

"Of all the causes of unhappiness, perhaps few bring about more distress in the world than the habit, which even good people allow themselves in, of putting an ungentle construction upon the ways and words of the people they live with. This habit has another bad effect, especially upon young people, who are greatly influenced by the opinion of their fellows. They think So-and-so will laugh at them for doing a certain obliging action, so they refrain from following the good impulses of a good heart. Kindness which is simple thinks none of these things, nor does it put evil constructions upon the thoughts that others may think in the given circumstances. 'Be ye kind one to another' is not an easy precept, but—

" 'All worldly joys go less
To the one joy of doing kindnesses'
—HERBERT" (Vol. 4, Book 1, p. 102).

3. Encourage your child to defend another's character, even in that person's absence, rather than malign him behind his back.

"His love of justice shows in the demand for 'fair play' for others now; he will

"Kindness is love, showing itself in act and word, look and manner."

not hear others spoken ill of in their absence, will not assign unworthy motives, or accuse another easily of unworthy conduct; he is just to the conduct, the character, the reputation of others. He puts himself involuntarily in the place of the other, and judges as he would be judged.

> " 'Teach me to feel another's woe,
>   To hide the faults I see;
>   That mercy I to others show,
>   That mercy show to me,'

is his unformed, unconscious prayer" (Vol. 5, p. 208).

4. Help siblings respond kindly to each other, even when faced with a brother's temper or personal injury.

"His benevolence, again, his kindness, will reach, not only to the distresses of others, but will show itself in forbearance towards tiresome tempers, in magnanimity in the forgiveness of injuries" (Vol. 5, p. 208).

5. Motivate your child with the idea that he might hold the happiness of others in his hands.

"His habits of kind and friendly behaviour will, by degrees, develop into principles of action; until at last his character is established, and he comes to be known as a just and virtuous man. Towards this great result the parents can do little more than keep the channels open, and direct the streams; they draw the attention of their son to the needs and claims of others, and point out to him from time to time the ways in which he holds the happiness of others in his hands" (Vol. 5, p. 208).

6. Be careful what messages your child receives from outside influences that would encourage selfishness.

"It is needless to say how a selfish or worldly maxim thrown in—'Take care of yourself,' 'Look after your own interests,' 'Give tit for tat,'—may obstruct the channel or choke the spring" (Vol. 5, p. 208).

Questions to Ask about Kindness

- Am I encouraging my child to think the best of other people?
- Is my child learning not to assume that others will laugh at him for his kindness?
- Is my child progressing in defending and protecting other people's good character in their absence?
- Am I helping my child to respond kindly to siblings or others with tiresome tempers?
- Is my child learning to respond kindly even when injured by another?
- Is my child inspired by the idea of making others happy by showing kindness?
- Is my child receiving selfish messages from any outside influences? If so, how can I counteract those selfish messages with messages of kindness?

"His habits of kind and friendly behaviour will, by degrees, develop into principles of action; until at last his character is established."

More Quotes on Kindness

"There is no beautifier of complexion, or form, or behavior, like the wish to scatter joy and not pain around us. 'Tis good to give a stranger a meal, or a night's lodging. 'Tis better to be hospitable to his good meaning and thought, and give courage to a companion. We must be as courteous to a man as we are to a picture, which we are willing to give the advantage of a good light."—Ralph Waldo Emerson

"I always prefer to believe the best of everybody—it saves so much trouble."—Rudyard Kipling

"Always try to be a little kinder than is necessary."—James M. Barrie

"A warm smile is the universal language of kindness."—William Arthur Ward

"Kind words can be short and easy to speak, but their echoes are truly endless."—Mother Teresa

"Be ye kind one to another."—Ephesians 4:32

"Charity suffereth long, and is kind."—1 Corinthians 13:4

Here's a great summary phrase: Respect the older; protect the younger.

Manners
Social rules of conduct shown in the prevalent customs

"Jacob, I've noticed that you sometimes start talking to Mommy when Mommy is already talking to or listening to someone else. That's called 'interrupting.' I want you to learn to wait your turn. So from now on I'm going to help you remember not to interrupt," Melanie explained.

Jacob sat next to her on the couch, listening carefully.

"Here's what we'll do," continued Melanie. "When you want to tell me something, first use your eyes and ears to see if I'm already talking to or listening to someone else. If I am, gently lay your hand on my arm. That will be our little signal that you want to tell me something. I'll put my finger up like this and hold it where you can see it, so you'll know that I felt your hand and I'll get to you just as soon as I can. When it's your turn to talk, I'll turn my head and look at you. Now let's practice."

Melanie started talking to a pretend neighbor in a chair across the room and waited for Jacob's tap on her arm.

This little signal has helped many children learn the good manner of not interrupting. (And helped many mothers remember that their children are waiting to tell them something!)

"Mothers work wonders once they are convinced that wonders are demanded of them."

Home is a great place to practice good manners. Of course, each mother will have a different level of etiquette that she expects her children to learn, but basic good manners should never be neglected.

Charlotte's Thoughts on Manners

1. Help your child role-play various situations and appropriate manners in each.

"Just let them go through the drill of good manners: let them rehearse little scenes in play,—Mary, the lady asking the way to the market; Harry, the boy who directs her, and so on. . . . They will invent a hundred situations, and the behaviour proper to each, and will treasure hints thrown in for their guidance; but this sort of drill should be attempted while children are young, before the tyranny of *mauvaise honte* sets in" (Vol. 1, pp. 132, 133).

2. Encourage good posture and appropriate actions as part of manners.

"Let them go through a position drill—eyes right, hands still, heads up. . . . Encourage them to admire and take pride in light springing movements, and to eschew a heavy gait and clownish action of the limbs" (Vol. 1, p. 133).

Mauvaise honte means "bad or silly shame; bashfulness, sheepishness."

Questions to Ask about Manners

- Is my child practicing how to show good manners in various situations, such as answering the telephone, introducing people, and waiting his turn?
- Is my child progressing toward showing good manners in body language and actions, as well as in words?
- Does my child understand and demonstrate respect to those older than he is and protection to those younger?

Other Quotes on Manners

"Manners are the happy way of doing things."—Ralph Waldo Emerson

"Manners are like the zero in arithmetic; they may not be much in themselves, but they are capable of adding a great deal to the value of everything else."—Freya Stark

"Manners are a sensitive awareness of the feelings of others. If you have that awareness, you have good manners, no matter what fork you use."—Emily Post

"Manners are just a formal expression of how you treat people."—Molly Ivins

Modesty and Purity

Propriety in dress, speech, or conduct; being morally pure in conduct and intention

"My biggest problem with school was gym class," Donna admitted. "It wasn't

"No other part of the world's work is of such supreme difficulty, delicacy and importance, as that of parents in the right bringing up of their children."

Notes

Be sure to encourage modesty between family members.

Be careful not to convey to your child that his private parts are bad. You may want to use the illustration of keeping a special present wrapped up until the set time of celebration. Our children should keep their special private parts "under wraps" until they can celebrate marriage with their spouses.

"Few things are more sad than to see a beautiful body, made for health, strength, and happiness—made in the image of God—injured and destroyed by bad habits."

the exercising that bothered me, it was taking a shower afterwards. I never got used to showering in front of all the other girls."

"Did you ever think that maybe the problem wasn't with you?" Ellen asked. "The problem was with the system. Your sense of modesty was right, and you felt uncomfortable because that modesty was being violated."

Modesty and purity is another character trait that we want to become a habit for our children. As with many other Decency and Propriety habits, modesty can be taught by the attitudes we encourage in our home. Opportunities for discussing modesty and purity will occur as our children grow older, but we would do well to lay the foundation from the early years and have it ready to build upon as those later opportunities come.

Charlotte's Thoughts on Modesty and Purity

1. Keep your child covered, even on his way to and from a bath. Do not allow him to run around naked.

"The operations of the bath afford the mother opportunities to give necessary teaching and training in habits of decency, and a sense of modesty. To let her young child live and grow in Eden-like simplicity is, perhaps, the most tempting and natural course to the mother. But alas! we do not live in the Garden, and it may be well that the child should be trained from the first to the conditions under which he is to live" (Vol. 1, p. 128).

2. Teach your child to respect and protect his "private parts," and don't allow joking or teasing about anyone's private parts.

"To the youngest child, as to our first parents, there is that which is forbidden. In the age of unquestioning obedience, let him know that not all of his body does Almighty God allow him to speak of, think of, display, handle, except for purposes of cleanliness" (Vol. 1, p. 128).

3. Make modesty and purity a matter of obedience in order to protect your young child and a matter of honor to motivate your older child.

"This will be the easier to the mother if she speak of heart, lungs, etc., which, also, we are not allowed to look at or handle, but which have been so enclosed in walls of flesh and bone that we cannot get at them. That which is left open to us is so left, like that tree in the Garden of Eden, as a test of obedience; and in the one case, as in the other, disobedience is attended with certain loss and ruin.

"The sense of prohibition, of sin in disobedience, will be a wonderful safeguard against knowledge of evil to the child brought up in habits of obedience; and still more effective will be the sense of honour, of a charge to keep—the motive of the apostolic injunctions on this subject" (Vol. 1, p. 128).

4. Continue to encourage your older child to remain pure, and pray for him daily.

"Let the mother renew this charge with earnestness on the eve, say, of each birthday, giving the child to feel that by obedience in this matter he may glorify God with his body; let her keep watch against every approach of evil; and let her pray daily that each one of her children may be kept in purity for that day" (Vol. 1, pp. 128, 129).

5. *Challenge your child to purity, choosing your words carefully, and provide a life full of healthy interests and activities.*

"To ignore the possibilities of evil in this kind is to expose the child to frightful risks. At the same time, be it remembered that words which were meant to hinder may themselves be the cause of evil, and that a life full of healthy interests and activities is amongst the surest preventives of secret vice" (Vol. 1, p. 129).

6. *Motivate your child with Scripture and heroic examples about purity.*

"For Chastity we can have no impulse higher than 'Your bodies are the temples of the Holy Ghost'; but how inadequately do we present the thought! The inspiring ideas which should sustain all physical culture and training are very numerous, and teaching on such subjects as Chastity, Fortitude, Courage, Constancy, Prudence, Temperance, with the consideration of heroic examples, should strengthen the hands of parents and teachers for the better physical culture of their charges. Parents would do well to see to it that they turn out their children fit for service, not only by observing the necessary hygienic conditions, but by bringing their bodies under rule, training them in habits and inspiring them with the ideas of knightly service" (Vol. 3, p. 112).

Questions to Ask about Modesty and Purity

- Am I teaching my child to keep his body covered?
- Is my child learning not to joke or tease about a person's private parts?
- Am I teaching siblings to be modest when changing diapers, changing clothes, or taking a bath?
- Is my child learning that his private parts are special, not bad?
- Do I wear modest clothes?
- Am I careful to keep my body covered when my child is present?
- Am I making modesty a matter of obedience with my younger child?
- Is my older child becoming motivated toward modesty and purity by a sense of honor?
- Do I try to keep encouraging my older child to remain pure?
- Do I pray for my child daily in the area of purity?
- Do I seek to be careful in choosing words when I talk about purity?
- Do I encourage my older child to keep his life full of healthy interests and activities?
- Am I seeking to motivate my child with Scripture and heroic examples?

More Quotes on Modesty and Purity

"Modesty is not only an ornament, but also a guard to virtue."—Joseph Addison

Notes

Charlotte wrote directly to young people about purity and chastity in Volume 4, Book 1, pages 21–23 and Book 2, pages 21–40.

"Above all, 'watch unto prayer' and teach your child dependence upon divine aid in this warfare of the spirit; but, also, the absolute necessity for his own efforts."

"Remember that with her clothes, a woman puts off her modesty."—Herodotus

"Let no man despise thy youth; but be thou an example of the believers, in word, in conversation, in charity, in spirit, in faith, in purity."—1 Timothy 4:12

Neatness
Everything in a suitable place, so as to produce a good effect

"Mommy, see how I put the dolls on the shelf?" Susie proudly displayed her work. "I sat one on each side of the little table and put the little dishes out like they were having tea. Don't you think it looks nice?"

Orderliness is good, but you can take it one step further to cultivate another great habit. Think about not just putting items in their place, but arranging them in a way that is pleasing to look at. The habit that Charlotte called "neatness" is a mind-set that we might refer to as "good taste."

Charlotte's Thoughts on Neatness

1. Provide your child with pleasing and suitable surroundings.

"Neatness is akin to order, but is not quite the same thing: it implies not only 'a place for everything, and everything in its place,' but everything in a suitable place, so as to produce a good effect; in fact, *taste* comes into play. The little girl must not only put her flowers in water but arrange them prettily, and must not be put off with some rude kitchen mug or jug for them, or some hideous pink vase, but must have jar or vase graceful in form and harmonious in hue, though it be but a cheap trifle. In the same way, everything in the nursery should be 'neat'— that is, pleasing and suitable" (Vol. 1, pp. 130, 131).

2. Encourage your child to arrange his play things nicely.

"Children should be encouraged to make neat and effective arrangements of their own little properties" (Vol. 1, p. 131).

3. Get rid of any vulgar toys, pictures, or books that are in poor taste.

"Nothing vulgar in the way of print, picture-book, or toy should be admitted—nothing to vitiate a child's taste or introduce a strain of commonness into his nature" (Vol. 1, p. 131).

4. Display one or two well-chosen works of art, even if the prints are inexpensive copies, where your child can see them often.

"It would be hard to estimate the refining, elevating influence of one or two well-chosen works of art, in however cheap a reproduction" (Vol. 1, p. 131).

"Everything in the nursery should be 'neat'—that is, pleasing and suitable."

Questions to Ask about Neatness

- Am I teaching my child good taste through his surroundings?
- Do I encourage my child to arrange his play things nicely?
- Am I allowing my child to have any vulgar toys, pictures, or books that are in poor taste?
- Am I cultivating my child's taste by displaying well-chosen works of art?

More Quotes on Neatness

"Have nothing in your house that you do not know to be useful or believe to be beautiful."—William Morris

"Bad taste is a species of bad morals."—Christian Nestell Bovee

"Arranging a bowl of flowers in the morning can give a sense of quiet in a crowded day."—Anne Morrow Lindbergh

Order
To put things into their proper places; organize; straighten out so as to eliminate confusion

Pam got to her feet and stretched with a sigh. It had been a big job, but she knew it would be worth the time and effort she had spent over the last few days. Two days ago she had begun clearing all the toys off her daughter's shelves and sorting them. She had made three piles: give away, store away for later, and keep on the shelves—plus a big trashbag full of abandoned straws and torn paper-plate puppet faces. Yesterday she had packed up the piles for giving and storing and put them where they belonged. Then she had started arranging the toys that were left to fit on the shelves. This morning she had taken a picture of each shelf with its toys sitting in place. And now she had just finished printing the pictures very small, cutting them out, and taping them to the shelves.

"Now all that Hannah needs to do is put the toys back on the shelves just like in the pictures," she said with a smile. *And all you have to do is make it a part of her regular daily routine to pick up the toys,* she told herself. *Well, if I schedule it right before something she likes to do, it might make things easier for both of us.*

Orderliness comes more easily to some people than to others, but it is a habit that will serve your child well if you can establish it from the early years. An orderly environment promotes orderly thinking. Think about how distracting it can be when, in the middle of a great idea, you have to take five minutes to hunt for a pen and piece of clean paper on which to record that idea!

Orderliness has other advantages, as well. It promotes safety by keeping toys up off the floor where little (and big) feet won't trip over them. It saves money; if you're able to find what you're looking for, you won't go buy another one.

"Truly parents are happy people—to have God's children lent to them."

Notes

See page 28 to learn what was said about cleanliness.

Make sure you have a place for everything! If the child's toy shelves and containers are so full that they are overflowing, it's time to remove some toys. Extra toys can be given away, sold, or packed away for a season and then swapped with the other toys that are in use.

"Let him *always* put away his things as a matter of course, and it is surprising how soon a habit of order is formed."

Orderliness in the home, even in the nursery, is the training ground for your child's future orderly household. Make the effort to instill this habit now.

Charlotte's Thoughts on Order

1. Keep your child's room orderly.

"What has been said about cleanliness applies as much to order—order in the nursery, and orderly habits in the nurse" (Vol. 1, p. 129).

2. Give your child nice things to take care of, not just worn-out and broken items.

"The nursery should not be made the hospital for the disabled or worn-out furniture of the house; cracked cups, chipped plates, jugs and teapots with fractured spouts, should be banished. The children should be brought up to think that when once an article is made unsightly by soil or fracture it is spoiled, and must be replaced; and this rule will prove really economical, for when children and servants find that things no longer 'do,' after some careless injury, they learn to be careful. But, in any case, it is a real detriment to the children to grow up using imperfect and unsightly makeshifts" (Vol. 1, p. 129).

3. Don't allow sentimental emotions to prevent you from teaching your child to be orderly.

"The pleasure grown-up people take in waiting on children is really a fruitful source of mischief;—for instance, in this matter of orderly habits. Who does not know the litter the children leave to be cleared up after them a dozen times a day, in the nursery, garden, drawing-room, wherever their restless little feet carry them? We are a bit sentimental about scattered toys and faded nosegays, and all the tokens of the children's presence; but the fact is, that the lawless habit of scattering should not be allowed to grow upon children. Everybody condemns the mother of a family whose drawers are chaotic, whose possessions are flung about heedlessly; but at least some of the blame should be carried back to *her* mother. It is not as a woman that she has picked up a miserable habit which destroys the comfort, if not the happiness, of her home; the habit of disorder was allowed to grow upon her as a child, and her share of the blame is, that she has failed to cure herself" (Vol. 1, pp. 129, 130).

4. By the age of two, your child should be able to pick up and put away his toys.

"The child of two should be taught to get and to replace his playthings. Begin early. Let it be a pleasure to him, part of his play, to open his cupboard, and put back the doll or the horse each in its own place. Let him *always* put away his things as a matter of course, and it is surprising how soon a habit of order is formed, which will make it pleasant to the child to put away his toys, and irritating to him to see things in the wrong place" (Vol. 1, p. 130).

Questions to Ask about Order

• Am I teaching my child to keep his room orderly?

- Is my child learning to take care of nice things?
- Am I allowing my emotions to prevent me from training my child in the habit of picking up and putting away his play things?
- Has my two-year-old (and any older child) developed this habit of order?
- Am I providing adequate space in which to store my child's things?
- Am I teaching my child that simplicity makes orderliness easier?

More Quotes on Order

"If parents would only see the morality of order, that order in the nursery becomes scrupulousness in after life, and that the training necessary to form the habit is no more, comparatively, than the occasional winding of a clock, which ticks away then of its own accord and without trouble to itself, more pains would be taken to cultivate this important habit."—Charlotte Mason (Vol. 1, p. 130)

"A place for everything, and everything in its place."—Benjamin Franklin

"He who has no taste for order, will be often wrong in his judgment, and seldom considerate or conscientious in his actions."—Johann Kaspar Lavater

"Let all things be done decently and in order."—1 Corinthians 14:40

Regularity
Adhering to a schedule or routine

Half of the children were still sleeping when Anne walked down the hall that morning. She could hear two other children bickering about the bathroom, and one more met her at the end of the hall, complaining that he was hungry.

Whew! thought Anne. *I'm not so sure attending that summer festival last night was a good idea. We stayed up much later than usual, and I'm afraid I'm going to be playing referee a lot today since I have nothing scheduled to keep them occupied.*

Children seem to thrive on regularity and consistency throughout childhood. When they know what to expect, they just seem to function better. Charlotte's writings tell us that the effort of decision-making is one of the hardest and most stressful efforts people are called upon to do. When a child is faced with a whole day of uncertainty, it will take its toll.

By all means, leave room for spontaneity; don't become a slave of the clock. But a consistent and regular routine for a typical day's events will make the household run much more smoothly.

Charlotte's Thoughts on Regularity

1. As soon as possible, get your child on a regular schedule for bedtime.

"The young mother knows that she must put her baby to bed at a proper time,

"I have been brought to look upon habit as the means whereby the parent may make almost anything he chooses of his child."

Feel free to adjust your schedule as necessary in order to keep it operating as your servant, not your master. Different seasons of life demand different daily schedules.

regardless of his cries, even if she leave him to cry two or three times, in order that, for the rest of his baby life, he may put himself sweetly to sleep in the dark without protest" (Vol. 1, p. 131).

2. As soon as possible, get your child on a regular feeding schedule.

"Nothing tends more to generate a habit of self-indulgence than to feed a child, or to allow it to remain out of bed, at unseasonable times, merely because it cries" (Vol. 1, p. 132).

3. Keep a regular schedule, or routine, for the day's events even for your older child.

"The habit of regularity is as attractive to older children as to the infant. The days when the usual programme falls through are, we know, the days when the children are apt to be naughty" (Vol. 1, p. 132).

Questions to Ask about Regularity

- Am I helping my child to develop a regular bedtime?
- Am I training my child to eat at regular intervals throughout the day?
- Am I setting a regular schedule, or routine, for my older child's typical day?
- Am I teaching my child that a schedule is helpful yet flexible?

More Quotes on Regularity

"Schedules become increasingly important to family stability and to a baby's well-being as time goes by. Many children seem to do perfectly well without a schedule in early infancy, when they're extremely portable and can fall asleep or be fed anywhere. Later they often begin to respond to irregular mealtimes and sleep times with regular crying and crankiness."—Arlene Eisenberg, Heidi Murkoff, Sandee Hathaway

"The effort of decision, we have seen, is the greatest effort of life; not the doing of the thing, but the making up of one's mind as to which thing to do first."—Charlotte Mason (Vol. 1, p. 119)

Other Habits of Decency and Propriety

Charlotte mentioned some wonderful character traits only once or twice in her writings without elaborating on them. It's easy not to connect "habits" with "character traits" in our minds. But the two are inseparably linked: "Sow an act, reap a habit; sow a habit, reap a character; sow a character, reap a destiny."

Read on the following pages about the habits she only mentioned, coupled

"The habit of regularity is as attractive to older children as to the infant."

with their definitions and some quotes to encourage you as you lay down the rails that will build these character traits in your child.

Charlotte's Thoughts on Other Habits of Decency and Propriety

1. Almost all of these habits, or characteristics and virtues, can be summed up in the attitude of unselfish love. Focus on that characteristic and the others will come along with it.

"Let us teach these (temperance and thrift) by all means; but also, and equally, diligence, candour, kindness, all the graces that go to make up love and justice, all the habits that ensue in intelligence" (Vol. 5, p. 408).

2. Make these habits a way of life -- the atmosphere of your home. Remember that Education is an Atmosphere, as well as a Discipline and a Life.

"We have already considered a group of half physical habits—order, regularity, neatness—which the child imbibes, so to speak, in this way. But this is not all: habits of gentleness, courtesy, kindness, candour, respect for other people, or—habits quite other than these, are inspired by the child as the very atmosphere of his home, the air he lives in and must grow by" (Vol. 1, p. 137).

"Justice requires that we should take steady care every day to yield his rights to every person we come in contact with; that is, 'to do unto others as we would that they should do unto us: to hurt nobody by word or deed'; therefore we must show gentleness to the persons of others, courtesy to their words, and deference to their opinions, because these things are due. We must be true and just in all our dealing. Veracity, fidelity, simplicity, and sincerity must therefore direct our words. Candour, appreciation, discrimination must guide our thoughts. Fair-dealing, honesty, integrity must govern our actions" (Vol. 4, Book 1, p. 137).

3. Provide plenty of living examples and stories of heroes who exemplify these habits.

"Parents should take pains to have their own thoughts clear as to the manner of virtues they want their children to develop. Candour, fortitude, temperance, patience, meekness, courage, generosity, indeed the whole role of the virtues, would be stimulating subjects for thought and teaching, offering ample illustrations" (Vol. 3, p. 136).

Candor

Freedom from prejudice or malice;
fairness to the opinions of others;
frank, honest, or sincere expression

Quotes on Candor

"Candor is a proof of both a just frame of mind, and of a good tone of

> "Parents should take pains to have their own thoughts clear as to the manner of virtues they want their children to develop."

breeding. It is a quality that belongs equally to the honest man and to the gentleman."—James F. Cooper

"Gracious to all, to none subservient,
Without offense he spoke the word he meant."—Thomas Bailey Aldrich

"Friends, if we be honest with ourselves, we shall be honest with each other."—George Macdonald

"Nothing astonishes men so much as common sense and plain dealing."—Ralph Waldo Emerson

Courage
Mental or moral strength to venture, persevere, and withstand danger, fear, or difficulty

Quotes on Courage

"Courage is contagious. When a brave man takes a stand, the spines of others are stiffened."—Billy Graham

"Courage is not simply one of the virtues, but the form of every virtue at the testing point."—C. S. Lewis

"It is curious that physical courage should be so common in the world and moral courage so rare."—Mark Twain

"Courage is what it takes to stand up and speak; courage is also what it takes to sit down and listen."—Winston Churchill

"Have not I commanded thee? Be strong and of a good courage; be not afraid, neither be thou dismayed: for the Lord thy God is with thee whithersoever thou goest."—Joshua 1:9

"Wait on the Lord: be of good courage, and he shall strengthen thine heart: wait, I say, on the Lord."—Psalm 27:14

Charlotte wrote directly to young people about courage in Volume 4, Book 1, pages 112–117.

"Courage, too, should be something more than the impulse of the moment; it is a natural fire to be fed by heroic example and by the teaching that the thing to be done is always of more consequence than the doer."

Diligence
Steady, earnest, and energetic effort

Quotes on Diligence

"Learning is not attained by chance. It must be sought for with ardor and attended to with diligence."—Abigail Adams

"Laziness means more work in the long run."—C. S. Lewis

"Seest thou a man diligent in his business? he shall stand before kings; he shall not stand before mean men."—Proverbs 22:29

"And whatsoever ye do, do it heartily, as to the Lord, and not unto men."—Colossians 3:23

Fortitude
(This habit is discussed under Physical Habits on page 123.)

Generosity
Liberal in giving

Quotes on Generosity

"The miracle is this—the more we share, the more we have."—Leonard Nimoy

"If nature has made you a giver, your hands are born open, and so is your heart. And though there may be times when your hands are empty, your heart is always full, and you can give things out of that."—Frances Hodgson Burnett

"There is that scattereth, and yet increaseth; and there is that withholdeth more than is meet, but it tendeth to poverty. The liberal soul shall be made fat: and he that watereth shall be watered also himself."—Proverbs 11:24, 25

"You make a living by what you get. You make a life by what you give."—Winston Churchill

Charlotte wrote directly to young people about generosity in Volume 4, Book 1, pages 103–107.

"Every quality has its defect, every defect has its quality. Examine your child; he has qualities, he is generous; see to it that the lovable little fellow, who would give away his soul, is not also rash, impetuous, self-willed, passionate."

Gentleness
Mildness of manners or disposition; free from harshness, sternness, or violence

Quotes on Gentleness

"Nothing is so strong as gentleness, nothing so gentle as real strength."—St. Francis de Sales

"Is not birth, beauty, good shape, discourse, Manhood, learning, gentleness, virtue, youth, liberality, and such like, the spice and salt that season a man?"—William Shakespeare

"But the fruit of the Spirit is love, joy, peace, longsuffering, gentleness, goodness, faith, meekness, temperance: against such there is no law."—Galatians 5:22, 23

"And the servant of the Lord must not strive; but be gentle unto all men, apt to teach, patient."—2 Timothy 2:24

Meekness
Enduring injury without resentment

Quotes on Meekness

"The meek will he guide in judgment: and the meek will he teach his way."—Psalm 25:9

"Glances of true beauty can be seen in the faces of those who live in true meekness."—Henry David Thoreau

"Blessed are the meek: for they shall inherit the earth."—Matthew 5:5

"Take my yoke upon you, and learn of me; for I am meek and lowly in heart: and ye shall find rest unto your souls."—Matthew 11:29

"With all lowliness and meekness, with longsuffering, forbearing one another in love."—Ephesians 4:2

"To speak evil of no man, to be no brawlers, but gentle, shewing all meekness unto all men."—Titus 3:2

Patience
Bearing pains or trials calmly or without complaint; not hasty or impetuous; steadfast despite opposition, difficulty, or adversity

Quotes on Patience

"He that can have patience can have what he will."—Benjamin Franklin

"Follow after righteousness, godliness, faith, love, patience, meekness."—1 Timothy 6:11

"But let patience have her perfect work, that ye may be perfect and entire, wanting nothing."—James 1:4

"Be patient toward all men."—1 Thessalonians 5:14

"Patience and perseverance have a magical effect before which difficulties disappear and obstacles vanish."—John Quincy Adams

"Patience is the companion of wisdom."—St. Augustine

Respect for Other People
(This habit is discussed under Reverence on page 103.)

Temperance
Moderation in action, thought, or feeling; restraint

Quotes on Temperance

"Moral excellence comes about as a result of habit. We become just by doing just acts, temperate by doing temperate acts, brave by doing brave acts."—Aristotle

"And beside this, giving all diligence, add to your faith virtue; and to virtue knowledge; and to knowledge temperance; and to temperance patience; and to patience godliness; and to godliness brotherly kindness; and to brotherly kindness charity."—2 Peter 1:5–7

"And every man that striveth for the mastery is temperate in all things."—1 Corinthians 9:25

Charlotte wrote directly to young people about temperance in Volume 4, Book 1, pages 192 and 193 and Book 2, pages 12–20.

Thrift
Careful management, especially of money

Quotes on Thrift

"Thrift comes too late when you find it at the bottom of your purse."—Seneca

"The habits of the child are, as it were, so many little hammers beating out by slow degrees the character of the man."

Notes

"Waste is worse than loss. The time is coming when every person who lays claim to ability will keep the question of waste before him constantly. The scope of thrift is limitless."—Thomas Edison

"There are but two ways of paying debt: Increase of industry in raising income, increase of thrift in laying out."—Thomas Carlyle

"Do not let the endless succession of small things crowd great ideals out of sight and out of mind."

Chapter 4
Mental Habits

Mental habits require more direct training than habits of Decency and Propriety. "Let us pass on, now, to the consideration of a group of mental habits which are affected by direct training rather than by example" (Vol. 1, p. 137).

These habits will be a great help to a child, cultivating within him a fine-tuned mind that can be ready and reliable for years to come, and giving him an advantage over those whose minds are not as well disciplined. "The second part of our subject—the formation of intellectual habits—need not occupy us long. We know that the possession of some half-dozen such habits makes up what is well called ability. They make a man able to do that which he desires to do with his mental powers, and to labour at the cost of not a tenth part of the waste of tissue which the same work would exact of a person of undisciplined mental habits. We know, too, that the habits in question are acquired through training and are not bestowed as a gift" (Vol. 3, pp. 118, 119).

"I need not refer again to the genesis of a habit; but perhaps most of us set ourselves more definitely to form physical and moral than we do to form intellectual habits. I will only mention a few such, which should be matters of careful training during the period of childhood" (Vol. 3, pp. 119, 120).

In this chapter you will find Charlotte's comments on

Attention	**Observation**
Imagining	**Perfect Execution**
Meditation	**Reading for Instruction**
Memorizing	**Remembering**
Mental Effort	**Thinking**

Plus these habits that Charlotte mentioned but didn't elaborate on.

Accuracy

Concentration

Reflection

Thoroughness

"We know that the possession of some half-dozen such habits makes up what is well called ability."

Attention

*Turning the whole force of the mind
to the subject in hand;
the fixed gaze of the mind*

Carlene closed the book and set it in her lap. Hesitantly, she looked up at her son's and daughter's faces. Both looked blank. *Heather is daydreaming again,* she thought. *And Bill hasn't sat still during the whole time I've been reading.*

"Bill, you start the narration for us. Tell me everything you learned about Nero," Carlene invited with a forced smile.

"I don't know," Bill replied.

"Didn't you learn anything?" asked Carlene.

"Yes, but I forgot," answered Bill.

"What about you, Heather? Can you tell me about Nero?" Carlene shifted her gaze to her daughter.

Heather started and turned her head toward Carlene. "What did you say, Mom?" she inquired half-heartedly.

Carlene sighed. How could she teach them anything if they wouldn't pay attention?

How, indeed? The habit of attention is one that Charlotte spent a lot of time and ink on. It is the starting point for so much of learning! Obviously, you cannot force someone to pay attention. But there are several things you can do to encourage it and cultivate it as a habit in your child's life.

Charlotte's Thoughts on Attention

1. The habit of attention is of first importance because all the other intellectual gifts depend on it.

"First, we put the *habit of Attention*, because the highest intellectual gifts depend for their value upon the measure in which their owner has cultivated the habit of attention. To explain why this habit is of such supreme importance, we must consider the operation of one or two of the laws of thought. But just recall, in the meantime, the fixity of attention with which the trained professional man—the lawyer, the doctor, the man of letters—listens to a roundabout story, throws out the padding, seizes the facts, sees the bearing of every circumstance, and puts the case with new clearness and method; and contrast this with the wandering eye and random replies of the uneducated;—and you see that to differentiate people according to their power of attention is to employ a legitimate test" (Vol. 1, p. 137).

"It is impossible to overstate the importance of this habit of attention. It is, to quote words of weight, 'within the reach of every one, and should be made the primary object of all mental discipline'; for whatever the natural gifts of the child, it is only so far as the habit of attention is cultivated in him that he is able to make use of them" (Vol. 1, p. 146).

The habit of attention is one of the "Top Three" habits that Charlotte talked about most. The other two are obedience (p. 96) and truthfulness (p. 110).

"It is impossible to overstate the importance of this habit of attention."

"No intellectual habit is so valuable as that of attention; it is a mere habit but it is also the hall-mark of an educated person" (Vol. 6, p. 99).

2. The mind naturally makes multiple associations, but your child should learn to control his flitting thoughts.

"We will consider, then, the nature and the functions of attention. The mind—with the possible exception of the state of coma—is never idle; ideas are for ever passing through the brain, by day and by night, sleeping or walking, mad or sane. We take a great deal too much upon ourselves when we suppose that *we* are the authors and intenders of the thoughts we think. The most we can do is to give direction to these trains of thought in the comparatively few moments when we *are* regulating the thoughts of our hearts. We see in dreams—the rapid dance of ideas through the brain during lighter sleep—how ideas follow one another in a general way. In the wanderings of delirium, in the fancies of the mad, the inconsequent prattle of the child, and the babble of the old man, we see the same thing, *i.e.* the law according to which ideas course through the mind when they are left to themselves. You talk to a child about glass—you wish to provoke a proper curiosity as to how glass is made, and what are its uses. Not a bit of it; he wanders off to Cinderella's glass slipper; then he tells you about *his* godmother who gave him a boat; then about the ship in which Uncle Harry went to America; then he wonders why you do not wear spectacles, leaving you to guess that Uncle Harry does so. But the child's ramblings are not whimsical; they follow a law, the law of association of ideas, by which any idea presented to the mind recalls some other idea which has been at any time associated with it—as glass and Cinderella's slipper; and that, again some idea associated with it. Now this law of association of ideas is a good servant and a bad master. To have this aid in recalling the events of the past, the engagements of the present, is an infinite boon; but to be at the mercy of associations, to have no power to think what we choose when we choose, but only as something 'puts it in our head,' is to be no better than an imbecile" (Vol. 1, pp. 138, 139).

3. Homeschooling becomes wearisome when your child is constantly thinking about something other than his lessons.

"A vigorous effort of will should enable us at any time to fix our thoughts. Yes; but a vigorous self-compelling will is the flower of a developed character; and while the child has no character to speak of, but only natural disposition, who is to keep humming-tops out of a geography lesson, or a doll's sofa out of a French verb? Here is the secret of the weariness of the home schoolroom—the children are thinking all the time about something else than their lessons; or rather, they are at the mercy of the thousand fancies that flit through their brains, each in the train of the last. 'Oh, Miss Smith,' said a little girl to her governess, 'there are so *many* things more interesting than lessons to think about!'

"Where is the harm? In this: not merely that the children are wasting time, though that is a pity; but that they are forming a desultory habit of mind, and reducing their own capacity for mental effort" (Vol. 1, p. 139).

4. Encourage your infant to look at and play with an object a little longer than he is first inclined to.

"The help, then, is not the will of the child but in the *habit of attention*, a habit

If your child has already formed a habit of dawdling, see chapter 11 for suggestions on replacing that bad habit with a habit of attention.

"No intellectual habit is so valuable as that of attention."

to be cultivated even in the infant. A baby, notwithstanding his wonderful powers of observation, has no power of attention; in a minute, the coveted plaything drops from listless little fingers, and the wandering glance lights upon some new joy. But even at this stage the habit of attention may be trained: the discarded plaything is picked up, and, with 'Pretty!' and dumb show, the mother keeps the infant's eyes fixed for fully a couple of minutes—and this is his first lesson in attention" (Vol. 1, pp. 139, 140).

5. Captivate your older child's interest in an object; help him look at it long enough to get a real acquaintance with it before moving on.

"Later, as we have seen, the child is eager to see and handle every object that comes in his way. But watch him at his investigations: he flits from thing to thing with less purpose than a butterfly amongst the flowers, staying at nothing long enough to get the good out of it. It is the mother's part to supplement the child's quick observing faculty with the habit of attention. She must see to it that he does not flit from this to that, but looks long enough at one thing to get a real acquaintance with it.

"Is little Margaret fixing round eyes on a daisy she has plucked? In a second, the daisy will be thrown away, and a pebble or buttercup will charm the little maid. But the mother seizes the happy moment. She makes Margaret see that the daisy is a bright yellow eye with *white* eyelashes round it; that all the day long it lies there in the grass and looks up at the great sun, never blinking as Margaret would do, but keeping its eye wide open. And that is why it is called daisy, 'day's eye,' because its eye is always looking at the sun which makes the day. And what does Margaret think it does at night, when there is no sun? It does what little boys and girls do; it just shuts up its eye with its white lashes tipped with pink, and goes to sleep till the sun comes again in the morning. By this time the daisy has become interesting to Margaret; she looks at it with big eyes after her mother has finished speaking, and then, very likely, cuddles it up to her breast or gives it a soft little kiss. Thus the mother will contrive ways to invest every object in the child's world with interest and delight" (Vol. 1, p. 140).

6. Play a game of "What Did You See?" with your child.

"Winter walks, too, whether in town or country, give great opportunities for cultivating the habit of attention. The famous conjurer, Robert Houdin, relates in his autobiography, that he and his son would pass rapidly before a shop window, that of a toy-shop, for instance, and each cast an attentive glance upon it. A few steps further on each drew paper and pencil from his pocket, and tried which could enumerate the greater number of the objects momentarily seen in passing. The boy surprised his father in quickness of apprehension, being often able to write down forty objects, whilst his father could scarcely reach thirty; yet on their returning to verify his statement, the son was rarely found to have made a mistake. Here is a hint for a highly educational amusement for many a winter's walk" (Vol. 1, pp. 86, 87).

7. Never let your child dawdle over a lesson; put it aside for a dissimilar lesson, then return to it with freshened wits and try to make it bright and pleasant.

"But the tug-of-war begins with the lessons of the schoolroom. Even the child

"It is the mother's part to supplement the child's quick observing faculty with the habit of attention."

who has gained the habit of attention to *things*, finds *words* a weariness. This is a turning-point in the child's life, and the moment for mother's tact and vigilance. In the first place, never let the child *dawdle* over copybook or sum, sit dreaming with his book before him. When a child grows stupid over a lesson, it is time to put it away. Let him do another lesson as unlike the last as possible, and then go back with freshened wits to his unfinished task. If mother or governess have been unwary enough to let the child 'moon' over a lesson, she must just exert her wits to pull him through; the lesson must be done, of course, but must be made bright and pleasant to the child" (Vol. 1, p. 141).

8. Keep variety in the day's lessons and try to preserve your child's natural desire for knowledge.

"The teacher should have some knowledge of the principles of education; should know what subjects are best fitted for the child considering his age, and how to make these subjects attractive; should know, too, how to vary the lessons, so that each power of the child's mind should rest after effort, and some other power be called into play. She should know how to incite the child to effort through his desire of approbation, of excelling, of advancing, his desire of knowledge, his love of his parents, his sense of duty, in such a way that no one set of motives be called unduly into play to the injury of the child's character. But the danger she must be especially alive to, is the substitution of any other natural desire for that of knowledge, which is equally natural, and is adequate for all the purposes of education" (Vol. 1, p. 141).

"Of course, the most obvious means of quickening and holding the attention of children lies in the attractiveness of knowledge itself, and in the real appetite for knowledge with which they are endowed. But how successful faulty teachers are in curing children of any desire to know, is to be seen in many a schoolroom" (Vol. 1, p. 145).

9. Schedule short, alternating lessons with a definite time-table in which to finish them.

"Let us look in at a home schoolroom managed upon sound principles. In the first place, there is a time-table, written out fairly, so that the child knows what he has to do and how long each lesson is to last. This idea of definite work to be finished in a given time is valuable to the child, not only as training him in habits of order, but in diligence; he learns that one time is *not* 'as good as another'; that there is no right time left for what is not done in its own time; and this knowledge alone does a great deal to secure the child's *attention* to his work. Again, the lessons are short, seldom more than twenty minutes in length for children under eight; and this, for two or three reasons. The sense that there is not much time for his sums or his reading, keeps the child's wits on the alert and helps to fix his attention; he has time to learn just so much of any one subject as it is good for him to take in at once: and if the lessons be judiciously alternated—sums first, say, while the brain is quite fresh; then writing, or reading—some more or less mechanical exercise, by way of a rest; and so on, the programme varying a little from day to day, but the same principle throughout—a 'thinking' lesson first, and a 'painstaking' lesson to follow,—the child gets through his morning

"When a child grows stupid over a lesson, it is time to put it away."

Notes

Here are the approximate grade breakdowns and lesson times used in Charlotte Mason's schools:
• *First through Third Grades: 10–20 minutes*
• *Fourth through Sixth Grades: 20–30 minutes*
• *Seventh through Ninth Grades: 30–45 minutes (though a couple of subjects, like mental math, were still at the 10-minute limit)*

See page 131 for a description of drill, or Swedish Drill.

See chapter 8 for Charlotte's thoughts on family reading.

"The power of reading with perfect attention will not be gained by the child who is allowed to moon over his lessons."

lessons without any sign of weariness" (Vol. 1, p. 142).

"The power of reading with perfect attention will not be gained by the child who is allowed to moon over his lessons. For this reason, reading lessons must be short; ten minutes or a quarter of an hour of fixed attention is enough for children of the ages we have in view, and a lesson of this length will enable a child to cover two or three pages of his book. The same rule as to the length of a lesson applies to children whose lessons are read to them because they are not yet able to read for themselves" (Vol. 1, p. 230).

"Considering that under the head of 'Education by Books' some half-dozen groups of subjects are included, with several subjects in each group, the practical teacher will be inclined to laugh at what will seem to him Education in Utopia. In practice, however, we find that the use of books makes for short hours. No book-work or writing, no preparation or report, is done in the *Parents' Review* School, except between the hours of 9 and 11.30 for the lowest class, to 9 and 1 for the highest, with half an hour's interval for drill, etc.

"From one to two hours, according to age and class, are given in the afternoons to handicrafts, field-work, drawing, etc.; and the evenings are absolutely free, so that the children have leisure for hobbies, family reading, and the like. We are able to get through a greater variety of subjects, and through more work in each subject, in a shorter time than is usually allowed, because children taught in this way get the habit of close attention and are carried on by steady interest" (Vol. 3, p. 240).

"Child or man, we spend half our time in being bored; and we are bored because our thoughts wander from the thing in hand—we are inattentive. When for a moment we do brace ourselves to an act of attention, the invigorating effect of such act is surprising. We are alive; and it is so good to be alive that we seek the fitful stimulus of excitement—to be the more listless after than before, because we have been stimulated and not invigorated. Being bored becomes a habit; we secretly look forward with longing to the end of every occupation or amusement, and are ready to take up with any 'crank' that promises distraction and fuller living, for however short a time. When we have used up that interest, another may occur.

"That we cannot find life enough for our living is perhaps one of these 'shoots of everlastingnesse' (not always 'bright') which remind us that we are the 'children of an infinite hope.' But we may not check these growing pains by any means which stunt our growth; and, to begin with the children, we may do something to keep them from getting into the habit of being bored. As it is, the best children pay attention probably for about one-third of a given lesson; for the rest of the time they are at the mercy of volatile thoughts, and at the end they are fagged, not so much by the lesson as by the throng of vagrant fancies which has played upon their inattentive minds.

"How, if we tried the same quantity of work in one-third of the time with the interest which induces fixed attention? This would enable us to reduce working-hours by one-third, and at the same time to get in a good many more subjects, having regard to a child's real need for knowledge of many kinds: the children would not be bored, they would discover the delightfulness of knowledge, and we should all benefit" (Vol. 5, pp. 409, 410).

10. Use natural consequences to motivate your child not to dawdle.

"Even with regular lessons and short lessons, a further stimulus may be occasionally necessary to secure the attention of the child. His desire of approbation may ask the stimulus, not only of a word of praise, but of something in the shape of a reward to secure his utmost efforts. Now, rewards should be dealt out to the child upon principle: they should be the *natural consequences* of his good conduct.

"What is the natural consequence of work well and quickly done? Is it not the enjoyment of ampler leisure? The boy is expected to do two right sums in twenty minutes: he does them in ten minutes; the remaining ten minutes are his own, fairly earned, in which he should be free for a scamper in the garden, or any delight he chooses. His writing task is to produce six perfect *m*'s: he writes six lines with only one good *m* in each line, the time for the writing lesson is over and he has none for himself; or, he is able to point out six good *m*'s in his first line, and he has the rest of the time to draw steamboats and railway trains. This possibility of letting the children occupy themselves variously in the few minutes they may gain at the end of each lesson, is compensation which the home schoolroom offers for the zest which the sympathy of numbers, and emulation, are supposed to give to school work" (Vol. 1, pp. 142, 143).

11. Any grades or good marks should be given for conduct rather than for cleverness.

"As for emulation, a very potent means of exciting and holding the attention of children, it is often objected that a desire to excel, to do better than others, implies an unloving temper, which the educator should rather repress than cultivate. Good marks of some kind are usually the rewards of those who do best, and it is urged that these good marks are often the cause of ungenerous rivalry. Now, the fact is, the children are being trained to live in the world, and in the world we all *do* get good marks of one kind or another, prize, or praise, or both, according as we excel others, whether in football or tennis, or in picture-painting or poem-making. There are envyings and heart-burnings amongst those who come in second best; so it has been from beginning, and doubtless will be to the end. If the child is to go out into an emulous world, why, it may possibly be well that he should be brought up in an emulous school. But here is where the mother's work comes in. She can teach her child to be first without vanity, and to be last without bitterness; that is, she can bring him up in such a hearty outgoing of love and sympathy that joy in his brother's success takes the sting out of his own failure, and regret for his brother's failure leaves no room for self-glorification. Again, if a system of marks be used as a stimulus to attention and effort, the good marks should be given for *conduct* rather than for *cleverness*—that is, they should be within everybody's reach: every child may get his mark for punctuality, order, attention, diligence, obedience, gentleness; and therefore, marks of this kind may be given without danger of leaving a rankling sense of injustice in the breast of the child who fails. Emulation becomes suicidal when it is used as the incentive to intellectual effort, because the desire for knowledge subsides in proportion as the desire to excel becomes active. As a matter of fact,

"This act, of bringing the whole mind to bear, may be trained into a *habit* at the will of the parent or teacher, who attracts and holds the child's attention by means of a sufficient motive."

marks of any sort, even for conduct, distract the attention of children from their proper work, which is in itself interesting enough to secure good behaviour as well as attention" (Vol. 1, pp. 143, 144).

"Marks, prizes, places, rewards, punishments, praise, blame, or other inducements are not necessary to secure attention, which is voluntary, immediate and surprisingly perfect" (Vol. 6, p. 7).

12. Attention is not a faculty of the mind, but a habit of the will that any child may be trained in.

"It is evident that *attention* is no 'faculty' of the mind; indeed, it is *very* doubtful how far the various operations of the mind should be described as 'faculties' at all. *Attention* is hardly even an operation of the mind, but is simply the act by which the whole mental force is applied to the subject in hand. This act, of bringing the whole mind to bear, may be trained into a *habit* at the will of the parent or teacher, who attracts and holds the child's attention by means of a sufficient motive" (Vol. 1, p. 145).

13. Enlist your older child's will to make himself pay attention by explaining how he can consciously focus his flitting thoughts.

"As the child gets older, he is taught to bring *his own will* to bear; *to make himself* attend in spite of the most inviting suggestions from without. He should be taught to feel a certain triumph in compelling himself to fix his thoughts. Let him know what the real difficulty is, how it is the nature of his mind to be incessantly thinking, but how the thoughts, if left to themselves, will always run off from one thing to another, and that the struggle and the victory required of him is to fix his thoughts upon the task in hand. 'You have done your *duty*,' with a look of sympathy from his mother, is a reward for the child who has made this effort in the strength of his growing will" (Vol. 1, pp. 145, 146).

14. Be on the watch from the beginning against your child's forming the habit of inattention.

"If it were only as it saves wear and tear, a perpetual tussle between duty and inclination, it is worth while for the mother to lay herself out to secure that her child never does a lesson into which he does not put his heart. And that is no difficult undertaking; the thing is, to be on the watch from the beginning against the formation of the contrary habit of *in*attention" (Vol. 1, p. 146).

15. Be careful not to require too much work or too difficult of work from your child.

"But it cannot be too much borne in mind that attention is, to a great extent, the product of the educated mind; that is, one can only attend in proportion as one has the intellectual power of developing the topic" (Vol. 1, p. 146).

"A great deal has been said lately about overpressure, and we have glanced at one or two of the causes whose effects go by this name. But truly, one of the most fertile causes of an overdone brain is a failure in the habit of attention. I suppose we are all ready to admit that it is not the things we *do*, but the things we

It's a good idea to severely limit your child's TV watching, or eliminate it entirely. Many TV programs and commercials sabotage attention spans by changing the camera angle or picture on the screen every one or two seconds.

"Be on the watch from the beginning against the formation of the contrary habit of *in*attention."

fail to do, which fatigue us, with the sense of omission, with the worry of hurry in overtaking our tasks. And this is almost the only cause of failure in work in the case of the healthy schoolboy or schoolgirl: wandering wits hinder a lesson from being fully taken in at the right moment; that lesson becomes a bugbear, continually wanted henceforth and never there; and the sense of loss tries the young scholar more than would the attentive reception of a dozen such lessons" (Vol. 1, pp. 146, 147).

16. *Require your child to narrate after a single reading of the material.*

"I have already spoken of the importance of a single reading. If a child is not able to narrate what he has read once, let him not get the notion that he may, or that he must, read it again. A look of slight regret because there is a gap in his knowledge will convict him" (Vol. 1, pp. 229, 230).

"The simplest way of dealing with a paragraph or a chapter is to require the child to narrate its contents after a single attentive reading,—*one* reading, however slow, should be made a condition; for we are all too apt to make sure we shall have another opportunity of finding out 'what 'tis all about' There is the weekly review if we fail to get a clear grasp of the news of the day; and, if we fail a second time, there is a monthly or a quarterly review or an annual summing up: in fact, many of us let present-day history pass by us with easy minds, feeling sure that, in the end, we shall be *compelled* to see the bearings of events. This is a bad habit to get into; and we should do well to save our children by not giving them the vague expectation of second and third and tenth opportunities to do that which should have been done at first" (Vol. 3, pp. 179, 180).

"A single reading is insisted on, because children have naturally great power of attention; but this force is dissipated by the re-reading of passages, and also, by questioning, summarizing, and the like" (Vol. 6, p. xxx).

"All school work should be conducted in such a manner that children are aware of the responsibility of learning; it is their business to know that which has been taught. To this end the subject matter should not be repeated. We ourselves do not attend to the matters in our daily paper which we know we shall meet with again in a weekly review, nor to that if there is a monthly review in prospect; these repeated aids result in our being persons of wandering attention and feeble memory. To allow repetition of a lesson is to shift the responsibility for it from the shoulders of the pupil to those of the teacher who says, in effect,—"I'll see that you know it," so his pupils make no effort of attention. Thus the same stale stuff is repeated again and again and the children get bored and restive, ready for pranks by way of a change" (Vol. 6, pp. 74, 75).

"A *single reading* is a condition insisted upon because a naturally desultory habit of mind leads us all to put off the effort of attention as long as a second or third chance of coping with our subject is to be hoped for. It is, however, a mistake to speak of the 'effort of attention.' Complete and entire attention is a natural function which requires no effort and causes no fatigue; the anxious labour of mind of which we are at times aware comes when attention wanders and has again to be brought to the point; but the concentration at which most

You can reinforce this principle of your child's learning to pay attention the first time by being careful to give instructions or comments only once in everyday situations. Many children get in the bad habit of automatically asking, "What?" or "What did you say?" every time someone says something to them. Don't get caught in the trap of repeating yourself.

"It is impossible to fix attention on that which we have heard before and know we shall hear again."

teachers aim is an innate provision for education and is not the result of training or effort. Our concern is to afford matter of a sufficiently literary character, together with the certainty that no second or third opportunity for knowing a given lesson will be allowed" (Vol. 6, pp. 171, 172).

"A second reading would be fatal because no one can give full attention to that which he has heard before and expects to hear again. Attention will go halt all its days if we accustom it to the crutch" (Vol. 6, p. 258).

"I dwell on the single reading because, let me repeat, it is impossible to fix attention on that which we have heard before and know we shall hear again" (Vol. 6, p. 261).

17. Any homework should also be completed well within an assigned time; however, students following the Charlotte Mason methods rarely have homework.

"The younger children, who have fewer or no home tasks, and take less time for practising, will have the more for play. But, if the schoolgirl is to get two or three hours intact, she will owe it to her mother's firmness as much as to her good management. In the first place, that the school tasks be done, and done well, *in the assigned time*, should be a most fixed law. The young people will maintain that it is impossible, but let the mother insist; she will thereby cultivate the habit of *attention*, the very key to success in every pursuit, as well as secure for her children's enjoyment the time they would dissipate if left to themselves. It seldom happens that home work is given which should occupy more than an hour to an hour and a half, and a longer time is spent in the habit of mental dawdling—a real wasting of brain substance. It is a mistake to suppose that efforts in this direction run counter to the intention of the teachers; on the contrary, the greatest impediment they meet with is that mental inertness in the children, who will rather dawdle for an hour over a task than brace the attention for five minutes' steady effort. There is promise that a certain strain will, by-and-by, be taken off home life by the removal of home work or evening 'preparation' from the school curriculum. Teachers will gradually discover that if they let their pupils work from fitting books in the three or four school hours, more ground will be covered in less time, and the occasion for home tasks (or evening work in schools) will disappear" (Vol. 5, pp. 194, 195).

18. Enforcing a time-table for other everyday activities can reinforce the concept of natural consequences.

"Firmness on the mother's part in enforcing promptness in the taking off and putting on of outdoor clothes, etc., and punctuality at meals, and in not allowing one occupation to overlap another, secures many a half-hour of pleasant leisure for the young people, and has the double advantage of also making them feel themselves under a firm *home rule*" (Vol. 5, pp. 195, 196).

19. Encourage your child to give full attention by using lots of good books and minimal oral teaching.

"Children no more come into the world without provision for dealing with

"We are bored because our thoughts wander from the thing in hand—we are inattentive."

knowledge than without provision for dealing with food. They bring with them not only that intellectual appetite, the desire of knowledge, but also an enormous, an unlimited power of attention to which the power of retention (memory) seems to be attached, as one digestive process succeeds another, until the final assimilation. "Yes," it will be said, "they are capable of much curiosity and consequent attention but they can only occasionally be beguiled into attending to their lessons." Is not that the fault of the lessons, and must not these be regulated as carefully with regard to the behaviour of mind as the children's meals are with regard to physical considerations?

"Let us consider this behaviour in a few aspects. The mind concerns itself only with thoughts, imaginations, reasoned arguments; it declines to assimilate the facts unless in combination with its proper pabulum; it, being active, is wearied in the passive attitude of a listener, it is as much bored in the case of a child by the discursive twaddle of the talking teacher as in that of a grown-up by conversational twaddle; it has a natural preference for literary form; given a more or less literary presentation, the curiosity of the mind is enormous and embraces a vast variety of subjects" (Vol. 6, pp. 14, 15).

"Attention is unfailing, prompt and steady when matter is presented suitable to a child's intellectual requirements, if the presentation be made with the conciseness, directness, and simplicity proper to literature" (Vol. 6, p. 17).

"We know that young people are enormously interested in the subject and give concentrated attention if we give them the right books. We are aware that our own discursive talk is usually a waste of time and a strain on the scholars' attention" (Vol. 6, p. 171).

"Give children the sort of knowledge that they are fitted to assimilate, served in a literary medium, and they will pay great attention" (Vol. 6, p. 257).

20. *The habit of attention can produce a lifelong habit of study.*

"We might hope that, instead of shutting up our books when we leave school or college, each of us, under ninety say, would have his days varied and the springs of life renewed by periods of definite study: we should all be students, the working-man as well as the man of leisure. The writer knew a man of ninety who then began to study Spanish. We know how our late Queen began the study of Hindustani at seventy, and we all know of work of great value accomplished by aged persons.

"But this highly varied intellectual work must not have the passing character of an amusement (is not this the danger of lectures?). Continuation and progression must mark every study, so that each day we go on from where we left off, and know that we are covering fresh ground. Perhaps some day we shall come to perceive that moral and spiritual progression are also for us, not by way of distinction, but for us in common with all men, and because we are human beings.

"Much and varied knowledge, the habit of study (begun early and continued through life), some acquaintance with the principles of an ordered moral life, some knowledge of economic science, should help in the making of well-ordered, well-balanced persons, capable of living without weariness, and without a

"We know that young people are enormously interested in the subject and give concentrated attention if we give them the right books."

disordered desire for notice from other people" (Vol. 5, pp. 410, 411).

Questions to Ask about Attention

- Am I working on the habit of attention as a top priority?
- Is my child working toward making appropriate mental associations without letting those associative thoughts control him?
- Do I have my child's attention during homeschool lessons?
- Am I encouraging my child to look at an object longer than is his natural inclination?
- Do I sometimes play "What Did You See?" with my child?
- Am I learning to put aside any lesson that my child is dawdling over, provide a change of pace, then return and attempt to make it bright and pleasant?
- Do I try to vary the day's lessons and encourage my child's desire for knowledge?
- Are our lessons short with a definite time-table scheduled?
- Am I progressing in using natural consequences to motivate my child?
- Do I emphasize conduct and character over cleverness?
- Am I mistakenly excusing my child's inattentiveness as lack of ability instead of treating it as a bad habit?
- Am I helping my older child learn how to fix his thoughts on the matter at hand?
- Am I careful to avoid things that might encourage inattentiveness in my child?
- Have I been expecting too much work or too difficult of work from my child?
- Do I require my child to narrate after a single reading?
- Do I require any homework to be done within a set time?
- Am I trying to use the time-table idea and natural consequences with everyday activities?
- Is my child making progress toward not being bored constantly?
- Am I trying to use good books and minimal oral teaching in lessons?
- Am I modeling a lifelong habit of study and learning?

More Quotes on Attention

"If I have ever made any valuable discoveries, it has been owing more to patient attention, than to any other talent."—Isaac Newton

"To the attentive eye, each moment of the year has its own beauty, and in the same field, it beholds, every hour, a picture which was never seen before, and which shall never be seen again"—Ralph Waldo Emerson

"My son, attend to my words; incline thine ear unto my sayings. Let them not depart from thine eyes; keep them in the midst of thine heart."—Proverbs 4:20, 21

"Attention is the power and habit of concentrating every faculty on the thing in hand. Now this habit of attention, parents, mothers especially, are taught to encourage and cultivate in their children from early infancy."

Imagining
Forming a mental image of something that is not present

Pam lay in her stifling bunk, listening for that telltale high-pitched buzz in the dark. She wasn't sure she liked camping after all. It was bad enough to be hot and sweaty with no air conditioning, but that hole in the screen was really the frosting on the cake! It was unfair to have a battalion of blood-sucking insects attack when you couldn't see them and you were trying to go to sleep!

Then out of the darkness Pam heard her daughter call quietly, "Mom?"

"Yes, dear."

"I wonder if Jesus had mosquitoes biting Him when He hung on the cross," the little girl voiced her thoughts. "It would have been awful not to be able to swat at them."

Pam's daughter had traveled in her thoughts to another time and place. Her imagination had made the scene become real, and she would never forget it. Imagining is a wonderful tool to have at your disposal when learning about other times and places! Read on for Charlotte's thoughts on this habit.

Charlotte wrote directly to young people about imagination in Volume 4, Book 1, pages 48–53.

Charlotte's Thoughts on Imagining

1. Alternate your child's lessons and activities between physical mechanics (like writing), strictly intellectual (like oral math), imagination (like picture study), and reason (like science).

"All their lessons will afford scope for some slight exercise of the children's thinking power, some more and some less, and the lessons must be judiciously alternated, so that the more mechanical efforts succeed the more strictly intellectual, and that the pleasing exercise of the imagination, again, succeed efforts of reason" (Vol. 1, p. 151).

"The brain, or some portion of the brain, becomes exhausted when any given function has been exercised too long. The child has been doing sums for some time, and is getting unaccountably stupid: take away his slate and let him read history, and you find his wits fresh again. Imagination, which has had no part in the sums, is called into play by the history lesson, and the child brings a lively unexhausted power to his new work. School time-tables are usually drawn up with a view to give the brain of the child variety of work; but the secret of weariness children often show in the home schoolroom is, that no such judicious change of lessons is contrived" (Vol. 1, p. 24).

"Every child should leave school with at least a couple of hundred pictures by great masters hanging permanently in the halls of his imagination, to say nothing of great buildings, sculpture, beauty of form and colour in things he sees. Perhaps we might secure at least a hundred lovely landscapes too,—sunsets, cloudscapes, star-light nights" (Vol. 6, p. 43).

"Imagination has the property of magical expansion, the more it holds the more it will hold."

Notes

You can search for good books by age level in the CM Bookfinder at http://apps. simplycharlottemason.com/

2. Let your child have funny books, but do not give him too much nonsense reading.

"By the way, it is a pity when the sense of the ludicrous is cultivated in children's books at the expense of better things. *Alice in Wonderland* is a delicious feast of absurdities, which none of us, old or young, could afford to spare; but it is doubtful whether the child who reads it has the delightful imaginings, the realising of the unknown, with which he reads *The Swiss Family Robinson*.

"This point is worth considering in connection with Christmas books for the little people. Books of 'comicalities' cultivate no power but the sense of the incongruous; and though life is the more amusing for the possession of such a sense, when cultivated to excess it is apt to show itself a flippant habit. *Diogenes and the Naughty Boys of Troy* is irresistible, but it is not the sort of thing the children will live over and over, and 'play at' by the hour, as we have all played at Robinson Crusoe finding the footprints. They must have 'funny books,' but do not give the children too much nonsense-reading" (Vol. 1, pp. 151, 152).

3. Nurture your child's imagination with good story books.

"Now imagination does not descend, full-grown, to take possession of an empty house; like every other power of the mind, it is the merest germ of a power to begin with, and grows by what it gets; and childhood, the age of faith, is the time for its nourishing. The children should have the joy of living in far lands, in other persons, in other times—a delightful double existence; and this joy they will find, for the most part, in their story-books" (Vol. 1, p. 153).

4. Provide history and geography lessons that capture your child's imagination.

"Their lessons, too, history and geography, should cultivate their conceptive powers. If the child do not live in the times of his history lesson, be not at home in the climes his geography book describes, why, these lessons will fail of their purpose. But let lessons do their best, and the picture-gallery of the imagination is poorly hung if the child have not found his way into the realms of fancy" (Vol. 1, p. 153).

"The peculiar value of geography lies in its fitness to nourish the mind with ideas, and to furnish the imagination with pictures" (Vol. 1, p. 272).

"Imagination does not stir at the suggestion of the feeble, much-diluted stuff that is too often put into children's hands" (Vol. 1, p. 294).

"Let a child have the meat he requires in his history readings, and in the literature which naturally gathers round this history, and imagination will bestir itself without any help of ours; the child will live out in detail a thousand scenes of which he only gets the merest hint" (Vol. 1, pp. 294, 295).

"But we must read History and think about it to understand how these things can be; and we owe a great debt of gratitude to the historians, of whom Herodotus has been called the 'father,' who called in Imagination to picture for them the men and events of the past (about which they had read and searched

"They must have 'funny books,' but do not give the children too much nonsense-reading."

diligently), so that everything seemed to take place again before their eyes, and they were able to write of it for us. But their seeing and writing is not of much use to us unless, in our case, Lord Intellect invites Imagination to go forth with him, and we think of things and figure them to ourselves, until at last they are real and alive to us" (Vol. 4, Book 1, p. 38).

"It would appear that nature opens to all children, one way or other, a perception of time past, History, and of space remote, Geography, as if these ideas were quite necessary nutriment for the mind of a child; and what is to be said for a school education that either eliminates this necessary food altogether, or serves it up in dry-as-dust morsels upon which the imagination cannot work?" (Vol. 5, p. 283).

5. *Allow your child to illustrate stories or poems.*

"They produce, also, illustrations of tales or poems, which leave much to seek in the matter of drawing, and are of little value as art instruction, but are useful imaginative exercises" (Vol. 3, p. 239).

Questions to Ask about Imagining

- Am I trying to alternate my child's lessons and activities between physical, intellectual, imagination, and reasoning skills?
- Am I careful not to give my child excessive nonsense books?
- Does my child have good story books?
- Am I taking steps toward making our history and geography lessons capture my child's imagination?
- Do I allow my child to illustrate stories or poems?

More Quotes on Imagining

"Using your imagination is the one time in life you can really go anywhere."—Ann Patchett

"The world is but a canvas to the imagination."—Henry David Thoreau

"There are no days in life so memorable as those which vibrated to some stroke of the imagination."—Ralph Waldo Emerson

"The soul never thinks without a mental picture."—Aristotle

"To see a thing clearly in the mind makes it begin to take form."—Henry Ford

Meditation
Following out a subject to all its issues

Randy thought again about the job ahead. There had to be a better way to get

"Imagination is stored with those images supplied day by day."

Do not confuse this type of meditation with an Eastern-religion-style meditation that advises you to empty your mind. The meditation endorsed here is one that requires active use of your mind in examining an issue from all sides and considering its various aspects carefully.

all that hay up into the top loft without involving three people, each pitching it to the next level. Then Randy remembered the grappling fork his dad had built years ago.

That one was for hauling logs, Randy thought. *But couldn't I modify it to work with hay? And what do we have laying around the farm that I could use to make one?*

Randy started off at a brisk walk for the back of the barn. He had seen an old loader back there.

Taking one concept and seeing how it might apply to various situations is a key to growing—both intellectually and spiritually. Charlotte called that skill "meditation."

Charlotte's Thoughts on Meditation

1. Meditation asks, "What if?"

"Meditation is also a habit to be acquired, or rather preserved, for we believe that children are born to meditate, as they are to reflect; indeed, the two are closely allied. In reflecting we ruminate on what we have received. In meditating we are not content to go over the past, we allow our minds to follow out our subject to all its issues" (Vol. 3, pp. 120, 121).

2. Meditating is necessary for intellectual progress.

"It has long been known that progress in the Christian life depends much upon meditation; intellectual progress, too, depends, not on mere reading or the laborious getting up of a subject which we call study, but on that active surrender of all the powers of the mind to the occupation of the subject in hand, which is intended by the word meditation" (Vol. 3, p. 121).

"No one can tell what particular morsel a child will select for his sustenance. One small boy of eight may come down late because—'I was meditating upon Plato and couldn't fasten my buttons,' and another may find his meat in 'Peter Pan'! But all children must read widely, and know what they have read, for the nourishment of their complex nature" (Vol. 6, p. 59).

Questions to Ask about Meditation

- Do I encourage my child to explore "What if?" scenarios in his mind?
- Am I trying to encourage both Biblical and intellectual meditation?

More Quotes on Meditation

"This book of the law shall not depart out of thy mouth; but thou shalt meditate therein day and night, that thou mayest observe to do according to all that is written therein: for then thou shalt make thy way prosperous, and then thou shalt have good success."—Joshua 1:8

"The important thing is not to stop questioning. Curiosity has its own reason for existing. One cannot help but be in awe when he contemplates the mysteries

"Children are born to meditate, as they are to reflect."

of eternity, of life, of the marvelous structure of reality. It is enough if one tries merely to comprehend a little of this mystery every day. Never lose a holy curiosity."—Albert Einstein

"Reading makes a full man,
Meditation a profound man,
Discourse a clear man."—Benjamin Franklin

"Meditate upon these things; give thyself wholly to them; that thy profiting may appear to all."—1 Timothy 4:15

"But his delight is in the law of the Lord; and in his law doth he meditate day and night."—Psalm 1:2

Memorizing
Storing information in the mind

As the van turned into the subdivision, Allison called out cheerfully, "Here we are at our house: 125 Montana Street in Ourville, Connecticut."

Timmy's big round eyes looked at her from his car seat, just as they did every time she pulled onto their street and called out their address. *I wonder if he knows it yet,* Allison thought to herself.

Memorizing doesn't have to be a tedious task. We often memorize material incidentally just by hearing it repeated often over a period of time. You can use the same gentle approach to help your child memorize Scripture or poetry, or whatever you want him to learn.

Charlotte's Thoughts on Memorizing

1. Just because your child recites a Scripture verse or a poem or his telephone number once, don't assume he has it in his long-term memory to recall at will.

"Recitation and committing to memory are not necessarily the same thing" (Vol. 1, p. 224).

2. Reading aloud a poem or passage of Scripture often can help your child commit it to memory without ever "working at" memorizing it.

"It is well to store a child's memory with a good deal of poetry, learnt without labour. Some years ago I chanced to visit a house, the mistress of which had educational notions of her own, upon which she was bringing up a niece. She presented me with a large foolscap sheet written all over with the titles of poems, some of them long and difficult: *Tintern Abbey*, for example. She told me that her niece could repeat to me any of those poems that I liked to ask for, and that she had never learnt a single verse by heart in her life. The girl did repeat several of

"It is well to store a child's memory with a good deal of poetry, learnt without labour."

Notes

For a great Scripture Memory System based on this approach, visit the Bonus Features page for this book at http://simplycharlottemason. com/books/layingdowntherails/

the poems on the list, quite beautifully and without hesitation; and then the lady unfolded her secret. She thought she had made a discovery, and I thought so too. She read a poem through to E.; then the next day, while the little girl was making a doll's frock, perhaps, she read it again; once again the next day, while E.'s hair was being brushed. She got in about six or more readings, according to the length of the poem, at odd and unexpected times, and in the end E. could say the poem which she had *not* learned.

"I have tried the plan often since, and found it effectual. The child must not try to recollect or to say the verse over to himself, but, as far as may be, present an open mind to receive an impression of interest. Half a dozen repetitions should give children possession of such poems as—'Dolly and Dick,' 'Do you ask what the birds say?' 'Little lamb, who made thee?' and the like. The gains of such a method of learning are, that the edge of the child's enjoyment is not taken off by weariful verse by verse repetitions, and, also, that the habit of making mental images is unconsciously formed" (Vol. 1, pp. 224, 225).

"The learning by heart of Bible passages should begin while the children are quite young, six or seven. It is a delightful thing to have the memory stored with beautiful, comforting, and inspiring passages, and we cannot tell when and how this manner of seed may spring up, grow, and bear fruit; but the learning of the parable of the Prodigal son, for example, should not be laid on the children as a burden. The whole parable should be read to them in a way to bring out its beauty and tenderness; and then, day by day, the teacher should recite a short passage, perhaps two or three verses, saying it over some three or four times until the children think they know it. Then, but not before, let them recite the passage. Next day the children will recite what they have already learned, and so on, until they are able to say the whole parable" (Vol. 1, p. 253).

3. Select simple yet noble poetry, and attempt to memorize only a little to begin with.

"Let the child lie fallow till he is six, and then, in this matter of memorising, as in others, attempt only a little, and let the poems the child learns be simple and within the range of his own thought and imagination. At the same time, when there is so much noble poetry within a child's compass, the pity of it, that he should be allowed to learn twaddle!" (Vol. 1, p. 226).

Questions to Ask about Memorizing

- Do I have a good system in place for reviewing material committed to memory?
- Am I helping my child memorize Scripture or poetry without "working at it"?
- Am I trying to select simple yet noble poetry instead of twaddle?

More Quotes on Memorizing

"Thy word have I hid in mine heart, that I might not sin against thee."— Psalm 119:11

"And thou shalt love the Lord thy God with all thine heart, and with all thy

"There is so much noble poetry within a child's compass, the pity of it, that he should be allowed to learn twaddle!"

soul, and with all thy might. And these words, which I command thee this day, shall be in thine heart: and thou shalt teach them diligently unto thy children, and shalt talk of them when thou sittest in thine house, and when thou walkest by the way, and when thou liest down, and when thou risest up."—Deuteronomy 6:5–7

Mental Effort
Exerting oneself to apply the mind

"What's this book of puzzles for, Grandma?" asked Bob.

"I try to do a word puzzle or math puzzle every day, Bobby-dear," Grandma answered.

"Why?" Bob wrinkled his brow, trying to understand.

"Well, you exercise your legs and arms, don't you?" questioned Grandma.

"Oh, yes. I want to have strong muscles!" exclaimed Bob.

Grandma smiled. "And I want to have a strong mind, so I exercise it every day."

Too many children (and adults) have soft, flabby minds from not giving them a daily workout. Instill this habit in your child now, and it will serve him well for the rest of his life.

Charlotte's Thoughts on Mental Effort

1. Invigorate your child's brain with daily mental work.

"Most of us have met with a few eccentric and a good many silly persons, concerning whom the question forces itself, Were these people born with less brain power than others? Probably not; but if they were allowed to grow up without the daily habit of appropriate moral and mental *work*, if they were allowed to dawdle through youth without regular and sustained efforts of thought or will, the result would be the same, and the brain which should have been invigorated by daily exercise has become flabby and feeble as a healthy arm would be after carried for years in a sling" (Vol. 1, p. 21).

"Do not let the children pass a day without distinct efforts, intellectual, moral, volitional; let them brace themselves to understand; let them compel themselves to do and to bear; and let them do right at the sacrifice of ease and pleasure: and this for many higher reasons, but, in the first and lowest place, that the mere physical organ of mind and will may grow vigorous with work" (Vol. 1, p. 22).

2. Be alert yourself and expect quick comprehension and rapid work from your child.

"The habits of mental activity and of application are trained by the very means employed to cultivate that of attention. The child may *plod* diligently through his work who might be trained to *rapid* mental effort. The teacher herself must be

"Do not let the children pass a day without distinct efforts, intellectual, moral, volitional."

Notes

alert, must expect instant answers, quick thought, rapid work. The tortoise *will* lag behind the hare, but the tortoise must be trained to move, every day, a trifle quicker. Aim steadily at securing quickness of apprehension and execution, and that goes far towards getting it" (Vol. 1, p. 149).

3. Motivate your child with pleasing lessons, natural rewards, and the honor of steady effort.

"The child must not be allowed to get into the mood in which he says, 'Oh, I am *so* tired of sums,' or 'of history.' His zeal must be stimulated; there must always be a pleasing vista before him; and steady, untiring application to work should be held up as honourable, while fitful, flagging attention and effort are scouted" (Vol. 1, pp. 149, 150).

"Engage the child upon little problems within his comprehension from the first, rather than upon set sums. The young governess delights to set a noble 'long division sum,'— 953,783,465÷873—which shall fill the child's slate, and keep him occupied for a good half-hour; and when it is finished, and the child is finished too, done up with the unprofitable labour, the sum is not right after all: the two last figures in the quotient are wrong, and the remainder is false. But he cannot do it again—he must not be discouraged by being told it is wrong; so, 'nearly right' is the verdict, a judgment inadmissible in arithmetic. Instead of this laborious task, which gives no scope for mental effort, and in which he goes to sea at last from sheer want of attention, say to him—

" 'Mr Jones sent six hundred and seven, and Mr Stevens eight hundred and nineteen, apples to be divided amongst the twenty-seven boys at school on Monday. How many apples apiece did they get?'

"Here he must ask himself certain questions. 'How many apples altogether? How shall I find out? Then I must divide the apples into twenty-seven heaps to find out each boy's share.' That is to say, the child perceives what rules he must apply to get the required information. He is interested; the work goes on briskly: the sum is done in no time, and is probably right, because the attention of the child is concentrated on his work. Care must be taken to give the child such problems as he can work, but yet which are difficult enough to cause him some little mental effort" (Vol. 1, pp. 254, 255).

4. Teach your child to take satisfaction in exerting mental effort.

"*Intellectual Volition*, the power, that is, of making ourselves think of a given subject at a given time;—most of us know how trying our refractory minds are in this matter, but, if the child is accustomed to take pleasure in the effort as effort, the man will find it easy to make himself think of what he will" (Vol. 3, p. 120).

"The habit of work, the power of work, rapidity in work, the set of the will to a given task, are 'the making' of man and woman; that the boy who has done the definite work necessary to pass a given examination is, *other things being equal*, worth twenty per cent more than he who has not been able to pull his forces together" (Vol. 5, p. 180).

5. Don't allow your child to read books that require no mental effort.

"Guard the nursery; let nothing in that has not the true literary flavour; let the

> "Aim steadily at securing quickness of apprehension and execution, and that goes far towards getting it."

children grow up on a few books read over and over, and let them have none, the reading of which does not cost an appreciable mental effort" (Vol. 5, p. 215).

6. *Encourage your child to narrate what he has read or heard.*

"As for all the teaching in the nature of 'told to the children,' most children get their share of that whether in the infant school or at home, but this is practically outside the sphere of that part of education which demands a conscious mental effort, from the scholar, the mental effort of telling again that which has been read or heard. That is how we all learn, we tell again, to ourselves if need be, the matter we wish to retain, the sermon, the lecture, the conversation. The method is as old as the mind of man, the distressful fact is that it has been made so little use of in general education" (Vol. 6, pp. 159, 160).

7. *Require both boys and girls to do mental work.*

"Here comes in for consideration the question of 'overpressure,' a possibility—too serious to be passed over without investigation—which parents naturally dread more for their girls than their boys. In the first place, work, regular disciplinary exercise, is so entirely wholesome for the brain, that girls, even more than boys, should be the better for definite work with a given object. It cannot be too strongly put, that, as a matter of health, growing girls cannot afford to be idle, *mentally*; it is just as pernicious that they should dawdle through their lessons as that they should lounge through the day. There is no more effectual check to the tendency to hysteria and other nervous maladies common to growing girls than the habit of steady brain-work" (Vol. 5, pp. 180, 181).

8. *Make sure your child's work is reasonable and balanced with time for leisure.*

"But then, it must be work under conditions: fit quantities at fit times, with abundant leisure for exercise and recreation" (Vol. 5, p. 181).

Questions to Ask about Mental Effort

- Do I encourage my child to do daily mental work, whether we have formal lessons or not?
- Am I alert during lessons?
- Is my child making progress toward quick comprehension and rapid answers?
- Do I try to provide pleasing lessons?
- Do I hold up steady work as an honorable thing?
- Is my child learning to take satisfaction in exerting mental effort?
- Am I allowing my child to read books that require no mental effort?
- Do I encourage my child to narrate what he has read or heard?
- Do I require mental work from girls as well as boys?
- Am I trying to provide a balance between work and leisure?

More Quotes on Mental Effort

"Just as iron rusts from disuse, even so does inaction spoil the intellect."—Leonardo da Vinci

"No doubt we do give intellectual food, but too little of it; let us have courage and we shall be surprised, as we are now and then, at the amount of intellectual strong meat almost any child will take at a meal and digest at his leisure."

"Let me tell you the secret that has led me to my goal. My strength lies solely in my tenacity."—Louis Pasteur

"The difference between the impossible and the possible lies in a person's determination."—Tommy Lasorda

"No problem can withstand the assault of sustained thinking."—Voltaire

Observation
Seeing fully and in detail

Let's join Charlotte Mason's description of a mother with her little children who are enjoying an afternoon in the English countryside. The children have just been turned loose for a lovely time of running, shouting, and playing.

"By-and-by the others come back to their mother, and, while wits are fresh and eyes are keen, she sends them off on an exploring expedition—Who can see the most, and tell the most, about yonder hillock or brook, hedge or copse. This is an exercise that delights children, and may be endlessly varied, carried on in the spirit of a game, and yet with the exactness and carefulness of a lesson.

" 'Find out all you can about that cottage at the foot of the hill; but do not pry about too much.' Soon they are back, and there is a crowd of excited faces, and a hubbub of tongues, and random observations are shot breathlessly into the mother's ear. 'There are bee-hives.' 'We saw a lot of bees going into one.' 'There is a long garden.' 'Yes, and there are sunflowers in it.' 'And hen-and-chicken daisies and pansies.' 'And there's a great deal of a pretty blue flower with rough leaves, mother; what do you suppose it is?' 'Borage for the bees, most likely; they are very fond of it.' 'Oh, and there are apple and pear and plum trees on one side; there's a little path up the middle, you know.' 'On which hand side are the fruit trees?' 'The right—no, the left; let me see, which is my thimble-hand? Yes, it is the right-hand side.' 'And there are potatoes and cabbages, and mint and things on the other side.' 'Where are the flowers, then?' 'Oh, they are just the borders, running down each side of the path.' 'But we have not told mother about the wonderful apple tree; I should think there are a million apples on it, all ripe and rosy!' 'A *million*, Fanny?' 'Well, a great many, mother; I don't know how many.' And so on, indefinitely; the mother getting by degrees a complete description of the cottage and its garden.

"This is all play to the children, but the mother is doing invaluable work; she is training their powers of observation and expression, increasing their vocabulary and their range of ideas by giving them the name and the uses of an object at the right moment,—when they ask, 'What is it?' and 'What is it for?' And she is training her children in truthful habits, by making them careful to see the fact and to state it exactly, without omission or exaggeration. The child who describes, 'A tall tree, going up into a point, with rather roundish leaves; not a pleasant tree for shade, because the branches all go up,' deserves to learn the name of the tree, and anything her mother has to tell her about it. But the little bungler, who

"The mother is doing invaluable work; she is training their powers of observation and expression."

fails to make it clear whether he is describing an elm or a beech, should get no encouragement; not a foot should his mother move to see his tree, no coaxing should draw her into talk about it, until, in despair, he goes off, and comes back with some more certain note—rough or smooth bark, rough or smooth leaves,—then the mother considers, pronounces, and, full of glee, he carries her off to see for herself" (Vol. 1, pp. 45–47).

Charlotte's Thoughts on Observation

1. Once in a while ask your child to look at a piece of landscape until he can see it perfectly in his mind's eye, then have him describe it to you in detail without looking.

"Get the children to look well at some patch of landscape, and then to shut their eyes and call up the picture before them, if any bit of it is blurred, they had better look again. When they have a perfect image before their eyes, let them say what they see. Thus: 'I see a pond; it is shallow on this side, but deep on the other; trees come to the water's edge on that side, and you can see their green leaves and branches so plainly in the water that you would think there was a wood underneath. Almost touching the trees in the water is a bit of blue sky with a soft white cloud; and when you look up you see that same little cloud, but with a great deal of sky instead of a patch, because there are no trees up there. There are lovely yellow water-lilies round the far edge of the pond, and two or three of the big round leaves are turned up like sails. Near where I am standing three cows have come to drink, and one has got far into the water, nearly up to her neck,' etc.

"This, too, is an exercise children delight in, but, as it involves some strain on the attention, it is fatiguing, and should only be employed now and then. It is, however, well worth while to give children the habit of getting a bit of landscape by heart in this way, because it is the effort of recalling and reproducing that is fatiguing; while the altogether pleasurable act of seeing, *fully and in detail*, is likely to be repeated unconsciously until it becomes a habit by the child who is required now and then to reproduce what he sees" (Vol. 1, pp. 48, 49).

2. Beautiful scenes stored in the mind can provide a wonderful "picture gallery" that calms and refreshes the soul.

"The children will delight in this game of 'picture-painting' all the more if the mother introduce it by describing some great picture-gallery she has seen—pictures of mountains, of moors, of stormy seas, of ploughed fields, of little children at play, of an old woman knitting,—and goes on to say, that though she does not paint her pictures on canvas and have them put in frames, she carries about with her just such a picture-gallery; for whenever she sees anything lovely or interesting, she looks at it until she has the picture in her 'mind's eye'; and then she carries it away with her, her own for ever, a picture 'on view' just when she wants it.

"It would be difficult to overrate this habit of seeing and storing as a means of after-solace and refreshment" (Vol. 1, pp. 49, 50).

3. The habit of observation and nature study form the groundwork for understanding science.

"Years hence, when the children are old enough to understand that science

"The altogether pleasurable act of seeing, *fully and in detail*, is likely to be repeated unconsciously until it becomes a habit by the child who is required now and then to reproduce what he sees."

itself is in a sense sacred and demands some sacrifices, all the 'common information' they have been gathering until then, and the habits of observation they have acquired, will form a capital groundwork for a scientific education. In the meantime, let them *consider* the lilies of the field and the fowls of the air" (Vol. 1, p. 63).

"And this is the process the child should continue for the first few years of his life. Now is the storing time which should be spent in laying up images of things familiar. By-and-by he will have to conceive of things he has never seen: how can he do it except by comparison with things he has seen and knows? By-and-by he will be called upon to reflect, understand, reason; what material will he have, unless he has a magazine of facts to go upon? The child who has been made to observe how high in the heavens the sun is at noon on a summer's day, how low at noon on a day in mid-winter, is able to conceive of the great heat of the tropics under a vertical sun, and to understand the climate of a place depends greatly upon the mean height the sun reaches above the horizon" (Vol. 1, p. 66).

4. Provide lots of varied opportunities for observation and direct your child to observe, especially nature.

"The *method* of this sort of instruction is shown in *Evenings at Home*, where 'Eyes and No-eyes' go for a walk. No-eyes come home bored; he has seen nothing, been interested in nothing: while Eyes is all agog to discuss a hundred things that have interested him. As I have already tried to point out, to get this sort of instruction for himself is simply the *nature* of a child: the business of the parent is to afford him abundant and varied opportunities, and to direct his observations, so that, knowing little of the principles of scientific classification, he is, unconsciously, furnishing himself with the materials for such classification. It is needless to repeat what has already been said on this subject; but, indeed, the future of the man or woman depends very largely on the store of real knowledge gathered, and the habits of intelligent observation acquired, by the child" (Vol. 1, p. 265).

"Object-lessons should be incidental; and this is where the family enjoys so great an advantage over the school. It is almost impossible that the school should give any but set lessons; but this sort of teaching in the family falls in with the occurrence of the object. The child who finds that wonderful and beautiful object, a 'paper' wasp's nest, attached to a larch-twig, has his object-lesson on the spot from father or mother. The grey colour, the round symmetrical shape, the sort of cup-and-ball arrangement, the papery texture, the comparative size, the comparative smoothness, the odour or lack of odour, the extreme lightness, the fact that it is not cold to the touch—these and fifty other particulars the child finds out unaided, or with no more than a word, here and there, to direct his observation. One does not find a wasp's nest every day, but much can be got out of every common object, and the commoner the better, which falls naturally under the child's observation, a piece of bread, a lump of coal, a sponge.

"In the first place, it is unnecessary in the family to give an exhaustive examination to every object; one quality might be discussed in this, another quality in that. We eat our bread and milk, and notice that bread is absorbent; and we overhaul our experience to discover other things which we know to be

"Let them *consider* the lilies of the field and the fowls of the air."

absorbent also; and we do what we can to compare these things as to whether they are less absorbent or more absorbent than bread. This is exceedingly important: the unobservant person states that an object is light, and considers that he has stated an ultimate fact: the observant person makes the same statement, but has in his mind a relative scale, and his judgment is of the more value because he compares, silently, with a series of substances to which this is relatively light" (Vol. 2, pp. 182, 183).

5. Most children naturally perceive what is around them to some extent, but the skill of methodical observation and accurate recall must be trained.

" 'Come and see the puff-puff, dear.' 'Do you mean the *locomotive*, grandmamma?' As a matter of fact, the child of four and five has a wider, more exact vocabulary in everyday use than that employed by his elders and betters, and is constantly adding to this vocabulary with surprising quickness; *ergo*, to give a child of this class a vocabulary is no part of direct education. Again, we know that nothing escapes the keen scrutiny of the little people. It is not their perceptive powers we have to train, but the habit of methodical observation and accurate record" (Vol. 2, p. 226).

Ergo means "therefore."

6. Train your child from his first reading lessons to notice how words are spelled as he reads.

"Accustom him from the first to shut his eyes and spell the word he has made. This is important. Reading is not spelling, nor is it necessary to spell in order to read well; but the good speller is the child whose eye is quick enough to take in the letters which compose it, in the act of reading off a word; and this is a habit to be acquired from the first: *accustom* him to *see* the letters in the word, and he will do so without effort.

"If words were always made on a given pattern in English, if the same letter always represented the same sounds, learning to read would be an easy matter; for the child would soon acquire the few elements of which all words would, in that case, be composed. But many of our English words are, each, a law unto itself: there is nothing for it, but the child must learn to know them at sight; he must recognise 'which,' precisely as he recognises '*B*,' because he has seen it before, been made to look at it with interest, so that the pattern of the word is stamped on his retentive brain. This process should go on side by side with the other—the learning of the powers of the letters; for the more variety you can throw into his reading lessons, the more will the child enjoy them. Lessons in word-making help him to take intelligent interest in *words*; but his progress in the art of reading depends chiefly on the 'reading at sight' lessons" (Vol. 1, pp. 203, 204).

"The whole secret of spelling lies in the habit of visualising words from memory, and children must be trained to visualise in the course of their reading" (Vol. 1, p. 243).

Questions to Ask about Observation

• Do I once in a while ask my child to look at a landscape until he can see it clearly, then describe it to me in detail?

"This is a habit to be acquired from the first: accustom him to see the letters in the word, and he will do so without effort."

- Am I taking steps toward building a "picture gallery" in my mind, as well as my child's mind, for future enjoyment?
- Am I laying the groundwork for science lessons by encouraging observation of nature?
- Am I trying to provide lots of varied opportunities and encouragement for my child to observe, especially nature?
- Am I careful not to mistake the natural perception my child has with methodical observation and accurate recall, which must be taught?
- Am I training my child to see how words are spelled as he reads?

More Quotes on Observation

"To acquire knowledge, one must study; but to acquire wisdom, one must observe."—Marilyn vos Savant

"It was one of the most bewitching sights in the world to observe a hill of beans thrusting aside the soil, or a rose of early peas just peeping forth sufficiently to trace a line of delicate green."—Nathaniel Hawthorne

"Go to the ant, thou sluggard; consider her ways, and be wise: which having no guide, overseer, or ruler, provideth her meat in the summer, and gathereth her food in the harvest."—Proverbs 6:6–8

Perfect Execution
*Working carefully with one's hands
with an aim at "perfect"*

Ava had grown up with the saying "Practice makes perfect." Yet, these days she was seriously questioning whether that saying were true. "I'm wondering whether it might not be more accurate to say, 'Practice makes permanent,'" Ava confided to her long-time friend, Terri.

"Why do you say that?" Terri wanted to know.

"Well, I practiced my handwriting on miles of paper when I was growing up, and look at my letters—they're definitely not perfect!" Ava pointed to the recipe card she was copying for Terri.

Terri laughed. "That's the truth! Your handwriting has never been very good, dear. So what's the big deal about making it perfect now?"

"I want to teach Sam how to write," Ava replied. "But I'm living proof that just having him repeat the letters won't make his handwriting good. I think we need to concentrate on making each stroke correctly first. What do you think? Does that make sense?"

"Absolutely!" agreed Terri. "Hey, maybe you could change the saying to 'Perfect practice makes perfect.'"

"That's it!" Ava smiled.

"Let the child accomplish something *perfectly* in every [writing] lesson."

Making a whole row of *A*'s doesn't improve a child's penmanship unless he makes each one perfectly. Simply repeating a mistake won't improve it! Charlotte advocated that adults encourage children to work carefully and aim for perfection before turning them loose to repeat their efforts over and over.

Charlotte's Thoughts on Perfect Execution

1. Encourage your child to form his numbers, letters, stitches, and any other handwork carefully.

" 'Throw perfection into all you do' is a counsel upon which a family may be brought up with great advantage. We English, as a nation, think too much of persons, and too little of *things, work, execution*. Our children are allowed to make their figures, or their letters, their stitches, their dolls' clothes, their small carpentry, anyhow, with the notion that they will do better by-and-by. Other nations—the Germans and the French, for instance—look at the question philosophically, and know that if the children get the *habit* of turning out imperfect work, the men and women will undoubtedly keep that habit up" (Vol. 1, p. 159).

"The habit of act rises from the habit of thought. The person who thinks, 'Oh, it will do'; 'Oh, it doesn't matter,' forms a habit of negligent and imperfect work" (Vol. 2, p. 234).

2. Do not excuse faulty work just because it is done by a child.

"I remember being delighted with the work of a class of about forty children, of six and seven, in an elementary school at Heidelberg. They were doing a writing lesson, accompanied by a good deal of oral teaching from a master, who wrote each word on the blackboard. By-and-by the slates were shown, and I did not observe *one faulty or irregular letter* on the whole forty slates. The same principle of 'perfection' was to be discerned in a recent exhibition of school-work held throughout France. No faulty work was shown, to be excused on the plea that it was the work of children" (Vol. 1, pp. 159, 160).

3. Be careful not to give your child a task that he cannot do perfectly.

"No work should be given to a child that he cannot execute *perfectly*, and then perfection should be required of him as a matter of course" (Vol. 1, p. 160).

4. It is better to require six perfectly-formed strokes than a whole page of sloppy ones.

"For instance, he is set to do a copy of strokes, and is allowed to show a slateful at all sorts of slopes and all sorts of intervals; his moral sense is vitiated, his *eye* is injured. Set him six strokes to copy; let him, not bring a slateful, but six perfect strokes, at regular distances and at regular slopes" (Vol. 1, p. 160).

5. Ask your child to point out imperfections in his work and persevere to correct them.

"If he produces a faulty pair, get *him* to point out the fault, and persevere until he has produced his task; if he does not do it to-day, let him go on to-morrow

Remember that there is a big difference between encouraging your child to do his best and frustrating him with too high of expectations for his abilities.

"If the children get the *habit* of turning out imperfect work, the men and women will undoubtedly keep that habit up."

and the next day, and when the six perfect strokes appear, let it be an occasion of triumph" (Vol. 1, p. 160).

6. Celebrate any handwork that is well done.

"So with the little tasks of painting, drawing, or construction he sets himself— let everything he does *be well done*. An unsteady house of cards is a thing to be ashamed of" (Vol. 1, p. 160).

7. Let your child accomplish something perfectly in every writing lesson, whether it be one line or one letter.

"I can only offer a few hints on the teaching of *writing*, though much might be said. First, let the child accomplish something *perfectly* in every lesson—a stroke, a pothook, a letter" (Vol. 1, p. 233).

8. Keep your child's writing lessons short: five or ten minutes.

"Let the writing lesson be short; it should not last more than five or ten minutes" (Vol. 1, p. 233).

9. Secure careful work first from your child; focus on practice later.

"Ease in writing comes by practice; but that must be secured later. In the meantime, the thing to be avoided is the habit of careless work—humpy *m*'s, angular *o*'s" (Vol. 1, pp. 233, 234).

10. Make sure your child can write well and easily in a medium-size handwriting before introducing smaller lines designed for small handwriting.

"Do not hurry the child into 'small hand'; it is unnecessary that he should labour much over what is called 'large hand,' but 'text-hand,' the medium size, should be continued until he makes the letters with ease. It is much easier for the child to get into an irregular scribble by way of 'small-hand,' than to get out of it again. In this, as in everything else, the care of the educator must be given, not only to the formation of good, but to the prevention of bad habits" (Vol. 1, p. 235).

Questions to Ask about Perfect Execution

- Am I encouraging my child to form all his handwork carefully?
- Do I tend to excuse my child's faulty work because he is a child?
- Am I careful not to assign my child a task that he cannot do perfectly?
- Am I requiring a little work well done rather than a lot of work sloppily done?
- Do I enlist my child's help to evaluate his work, point out imperfections, and work to correct them?
- Am I quick to celebrate any handwork well done by my child?
- Am I trying to let my child accomplish something perfectly in every writing lesson?
- Are our writing lessons short: five or ten minutes?

"In this, as in everything else, the care of the educator must be given, not only to the formation of good, but to the prevention of bad habits."

- Am I emphasizing careful work or just practice?
- Am I making sure that my child has mastered writing medium-size letters before moving on to smaller handwriting?

More Quotes on Perfect Execution

"High expectations are the key to everything."—Sam Walton

"Trifles make perfection, and perfection is no trifle."—Michelangelo

"Aim at perfection in everything, though in most things it is unattainable. However, they who aim at it, and persevere, will come much nearer to it than those whose laziness and despondency make them give it up as unattainable."—Lord Chesterfield

Reading for Instruction
Reading with the mind fully engaged so as to learn something

James thought he was a pretty educated person; after all, he read at least twelve books every year! But when James looked back at the list of titles, he found mostly mysteries and novels.

I can remember learning from only two books on this list, he grimly reflected. Both books dealt with bicycling and fitness—the hobby that had grabbed his attention last year. James smiled as he recalled the rush of information that had saturated his mind while reading those two books and the sense of accomplishment he had felt from gaining all that knowledge. He also remembered how everything around him had seemed to disappear as the books had absorbed his thoughts. It hadn't been as easy as reading a novel, but it had certainly been more helpful.

I need to find more books like that, James decided. *I guess not all books are created equal.*

The habit of reading for instruction is not the same as a love for reading. Reading for instruction requires active participation on the part of the reader's mind. But once this habit is set up, a person can teach himself just about anything.

Charlotte's Thoughts on Reading for Instruction

1. During your child's sixth through twelfth years, concentrate on cultivating this habit of reading for instruction.

"This period of a child's life between his sixth and his ninth year should be used to lay the basis of a liberal education, and of the *habit* of reading for instruction" (Vol. 1, Preface).

"The most common and the monstrous defect in the education of the day is that children fail to acquire the habit of reading."

Notes

"The most common and the monstrous defect in the education of the day is that children fail to acquire the habit of reading. Knowledge is conveyed to them by lessons and talk, but the studious habit of using books as a means of interest and delight is not acquired. This habit should be begun early; so soon as the child can read at all, he should read for himself, and to himself, history, legends, fairy tales, and other suitable matter. He should be trained from the first to think that one reading of any lesson is enough to enable him to narrate what he has read, and will thus get the habit of slow, careful reading, intelligent even when it is silent, because he reads with an eye to the full meaning of every clause" (Vol. 1, p. 227).

"The attention of his teachers should be fixed on two points—that he acquires the habit of reading, and that he does not fall into slipshod habits of reading" (Vol. 1, p. 226).

"Our great failure seems to me to be caused by the fact that we do not form the habit of reading books that are worth while in children while they are at school and are under twelve years of age" (Vol. 3, Preface).

"One must read to learn the meaning of life; and we should know in the end, who said what, and on what occasion! The characters in the books we know become our mentors or our warnings, our instructors always; but not if we let our mind behave as a sieve, through which the whole slips like water" (Vol. 4, Book 2, p. 72).

"The boy who has not formed the habit of getting nourishment out of his books in school-days does not, afterwards, see the good of reading. He has not acquired, in an intellectual sense, the art of reading, so he cannot be said to have lost it; and he goes through life an imperfect person, with the best and most delightful of his powers latent or maimed" (Vol. 5, p. 291).

"It is a pitiful thing when his education leaves a youth without the power or habit of reading, and also without an absorbing intellectual interest" (Vol. 5, pp. 295, 296).

"From their earliest days they should get the habit of reading literature which they should take hold of for themselves, much or little, in their own way" (Vol. 6, p. 191).

"The child must read to know" (Vol. 6, p. 304).

2. Read aloud to your older child only occasionally.

"It is a delight to older people to read aloud to children, but this should be only an occasional treat and indulgence, allowed before bedtime, for example. We must remember the natural inertness of a child's mind; give him the habit of being read to, and he will steadily shirk the labour of reading for himself; indeed, we all like to be spoon-fed with our intellectual meat, or we should read and think more for ourselves and be less eager to run after lectures" (Vol. 1, p. 228).

"The child must read to know."

3. Evaluate your child's comprehension of what he has read by asking for a narration, not asking direct questions about the subject matter or word definitions.

"When a child is reading, he should not be teased with questions as to the meaning of what he has read, the signification of this word or that; what is annoying to older people is equally annoying to children. Besides, it is not of the least consequence that they should be able to give the meaning of every word they read. A knowledge of meanings, that is, an ample and correct vocabulary, is only arrived at in one way—by the habit of reading. A child unconsciously gets the meaning of a new word from the context, if not the first time he meets with it, then the second or the third: but he is on the look-out, and will find out for himself the sense of any expression he does not understand. Direct questions on the subject-matter of what a child has read are always a mistake. Let him narrate what he has read, or some part of it. He enjoys this sort of consecutive reproduction, but abominates every question in the nature of a riddle. If there must be riddles, let it be his to ask and the teacher's to direct him to the answer. Questions that lead to a side issue or to a personal view are allowable because these interest children—'What would you have done in his place?' " (Vol. 1, pp. 228, 229).

"There is much difference between intelligent reading, which the pupil should do in silence, and a mere parrot-like cramming up of contents; and it is not a bad test of education to be able to give the points of a description, the sequence of a series of incidents, the links in a chain of argument, correctly, after a single careful reading. This is a power which a barrister, a publisher, a scholar, labours to acquire; and it is a power which children can acquire with great ease, and once acquired, the gulf is bridged which divides the reading from the non-reading community" (Vol. 3, p. 180).

"They have an enviable power of getting at the gist of a book or subject. Sometimes they are asked to write verses about a personage or an event; the result is not remarkable by way of poetry, but sums up a good deal of thoughtful reading in a delightful way" (Vol. 6, p. 242).

4. Select your child's lesson books carefully; they should convey that knowledge is attractive and delightful.

"A child has not begun his education until he has acquired the habit of reading to himself, with interest and pleasure, books fully on a level with his intelligence. I am speaking now of his lesson-books, which are all too apt to be written in a style of insufferable twaddle, probably because they are written by persons who have never chanced to meet a child. All who know children know that they do not talk twaddle and do not like it, and prefer that which appeals to their understanding. Their lesson-books should offer matter for their reading, whether aloud or to themselves; therefore they should be written with literary power. As for the matter of these books, let us remember that children can take in ideas and principles, whether the latter be moral or mechanical, as quickly and clearly as we do ourselves (perhaps more so); but detailed processes, lists and summaries, blunt the edge of a child's delicate mind. Therefore, the selection of their first lesson-

"A child has not begun his education until he has acquired the habit of reading to himself, with interest and pleasure, books fully on a level with his intelligence."

books is a matter of grave importance, because it rests with these to give children the idea that knowledge is supremely attractive and that reading is delightful. Once the habit of reading his lesson-books with delight is set up in a child, his education is—not complete, but—ensured" (Vol. 1, p. 229).

"A book that is worth reading, whether it be a novel or a homily, contains the best thought of the writer, and we can only get at his meaning by serious thinking" (Vol. 4, Book 1, pp. 183, 184).

"It is not important that many books should be read; but it is important that only good books should be read; and read with such ease and pleasant leisure, that they become to the hearers so much mental property for life" (Vol. 5, p. 223).

"Why in the world should we not give children, while they are at school, the sort of books they can live upon; books alive with thought and feeling, and delight in knowledge, instead of the miserable cram-books on which they are starved?" (Vol. 5, p. 291).

"It is as teachers know a matter of extreme difficulty to find the exactly right book for children's reading in each subject" (Vol. 6, p. 176).

5. A habit of reading for instruction is different from a love of reading.

"Sir Philip Magnus, in a recent address on Headwork and Handwork in Elementary Schools, says some things worth pondering. Perhaps he gives his workshop too big a place in the school of the future, but certainly he puts his finger on the weak point in the work of both elementary and secondary schools—the 'getting by heart scraps of knowledge, fragments of so-called science.' And we are with him in the emphasis he lays upon *reading and writing*; it is through these that even school 'studies' shall become 'for delight.' Writing, of course, comes of reading, and nobody can write well who does not read much. Sir Philip Magnus says, speaking of the schools of the future:—'We shall no longer require children to learn by constant repetition, scraps of history, geography, and grammar, nor try to teach them fragments of so-called science. The daily hours devoted to these tasks will be applicable to the creation of mental aptitudes, and will be utilised in showing the children how to obtain knowledge for themselves. . . In future the main function of education will be to train our hands and our sense organs and intellectual faculties, so that we may be placed in a position of advantage for seeking knowledge. . . The scope of the lessons will be enlarged. Children will be taught to read in order that they may desire to read, and to write that they may be able to write. . . It will be the teacher's aim to create in his pupils a desire for knowledge, and consequently a love of reading, and to cultivate in them, by a proper selection of lessons, the pleasure which reading may be made to yield. The main feature of the reading lesson will be to show the use of books, how they may be consulted to ascertain what other people have said or done, and how they may be read for the pleasure they afford. The storing of the memory with facts is no part of elementary school work. . . It is not enough that a child should learn how to write, he must know *what* to write. He must learn to describe clearly what he has heard or seen, to transfer to written language his sense-impressions, and to express concisely his own thoughts.'

"Once the habit of reading his lesson-books with delight is set up in a child, his education is—not complete, but—ensured."

"We should like to add a word to Sir Philip Magnus's conception, emphasising the *habit* of reading as a chief acquirement of school life. It is only those who have read who do read" (Vol. 3, pp. 232–234).

"We all know how the reading of a passage may stimulate in us thought, inquiry, inference, and thus get for us in the end some added knowledge" (Vol. 3, p. 241).

"Casual reading—that is, vague reading round a subject without the effort to know—is not in much better case: if we are to read and grow thereby, we must read to know, that is, our reading must be study—orderly, definite, purposeful" (Vol. 5, p. 382).

"People are naturally divided into those who read and think and those who do not read or think; and the business of schools is to see that all their scholars shall belong to the former class; it is worth while to remember that thinking is inseparable from reading which is concerned with the content of a passage and not merely with the printed matter" (Vol. 6, p. 31).

Questions to Ask about Reading for Instruction

- Am I concentrating on cultivating this habit in my six- to twelve-year-old child?
- Do I read aloud only occasionally to my older child?
- Am I evaluating my child's comprehension by asking for a narration?
- Do I try to select my child's lesson books carefully, making sure they present knowledge as attractive and delightful?
- Am I mistakenly assuming that my child's love for reading is the same as a habit of reading for instruction?

More Quotes on Reading for Instruction

"All men who have turned out worth anything have had the chief hand in their own education."—Sir Walter Scott

"Man's mind, once stretched by a new idea, never regains its original dimensions."—Oliver Wendell Holmes

Remembering
Recalling at will
knowledge stored in the memory

"We need to seed this section of the yard," Dad explained to Flo. "Let's get the measuring tape and see how big it is so we will know how much seed to get."
Flo helped hold the end of the tape measure and wrote down the numbers as

"People are naturally divided into those who read and think and those who do not read or think."

Dad called them out. After the last measurement had been recorded, Dad said, "So how much seed do we need?"

"Well," Flo answered. "I know we can figure out the answer by using these numbers, but I can't remember how to do it."

Dad looked puzzled. "I thought you passed the test on this just last week."

Flo nodded sheepishly.

There's a difference between remembering in order to pass a test and really remembering! True education consists of what we really remember. Here are some great suggestions for helping your student develop the habit of remembering over the long haul.

Charlotte's Thoughts on Remembering

1. What young children learn forms the groundwork for knowledge in future years.

"Memory is the storehouse of whatever knowledge we possess; and it is upon the fact of the stores lodged in the memory that we take rank as intelligent beings. The children learn in order that they may remember. Much of what we have learned and experienced in childhood, and later, we cannot reproduce, and yet it has formed the groundwork of after-knowledge; later notions and opinions have grown out of what we once learned and knew. That is our sunk capital, of which we enjoy the interest though we are unable to realise" (Vol. 1, p. 154).

2. Being able to recall a memory at will is our most valuable ability.

"Again, much that we have learned and experienced is not only retained in the storehouse of memory, but is our available capital, we can reproduce, *recollect* upon demand. This memory which may be drawn upon by the act of recollection is our most valuable endowment" (Vol. 1, pp. 154, 155).

3. Cramming for a test does not assure remembering and knowing.

"There is a third kind of (spurious) memory—facts and ideas floating in the brain which yet make no part of it, and are exuded at a single effort; as when a barrister produces all his knowledge of a case in his brief, and then forgets all about it; or when the schoolboy 'crams' for an examination, writes down what he has thus learned, and behold, it is gone from his gaze for ever: as Ruskin puts it, 'They cram to pass, and not to know; they *do* pass, and they *don't* know.' That the barrister, the physician, should be able thus to dismiss the case on which he has ceased to be occupied, the publisher the book he has rejected, is well for him, and this art of forgetting is not without its uses: but what of the schoolboy who has little left after a year's work but his place in a class-list?" (Vol. 1, p. 155)

4. Arrest your child's full attention on a fact, and he will remember it.

"It appears, both from common experience and from an infinite number of examples quoted by psychologists, that any object or idea which is regarded with *attention* makes the sort of impression on the brain which is said to fix it in the memory. In other words, give an instant's undivided attention to anything

"The children learn in order that they may remember."

whatsoever, and that thing will be remembered. In describing this effect, the common expression is accurate beyond its intention. We say, 'Such and such a sight or sound, or sensation, made a strong *impression* on me.' And that is precisely what has happened: arrest the attention upon any fact or incident, and that fact or incident is remembered; it is impressed, imprinted upon the brain substance. The inference is plain. You want a child to remember? Then secure his whole *attention*, the fixed gaze of his mind, as it were, upon the fact to be remembered; then he will have it: by a sort of photographic (!) process, that fact or idea is 'taken' by his brain, and when he is an old man, perhaps, the memory of it will flash across him" (Vol. 1, pp. 156, 157).

5. Link each lesson to the previous one in a mental train.

"But it is not enough to have a recollection flash across one incidentally; we want to have the power of recalling at will: and for this, something more is necessary than an occasional act of attention producing a solitary impression. Supposing, for instance, that by good teaching you secure the child's attention to the verb *avoir*, he will remember it; that is to say, some infinitely slight growth of brain tissue will record and retain that one French verb. But one verb is nothing; you want the child to learn *French*, and for this you must not only fix his attention upon each new lesson, but each must be so linked into the last that it is impossible for him to recall one without the other following in its train" (Vol. 1, p. 157).

"Let every lesson gain the child's entire attention, and let each new lesson be so interlaced with the last that the one *must* recall the other; that, again, recalls the one before it, and so on to the beginning" (Vol. 1, p. 158).

6. These mental links can be similarities or differences or anything else found in the nature of the lesson's subject.

"To acquire any knowledge or power whatsoever, and then to leave it to grow rusty in a neglected corner of the brain, is practically useless. Where there is no chain of association to draw the bucket out of the well, it is all the same as if there were no water there. As to how to form these links, every subject will suggest a suitable method. The child has a lesson about Switzerland to-day, and one about Holland to-morrow, and the one is linked to the other by the very fact that the two countries have hardly anything in common; what the one has, the other has not. Again, the association will be of *similarity*, and not of *contrast*. In our own experience we find that colours, places, sounds, odours recall persons or events; but links of this sensuous order can hardly be employed in education. The link between any two things must be found in the nature of the things associated" (Vol. 1, pp. 158, 159).

Questions to Ask about Remembering

- Am I trying to give my younger child opportunities to learn?
- Am I working toward my child's being able to recall a memory at will?
- Do I allow my child to cram for a test?
- Am I seeking to arrest my child's full attention on the fact I want him to remember?

"You want a child to remember? Then secure his whole *attention*, the fixed gaze of his mind, as it were, upon the fact to be remembered."

- Do I try to link each lesson to the previous one in order to help form associations in my child's memory?
- Am I improving in finding various kinds of links between subjects of lessons—whether similarities, differences, or something else?

More Quotes on Remembering

"I will remember the works of the Lord: surely I will remember thy wonders of old."—Psalm 77:11

Thinking
The actual labor of the brain; a real conscious effort of mind

"All right," announced Mom at the breakfast table. "We have these three errands that need to be done today. In which order shall we do them?"

Mom smiled inwardly as the four children's minds started to work on the puzzle. She had posed questions like this several times over the year, and it was gratifying to see their progress in rational and logical thinking. The little ones were picking up key points from listening to the older ones, and sometimes the younger ones found a hole in the older ones' logic.

Before long the children had the route planned, taking into account that groceries must be done last so the ice cream wouldn't melt before reaching home.

Everyday situations, as well as lesson times, are great opportunities to encourage logical thinking!

Charlotte's Thoughts on Thinking

1. Encourage your child to trace cause and effect, comparison and contrast, premise and conclusion in his lessons.

"The actual labour of the brain is known to psychologists under various names, and divided into various operations: let us call it *thinking*, which, for educational purposes, is sufficiently exact; but, by 'thinking,' let us mean a real conscious effort of mind, and not the fancies that flit without effort through the brain. This sort of thing, for instance, an example quoted by Archbishop Thompson in his *Laws of Thought*:—'when Captain Head was travelling across the pampas of South America, his guide one day suddenly stopped him, and pointing high into the air, cried out "A lion!" Surprised at such an exclamation, accompanied with such an act, he turned up his eyes, and with difficulty perceived, at an immeasurable height, a flight of condors, soaring in circles in a particular spot. Beneath this spot, far out of sight of himself or guide, lay the carcass of a horse, and over that carcass stood, as the guide well knew, a lion, whom the condors were eyeing with envy from their airy height. The signal of the birds was to him what the sight of the lion alone would have been to the

Charlotte wrote directly to young people about reasoning and common sense in Volume 4, Book 1, pages 56–65.

"Thinking, like writing or skating, comes by practice."

traveller—a full assurance of its existence. Here was an act of thought which cost the thinker no trouble, which was as easy to him as to cast his eyes upward, yet which from us, unaccustomed to the subject, would require many steps and some labour. The sight of the condors convinced him that there was some carcass or other; but as they kept wheeling far above it, instead of swooping down to their feast, he guessed that some beast had anticipated them. Was it a dog, or a jackal? No; the condors would not fear to drive away, or share with, either: it must be some large beast, and as there were lions in the neighbourhood, he concluded that one was here.' And all these steps of thought are summed up in the words 'A lion.'

"This is the sort of thing that the children should go through, more or less, in every lesson—a tracing of effect from cause, or of cause from effect; a comparing of things to find out wherein they are alike, and wherein they differ; a conclusion as to causes or consequences from certain premises" (Vol. 1, pp. 150, 151).

2. Thinking comes by practice.

"*Thinking*, like writing or skating, comes by practice. The child who never has thought, never does think, and probably never will think; for are there not people enough who go through the world without any deliberate exercise of their own wits? The child must think, get at the reason-why of things for himself, every day of his life, and more each day than the day before" (Vol. 1, pp. 153, 154).

3. When appropriate, ask your child "Why?" instead of always giving him the answer.

"Children and parents both are given to invert this educational process. The child asks 'Why?' and the parent answers, rather proud of this evidence of thought in his child. There is some slight show of speculation even in wondering 'Why?' but it is the slightest and most superficial effort the thinking brain produces. Let the parent ask 'Why?' and the child produce the answer, if he can. After he has turned the matter over and over in his mind, there is no harm in telling him—and he will remember it—the reason why. Every walk should offer some knotty problem for the children to think out—'Why does that leaf float on the water, and this pebble sink?' and so on" (Vol. 1, p. 154).

4. Challenge your child to form an opinion only after carefully thinking through the matter.

"We begin to see what is our duty about opinions. In the first place, we must have 'a thinking' about an immense number of things. So we must read, mark, learn, and inwardly digest; must listen and consider, being sure that one of the purposes we are in the world for is, to form right opinions about all matters that come in our way.

"Next, we must avoid the short road to opinions; we must not pick them up ready made at any street-corner; and next, we must learn—and this is truly difficult, a matter that takes us all our lives—to recognise a fallacy, that is, an argument which appears sound but does not bear examination. For example, 'We are all born equal'; so we are, with equal right to the pure air, to the beauty of earth and sky, to the protection of the laws of our country, and much besides. But the sense in which men use the phrase is,—that we are all born with an equal right to the property that is in the world. That is absurd, as the very word

"The child must think, get at the reason-why of things for himself, every day of his life, and more each day than the day before."

Numa was a Roman who, though he had many well-thought-out reasons why he should not be king, changed his mind when ambassadors convinced him with their reasoning.

'property' shows us: property means ownership, it is the own possession of the persons who hold it. We are ashamed even of a cuckoo that appropriates the own nest of another bird. But the question of fallacies is a big one, and all we need bear in mind now is, that popular cries, whether in the school or the country, very often rest upon fallacies or false judgments. So we must look all round the notions we take up.

"Next, before forming an opinion about anyone in place and power, we must try to realise and understand that person's position and all that belongs to it. One more thing, when we have arrived at an opinion we must remember that it is only 'a thinking,' and must hold it with diffidence; but because it is our thinking, our very own property that has come to us through pondering, we must hold it firmly, unless, like Numa, we are convinced that another view is sounder than our own.

"But, once again, we may not be sluggish in this matter of opinion. It is the chief part of Justice to think just thoughts about the matters that come before us, and the best and wisest men are those who have brought their minds to bear upon the largest number of subjects, and have learned to think just thoughts about them all" (Vol. 4, Book 1, pp. 185, 186).

Questions to Ask about Thinking

- Do I encourage my child to trace cause and effect, comparison and contrast, and premise and conclusion?
- Is my child working toward thinking logically?
- Am I asking my child to determine "Why?" sometimes, instead of always giving him the answer?
- Am I challenging my child to form an opinion only after careful thought?

More Quotes on Thinking

"Reading furnishes the mind only with materials of knowledge; it is thinking that makes what we read ours."—John Locke

"To be able to be caught up into the world of thought—that is to be educated."—Edith Hamilton

"Reader! Had you in your mind
Such stores as silent thought can bring,
O gentle Reader! You would find
A tale in everything."—Wordsworth

"Too often we . . . enjoy the comfort of opinion without the discomfort of thought."—John F. Kennedy

"We must look all round the notions we take up."

Other Mental Habits

Charlotte mentioned more mental habits only in passing. Here are those

Notes

habits along with their definitions, her brief comments, and some additional quotes.

Accuracy
*Freedom from mistake or error;
conforming to truth or to a standard*

See also Truthfulness on page 110.

Charlotte's Thoughts on Accuracy

"*Accuracy*, which is to be taught, not only through arithmetic, but through all the small statements, messages, and affairs of daily life" (Vol. 3, p. 120).

"The chief value of arithmetic, like that of the higher mathematics, lies in the training it affords the reasoning powers, and in the habits of insight, readiness, accuracy, intellectual truthfulness it engenders" (Vol. 1, p. 254).

Quotes on Accuracy

"Beware of the man who won't be bothered with details."—William Feather, Sr.

"Oh, the difference between nearly right and exactly right."—Horace J. Brown

Concentration
*Actively engaged on a given problem
rather than passively receptive*

Charlotte's Thoughts on Concentration

"*Concentration*, which differs from attention in that the mind is actively engaged on some given problem rather than passively receptive" (Vol. 3, p. 120).

Quotes on Concentration

"I never could have done what I have done without the habits of punctuality, order, and diligence, without the determination to concentrate myself on one subject at a time . . ."—Charles Dickens

"Concentration is the factor that causes the great discrepancy between men and the results they achieve . . . the difference in their power of calling together all the rays of their ability and concentrating on one point."—Orison Swett Marden

"Habit is to life what rails are to transport cars."

"If you chase two rabbits, both will escape."—Proverb

"What do I mean by concentration? I mean focusing totally on the business at hand and commanding your body to do exactly what you want it to do."—Arnold Palmer

Reflection
Ruminating on what we have received

Charlotte's Thoughts on Reflection

"*Reflection*, the ruminating power which is so strongly developed in children and is somehow lost with much besides of the precious cargo they bring with them into the world. There is nothing sadder than the way we allow intellectual impressions to pass over the surface of our minds, without any effort to retain or assimilate" (Vol. 3, p. 120).

"In reflecting we ruminate on what we have received" (Vol. 3, p. 121).

"Children must be allowed to ruminate, must be left alone with their own thoughts" (Vol. 3, p. 162).

Quotes on Reflection

"Reading without reflecting is like eating without digesting."—Edmund Burke

Thoroughness
Dissatisfaction with a slipshod, imperfect grasp of a subject

Charlotte's Thoughts on Thoroughness

"*Thoroughness*, the habit of dissatisfaction with a slipshod, imperfect grasp of a subject, and of mental uneasiness until a satisfying measure of knowledge is obtained;—this habit is greatly encouraged by a reference to an encyclopædia, to clear up any doubtful point, when it turns up" (Vol. 3, p. 120).

Quotes on Thoroughness

"To be conscious that you are ignorant is a great step to knowledge."—Benjamin Disraeli

"Knowledge is of two kinds. We know a subject ourselves, or we know where

Guide your child in learning how to research a topic at the library or on the Internet.

"There is a sort of artistic pleasure in putting the fine touches to character."

we can find information on it."—Samuel Johnson

"Mankind have a great aversion to intellectual labor; but even supposing knowledge to be easily attainable, more people would be content to be ignorant than would take even a little trouble to acquire it."—Samuel Johnson

"The point of view it seems well to take is, that all beautiful and noble possibilities are present in varying degree in everyone, but that each person is subject to assault and hindrance in various ways of which he should be aware."

Chapter 5
Moral Habits

When we think of a person's character, we usually are thinking of these "moral" traits that are displayed consistently in that person's life—traits that have become habitual. In this chapter you will find Charlotte's comments on these habits:

Integrity (in four aspects)

> **Priorities**
>
> **Finishing**
>
> **Use of Time**
>
> **Borrowed Property**

Obedience

Personal Initiative

Reverence

Self-Control

Sweet, Even Temper

Truthfulness

Usefulness

Charlotte laid the groundwork for moral habits in Volume 1, *Home Education*, and then expanded upon them in the other books. Among her specific suggestions, she also gave these general thoughts on how to teach moral habits.

1. Don't debate whether moral habits are right or wrong; always present morals as right.

" 'The teacher should always take the moral habit for granted. He should never give his pupils to understand that he and they are about to examine whether, for instance, it is wrong or not wrong to lie. The commandment against lying is assumed, and its obligation acknowledged at the outset.' This we heartily agree with, and especially we like the apparently inadvertent use of the word 'commandment,' which concedes the whole question at issue—that is, that the idea of duty is a relative one depending on an Authority supreme and intimate, which embraces the thoughts of the heart and the issues of the life" (Vol. 2, p. 114).

"Only at home can children be trained in the chivalrous temper of 'proud submission and dignified obedience'; and if the parents do not inspire and foster deference, reverence, and loyalty, how shall these crowning graces of character thrive in a hard and emulous world?"

2. Give common-sense reasons, as well as Biblical reasons, for moral habits. Don't limit your approach to only laws and punishments.

"Moral teaching must be as simple, direct and definite as the teaching which appeals to the intellect; presented with religious sanctions, quickened by religious impulses, but not limited to the prohibitions of the law nor to the penalties which overtake the transgressor" (Vol. 2, p. 213).

3. Provide plenty of living examples and stories of heroes who exemplify these habits, and reinforce these ideas—conscientiously but casually —in front of your child.

"Moral habits, the way to form them and the bounden duty of every parent to send children into the world with a good outfit of moral habits, is a subject so much to the front in our thoughts, that I need not dwell further upon it here. The moral impulse having been given by means of some such inspiring idea as we have considered, the parent's or teacher's next business is to keep the idea well to the front, with tact and delicacy, and without insistence, and to afford apparently casual opportunities for moral effort on the lines of the first impulse" (Vol. 3, p. 135).

Integrity
Firm adherence to a code of values; being a good steward of all that we possess

"Mommy, what is 'integrity'?" asked Shelly.

"Well, do you remember in math we were talking about integers?" Mom replied.

"Yes," Shelly answered with a questioning look on her face.

Mom smiled. "Both words come from the same root. What is an integer?"

"A number that is whole, not divided into fractions," Shelly recalled.

"Exactly," said Mom. "And a person with integrity is consistent in his whole life. He has the same standards of behavior for every area. His life is not divided by changing standards in different areas. Does that make sense?"

"I think so," Shelly replied. "But what kind of standards and what areas of life do you mean? I think I would understand better if you gave me an example."

"Usually a person of integrity has the standard of always doing what is right. So he would be careful to do what is right in the areas of his work, his finances, his relationships with friends, his family responsibilities—get the idea?"

"I see," nodded Shelly. "He does what is right over all and through and through."

"Right. In all areas and in both big stuff and little matters," Mom affirmed.

Integrity includes so many aspects of a person's life! Charlotte mentioned several aspects under the umbrella of Integrity, in four of which she used the word "habit": priorities, finishing a task, use of time, and borrowed property. If you think about it, those four aspects can tell you a lot about a person's character.

"Moral teaching must be as simple, direct and definite."

Charlotte's Thoughts on Integrity

1. Help your child learn how to set priorities and practice prioritizing his work.

"To find 'ye nexte thynge' is not, after all, so simple. It is often a matter of selection. There are twenty letters to write, a dozen commissions to do, a score of books you want to read, and much ordering and arranging of shelves and drawers that you would like to plunge into at once.

"It has been amusingly said, 'Never do to-day what you can put off till to-morrow.' The dilatory, procrastinating person rejoices over a counsel he can follow! But not so fast, friend; this easy-going rule of life means '*putting first things first.*' Now, the power of ordering, organising, one's work which this implies distinguishes between a person of intelligence and the unintelligent person who lets himself be swamped by details. The latter will grind steadily through the twenty letters, say, just as they come to hand. He has to leave his correspondence unfinished; and the three or four letters which it was necessary to answer by return are left over for another day.

"The power to distinguish what *must* be done at once, from what *may* be done, comes pretty much by habit. At first it requires attention and thought. But mind and body get into the way of doing most things; and the person, whose mind has the habit of singling out the important things and doing them first, saves much annoyance to himself and others, and has gained in Integrity" (Vol. 4, Book 1, pp. 171, 172).

2. Direct your child to finish one project before beginning something new.

"What is worth beginning is worth finishing, and what is worth doing is worth doing well. Do not let yourself begin to make a dozen things, all of them tumbling about unfinished in your box. Of course there are fifty reasons for doing the new thing; but here is another case where we must curb that filly, Inclination. It is worth while to make ourselves go on with the thing we are doing until it is finished. Even so, there is the temptation to scamp in order to get at the new thing; but let us do each bit of work as perfectly as we know how, remembering that each thing we turn out is a bit of ourselves, and we must leave it whole and complete; for this is Integrity.

"The idle, the careless, and the volatile may be engaging enough as companions, but they do not turn out honest work, and are not building up for themselves integrity of character. This rests upon the foundations of diligence, attention, and perseverance. In the end, integrity makes for gaiety, because the person who is honest about his work has time to play, and is not secretly vexed by the remembrance of things left undone or ill done" (Vol. 4, Book 1, p. 172).

"Closely connected with this habit of 'perfect work' is that of finishing whatever is taken in hand. The child should rarely be allowed to set his hand to a new undertaking until the last is finished" (Vol. 1, p. 160).

3. Help your child learn to make good use of his time every day.

"It is a bad thing to think that time is our own to do what we like with. We are all employed; we all have duties, and a certain share of our time must be given to those duties. It is astonishing how much time there is in a day, and how many

"What is worth beginning is worth finishing, and what is worth doing is worth doing well."

things we can get in if we have a mind. It is also astonishing how a day, a week, or a year may slip through our fingers, and nothing done. We say we have done no harm, that we have not *meant* to do wrong. We have simply let ourselves drift. Boys or girls will drift through life at school, men or women through life in the world, effecting nothing, because they have not taken hold. They fail in examinations, in their professions, in the duty of providing for a family, in the duty of serving their town or their country, not because they are without brains, nor because they are vicious, but because they do not see that *to use time* is a duty.

"They dawdle through the working day, hoping that some one will *make* them do the thing they ought. Now, this is a delusion. No one can *make* even a little child do things. If he is obedient, it is because he makes himself obey; if he is diligent, he makes himself work, and not all the king's horses and all the king's men can make the dawdler diligent; he himself must make himself do the thing he ought at the right time. This power of making oneself work is a fine thing. Every effort makes the next easier, and, once we mount upon that easy nag, Habit, why, it is a real satisfaction to do the day's work in the day, and be free to enjoy the day's leisure" (Vol. 4, Book 1, p. 173).

4. Teach your child that anything he borrows should be returned promptly and in good shape.

"The question of borrowing falls under the head of the care we owe to other people's property. From a black-lead pencil to an umbrella, young people borrow without stint; and there is so much community of property and good fellowship among them that the free use of each other's belongings is perhaps hardly to be objected to. One word, though, in the name of honesty! What we borrow we must return promptly, the thing being none the worse for our use of it. No degree of community of life excuses us from this duty. The friend we borrow from may take no heed of the fact that we do not return the object; but we suffer in our wholeness, our integrity, from all such lapses" (Vol. 4, Book 1, p. 178).

5. Explain that every lapse in these areas of integrity leaves its mark on our character.

"As we have seen, our work, our time, the material or property of which we have the handling, are all matters for the just and honest use of which we are accountable. We may be guilty of many lapses which no one notices, but every lapse makes an imperfection in our own character. We have less integrity after a lapse than before it; and the habit of permitting ourselves in small dishonesties, whether in the way of waste of time, slipshod work, or injured property, prepares the way for a ruinous downfall in after life. But we need fear no fall, for Integrity is, with us, a part of 'ourselves,' and only asks of us a hearing" (Vol. 4, Book 1, p. 178).

Questions to Ask about Integrity

- Is my child learning how to prioritize his work?
- Does my child finish a project before he begins a new one?
- Is my child making progress toward using his time wisely every day?
- Does my child return borrowed property promptly and in good repair?

"This power of making oneself work is a fine thing."

• Am I taking steps to teach my child how lapses in integrity affect his character?

More Quotes on Integrity

Priorities

"Organizing is what you do before you do something, so that when you do it, it's not all mixed up."—A. A. Milne

"But seek ye first the kingdom of God, and his righteousness; and all these things shall be added unto you."—Matthew 6:33

"Thou shalt love the Lord thy God with all thy heart, and with all thy soul, and with all thy mind, and with all thy strength: this is the first commandment. And the second is like, namely this, Thou shalt love thy neighbour as thyself. There is none other commandment greater than these."—Mark 12:30, 31

Finishing

"Do not plan for ventures before finishing what's at hand."—Euripides

"There is nothing so fatal to character as half finished tasks."—David Lloyd George

"There are two kinds of people, those who finish what they start and so on."—Robert Byrne

"Genius begins great works; labor alone finishes them."—Joseph Joubert

"For which of you, intending to build a tower, sitteth not down first, and counteth the cost, whether he have sufficient to finish it?"—Luke 14:28

Use of Time

"Those who make the worst use of their time are the first to complain of its shortness."—Jean de La Bruyere

"Look at a day when you are supremely satisfied at the end. It's not a day when you lounge around doing nothing. It's when you've had everything to do, and you've done it."—Margaret Thatcher

"If a man has any greatness in him, it comes to light—not in one flamboyant hour, but in the ledger of his daily work."—Beryl Markham

"Nine-tenths of wisdom consists in being wise in scheduling time."—Theodore Roosevelt

"You will always be glad at evening if you have spent the day well."—Thomas a Kempis

Notes

"Habit is inevitable. If we fail to ease life by laying down habits of right thinking and right acting, habits of wrong thinking and wrong acting fix themselves of their own accord."

Notes

"Never lose one moment of time, but improve it in the most profitable way possible."—Jonathan Edwards

Borrowed Property

"A man can get a reputation from very small things."—Sophocles

Obedience
Submitting to the restraint or command of authority

Amber glanced into the dining room and saw her four-year-old son holding the fragile candlestick. "Matthew, please put that candlestick down," she instructed in a quiet but firm voice.

"You can't get it from me," Matthew replied with a smirk and a mischievous twinkle in his eyes.

"You're right, Matthew, I can't," said Amber, "And I don't want to get it from you. I want you to choose to put it down because you know it's the right thing to do."

Matthew's expression changed as his mommy's words sunk in. Then he set down the candlestick. "I'm sorry," he said.

When children are little we must do all we can to form in them the habit of obedience, but we must also keep in mind that our goal is for them to eventually choose to obey of their own free will.

The habit of obedience is one of the "Top Three" habits that Charlotte talked about most. The other two are attention (p. 50) and truthfulness (p. 110).

Charlotte's Thoughts on Obedience

1. Make obedience a top priority, even more important than academics.

"First, and infinitely the most important, is the habit of *obedience*. Indeed, obedience is the whole duty of the child, and for this reason—every other duty of the child is fulfilled as a matter of obedience to his parents. Not only so: obedience is the whole duty of man; obedience to conscience, to law, to Divine direction" (Vol. 1, p. 161).

2. Treat willfulness as disobedience.

"It has been well observed that each of the three recorded temptations of our Lord in the wilderness is a suggestion, not of an act of overt sin, but of an act of *wilfulness*, that state directly opposed to obedience, and out of which springs all that foolishness which is bound up in the heart of a child" (Vol. 1, p. 161).

3. Realize that you are on assignment from God to teach your child obedience.

"Now, if the parent realise that obedience is no mere accidental duty, the fulfilling of which is a matter that lies between himself and the child, but that

"First, and infinitely the most important, is the habit of *obedience*."

he is the appointed agent to train the child up to the intelligent obedience of the self-compelling, law-abiding human being, he will see that he has no right to *forego* the obedience of his child, and that every act of disobedience in the child is a direct condemnation of the parent. Also, he will see that the motive to the child's obedience is not the arbitrary one of, 'Do this, or that, because I have said so,' but the motive of the apostolic injunction, 'Children, obey your parents in the Lord, *for this is right*' " (Vol. 1, p. 161).

4. *Remember that your ultimate goal is a child who desires to obey.*

"It is only in proportion as the will of the child is in the act of obedience, and he obeys because his sense of *right* makes him *desire* to obey in spite of temptations to disobedience—not of constraint, but willingly—that the habit has been formed which will, hereafter, enable the child to use the strength of his will against his inclinations when these prompt him to lawless courses. It is said that the children of parents who are most strict in exacting obedience often turn out ill; and that orphans and other poor waifs brought up under strict discipline only wait their opportunity to break out into license. Exactly so; because, in these cases, there is no gradual training of the child in the *habit* of obedience; no gradual enlisting of his *will* on the side of sweet service and a free-will offering of submission to the highest law: the poor children are simply bullied into submission to the *will*, that is, the *wilfulness*, of another; not at all, 'for it is *right*'; only because it is convenient" (Vol. 1, pp. 161, 162).

5. *Expect obedience and convey that expectation in a quiet, but firm, tone of voice.*

"There is no need to rate the child, or threaten him, or use any manner of violence, because the parent is *invested* with authority which the child intuitively recognises. It is enough to say, 'Do this,' in a quiet, authoritative tone, and *expect it to be done.* The mother often loses her hold over her children because they detect in the tone of her voice that she does not expect them to obey her behests; she does not think enough of her position; has not sufficient confidence in her own authority" (Vol. 1, p. 162).

6. *Insist on prompt, cheerful, and lasting obedience every time.*

"The mother's great stronghold is in the *habit* of obedience. If she begin by requiring that her children always obey her, why, they will always do so as a matter of course; but let them once get the thin end of the wedge in, let them discover that they can do otherwise than obey, and a woeful struggle begins, which commonly ends in the children doing that which is right in their own eyes.

"This is the sort of thing which is fatal: The children are in the drawing-room, and a caller is announced. 'You must go upstairs now.' 'Oh, mother dear, *do* let us stay in the window-corner; we will be as quiet as mice!' The mother is rather proud of her children's pretty manners, and they stay. They are *not* quiet, of course; but that is the least of the evils; they have succeeded in doing as they chose and not as they were bid, and they will not put their necks under the yoke again without a struggle. It is in little matters that the mother is worsted. 'Bedtime, Willie!' 'Oh, mamma, *just* let me finish this'; and the mother yields, forgetting that the case in point is of no consequence; the thing that matters is that the

Charlotte chose not to address in detail the subject of spanking. She did, however, mention it in a section of Home Education, *where she lamented the societal shift of authority and indulgent mind-set that were becoming the norm of her day: "For instance, according to the former code, a mother might use her slipper now and then, to good effect and without blame; but now, the person of the child is, whether rightly or wrongly, held sacred and the infliction of pain for moral purposes is pretty generally disallowed.*

"Again, the old rule for the children's table was, 'the plainer the better, and let hunger bring sauce'; now the children's diet must be at least as nourishing and as varied as that of their elders; and appetite, the craving for certain kinds of food, hitherto a vicious tendency to be repressed, is now within certain limitations the parents' most trustworthy guide in arranging a dietary for their children. . . .

"That children should do as they are bid, mind their books, and take pleasure as it offers when nothing stands in the way, sums up the old theory; now, the pleasures of children are apt to be made of more account than their duties.

"Formerly, they were brought up in subjection; now, the elders give place, and the world is made for the children" (Vol. 1, pp. 6, 7).

For more on #7, see the introductory story under Self-Discipline in Habits on page 142.

Charlotte wrote directly to young people about obedience in Volume 4, Book 2, page 145.

"The children who are trained to perfect obedience may be trusted with a good deal of liberty."

child should be daily confirming a *habit* of obedience by the unbroken repetition of acts of obedience. It is astonishing how clever the child is in finding ways of evading the spirit while he observes the letter. 'Mary, come in.' 'Yes, mother'; but her mother calls four times before Mary comes. 'Put away your bricks'; and the bricks are put away with slow, reluctant fingers. 'You must *always* wash your hands when you hear the first bell.' The child obeys for that once, and no more.

"To avoid these displays of wilfulness, the mother will insist from the first on an obedience which is prompt, cheerful, and lasting—save for lapses of memory on the child's part. Tardy, unwilling, occasional obedience is hardly worth the having; and it is greatly easier to give the child the *habit* of perfect obedience by never allowing him in anything else, than it is to obtain this mere formal obedience by a constant exercise of authority" (Vol. 1, pp. 162–164).

7. *Never give a command that you do not intend to see carried out to the full.*

"By-and-by, when he is old enough, take the child into confidence; let him know what a noble thing it is to be able to make himself do, in a minute, and brightly, the very thing he would rather not do. To secure this habit of obedience, the mother must exercise great self-restraint; she must never give a command which she does not intend to see carried out to the full. And she must not lay upon her children burdens, grievous to be borne, of command heaped upon command" (Vol. 1, p. 164).

8. *Be careful of giving so many commands that your child feels pestered.*

"The children who are trained to perfect obedience may be trusted with a good deal of liberty: they receive a few directions which they know they must not disobey; and for the rest, they are left to learn how to direct their own actions, even at the cost of some small mishaps; and are not pestered with a perpetual fire of 'Do this' and 'Don't do that!' " (Vol. 1, p. 164).

9. *Teach your child to appeal respectfully; be gracious enough to yield sometimes in matters that are not crucial.*

"Authority is neither harsh nor indulgent. She is gentle and easy to be entreated in all matters immaterial, just because she is immovable in matters of real importance; for these, there is always a fixed principle. It does not, for example, rest with parents and teachers to dally with questions affecting either the health or the duty of their children. They have no authority to allow children in indulgences—in too many sweetmeats, for example—or in habits which are prejudicial to health; nor to let them off from any plain duty of obedience, courtesy, reverence, or work. Authority is alert; she knows all that is going on and is aware of tendencies. She fulfils the apostolic precept—'He that ruleth (let him do it), with diligence.' But she is strong enough to fulfil that other precept also, 'He that showeth mercy (let him do it), with cheerfulness'; timely clemency, timely yielding, is a great secret of strong government. It sometimes happens that children, and not their parents, have right on their side: a claim may be made or an injunction resisted, and the children are in opposition to parent or teacher. It is well for the latter to get the habit of swiftly and imperceptibly reviewing the situation; possibly, the children may be in the right, and the parent may gather up his wits in time to yield the point graciously and send the little rebels away in a glow of love and loyalty" (Vol. 3, p. 17).

10. Begin teaching obedience by the time your child is one year old.

" 'I teach my children obedience by the time they are one year old,' the writer heard a very successful mother remark; and, indeed, that is the age at which to begin to give children the ease and comfort of the habit of obeying lawful authority" (Vol. 3, p. 18).

11. Remember that the child who learns to make himself do what he should (even when he doesn't feel like it) will be able to accomplish much in this life.

"It is an old story that the failures in life are not the people who lack good intentions; they are those whose physical nature has not acquired the habit of prompt and involuntary obedience. The man who can make himself do what he wills has the world before him, and it rests with parents to give their children this self-compelling power as a mere matter of habit" (Vol. 3, p. 20).

See also Self-Control on page 105.

12. Teach your child to respond to his conscience, but do not depend on it solely.

"But is it not better and higher, it may be asked, to train children to act always in response to the divine mandate as it makes itself heard through the voice of conscience? The answer is, that in doing this we must not leave the other undone. There are few earnest parents who do not bring the power of conscience to bear on their children, and there are emergencies enough in the lives of young and old when we have to make a spiritual decision upon spiritual grounds—when it rests with us to choose the good and refuse the evil, consciously and voluntarily, because it is God's will that we should" (Vol. 3, p. 20).

13. Give reasons for your commands when appropriate and helpful, but don't feel trapped into doing so every time.

"It is not advisable to answer children categorically when they want to know the why for every command, but wise parents steer a middle course. They are careful to form habits upon which the routine of life runs easily, and, when the exceptional event requires a new regulation, they may make casual mention of their reasons for having so and so done; or, if this is not convenient and the case is a trying one, they give the children the reason for all obedience—'for this is right.' In a word, authority avoids, so far as may be, giving cause of offence" (Vol. 3, p. 22).

14. Whenever possible, plan ahead to make transitions smooth by giving your child a predetermined amount of time to prepare for the change in activity.

"Another hint as to the fit use of authority may be gleaned from the methods employed in a well-governed state. The importance of *prevention* is fully recognised: police, army, navy, are largely preventive forces; and the home authority, too, does well to place its forces on the Alert Service. It is well to prepare for trying efforts: 'We shall have time to finish this chapter before the

"What is the object of family discipline, of that obedience which has been described as 'the whole duty of a child'? Is it not to ease the way of the child, while will is weak and conscience immature, by setting it on the habits of the good life where it is as easy to go right as for a locomotive to run on its lines?"

Notes

Vis inertiae means "the tendency to remain at rest." Abeyance means "temporarily stopped, or in suspension."

Do you understand how discipline brings freedom? Take an example of practicing the piano. If you discipline yourself to practice every day and keep your skills sharp, you will be prepared and able to play complicated works freely at a moment's notice. However, if you neglect practicing, you will not be free to play as you would like to.

"Little children must be trained in the obedience of habit; but every gallant boy and girl has learned to *choose* to obey all who are set in authority."

clock strikes seven'; or, 'we shall be able to get in one more round before bedtime.' Nobody knows better than the wise mother the importance of giving a child time to collect himself for a decisive moment. This time should be spent in finishing some delightful occupation; every minute of idleness at these critical junctures goes to the setting up of the *vis inertiae*, most difficult to overcome because the child's will power is in abeyance. A little forethought is necessary to arrange that occupations do come to an end at the right moment; that bedtime does not arrive in the middle of a chapter, or at the most exciting moment of a game. In such an event authority, which looks before and after, *might* see its way to allow five minutes' grace, but would not feel itself empowered to allow a child to dawdle about indefinitely before saying good-night" (Vol. 3, pp. 22, 23)

15. *Motivate your child with the truth that discipline brings freedom and that obedience is both delightful and dignified.*

"The result of an ordered freedom is obtained, that ordered freedom which rules the lives of 999 in 1000 of the citizens of the world; but the drawback to an indirect method of securing this result is that when, 'Do as you please,' is substituted for, 'Do as you're bid,' there is dissimulation in the air and children fail to learn that habit of 'proud subjection and dignified obedience' which distinguishes great men and noble citizens. No doubt it is pleasing that children should behave naturally, should get up and wander about, should sit still or frolic as they have a mind to, but they too, must 'learn obedience'; and it is no small element in their happiness and ours that obedience is both delightful and reposeful" (Vol. 6, p. 70).

16. *Train your child in the habit of obedience with the goal that he will ultimately choose to obey all authority.*

"Little children must be trained in the obedience of habit; but every gallant boy and girl has learned to *choose* to obey all who are set in authority" (Vol. 6, p. 134).

Questions to Ask about Obedience

- Do I make obedience top priority, even more important than academics?
- Am I treating willfulness the same as disobedience?
- Do I realize that I am on assignment from God to teach my child to obey?
- Is my child moving toward desiring to obey?
- Do I expect my child to obey me?
- Am I trying to use a quiet but firm tone of voice when telling my child to do something?
- Do I insist on prompt, cheerful, and lasting obedience every time?
- Am I learning not to give a command that I do not intend to see carried out to the full?
- Am I giving so many commands that my child feels pestered?
- Am I gracious enough to yield occasionally in matters that are not crucial if my child appeals respectfully?
- Am I seeking to teach my child obedience by the time he is one year old?

- Do I see my training my child in obedience as helping him accomplish much in his future life?
- Is my child learning to respond to his conscience?
- Am I giving reasons for my commands when appropriate, or do I feel trapped into giving a reason every time?
- Am I striving to make transitions between activities smooth by giving my child a set amount of time to prepare for the change?
- Is my child learning that discipline brings freedom and that obedience is delightful and dignified?
- Is my child moving toward choosing to obey all authority in his life?

More Quotes on Obedience

"The word *no* carries a lot more meaning when spoken by a parent who also knows how to say yes."—Joyce Maynard

"And Samuel said, Hath the Lord as great delight in burnt offerings and sacrifices, as in obeying the voice of the Lord? Behold, to obey is better than sacrifice, and to hearken than the fat of rams."—1 Samuel 15:22

"Children, obey your parents in all things: for this is well pleasing unto the Lord."—Colossians 3:20

"Obey them that have the rule over you, and submit yourselves."—Hebrews 13:17

Personal Initiative
Acting at one's own discretion, independently of outside influence or control

"I feel guilty if I don't spend hours playing with my child," Barbara admitted.
Lee smiled in an understanding way. "You certainly don't want to neglect your child, but it sounds like you don't realize what a favor you would be doing in giving your child time to play on his own," she responded.
"I would be doing him a favor?" Barbara was skeptical.
"Think about it. A child who is constantly amused and entertained by others will never learn how to keep himself occupied or think up his own amusements," Lee explained.
Barbara laughed. "Oh, he'll think up his own amusements, all right! He'll be drawing on the toilet seat with a marking pen!"
"Within boundaries," added Lee. "Freedom within boundaries is the key. It can be hard work to come up with one's own ideas. I remember when my children were growing up they would come to me and complain that they were bored. Well, I knew that comment simply meant that they didn't want to exert the effort to think of something to do on their own, so I kept a list of chores

"Tardy, unwilling, occasional obedience is hardly worth the having."

handy. When a child said he was bored, I assigned him a chore." Lee chuckled, remembering. "That stopped the 'I'm bored' routine very quickly!"

Encourage your child to take personal initiative by giving him lots of free time and opportunities to explore within your set boundaries.

Charlotte's Thoughts on Personal Initiative

1. Make sure your child has plenty of free time to play, explore, and grow.

"Danger lurks in the Kindergarten, just in proportion to the completeness and beauty of its organisation. It is possible to supplement Nature so skilfully that we run some risk of supplanting her, depriving her of space and time to do her own work in her own way. 'Go and see what Tommy is doing and tell him he mustn't,' is not sound doctrine. Tommy should be free to do what he likes with his limbs and his mind through all the hours of the day when he is not sitting up nicely at meals. He should run and jump, leap and tumble, lie on his face watching a worm, or on his back watching the bees in a lime tree" (Vol. 1, pp. 191, 192).

2. Be available to guide, inform, and give direction as needed.

"Nature will look after him and give him promptings of desire *to know* many things; and somebody must tell as he wants to know; and *to do* many things, and somebody should be handy just to put him in the way; and *to be* many things, naughty and good, and somebody should give direction" (Vol. 1, p. 192).

3. Don't sacrifice the habit of personal initiative because you are uptight about controlling all the other habits you want to cultivate in your child.

"The busy mother says she has no leisure to be that somebody [who informs and gives direction], and the child will run wild and get into bad habits; but we must not make a fetish of habit; education is a *life* as well as a discipline. Health, strength, and agility, bright eyes and alert movements, come of a free life, out-of-doors, if it may be; and as for habits, there is no habit or power so useful to man or woman as that of personal initiative" (Vol. 1, p. 192).

4. Encourage your child to invent his own games and find things to do within the boundaries you have set.

"The resourcefulness which will enable a family of children to invent their own games and occupations through the length of a summer's day is worth more in after life than a good deal of knowledge about cubes and hexagons, and this comes, not of continual intervention on the mother's part, but of much masterly inactivity" (Vol. 1, p. 192).

5. Allow your child freedom to express his personality in his school work within the boundaries you have set.

"In their work, too, we are too apt to interfere with children. We all know the delight with which any scope for personal initiative is hailed, the pleasure children take in doing anything which they may do their own way; anything, in fact, which allows room for skill of hand, play of fancy, or development of thought. With our present theories of education it seems that we cannot give much scope

You can read more about masterly inactivity in Volume 3, pages 25–35.

"Education is a *life* as well as a discipline."

for personal initiative. There is so much task-work to be done, so many things that must be, not learned, but learned about, that it is only now and then a child gets the chance to produce himself in his work. But let us use such opportunities as come in our way. A very interesting and instructive educational experiment on these lines has lately been tried at the School Field, Hackney, where Mr Sargent got together some eighty boys and girls under the conditions of an ordinary elementary school, except that the school was supported, not by the Education Department nor by the rates, but by the founder. The results seem to have been purely delightful; the children developed an amazing capacity for drawing, perhaps because so soon as they were familiar with the outlines of the flower and foliage of a given plant, for example, they were encouraged to form designs with these elements. The really beautiful floral designs produced by these girls and boys, after quite a short art training, would surprise parents whose children have been taught drawing for years with no evident result. These School Field children developed themselves a great deal on their school magazine also, for which they wrote tales and poems, and essays, not prescribed work, but self-chosen. The children's thought was stimulated, and they felt they had it in them to say much about a doll's ball, Peter, the school cat, or whatever other subject struck their fancy. 'They felt their feet,' as the nurses say of children when they begin to walk; and our non-success in education is a good deal due to the fact that we carry children through their school work and do not let them feel their feet" (Vol. 3, pp. 37, 38).

Questions to Ask about Personal Initiative

- Am I giving my child plenty of free time?
- Am I trying to be available to guide and inform as needed?
- Am I encroaching on my child's developing initiative by trying to control every moment of his day?
- Is my child learning to invent his own games and occupations within my set boundaries, or is he depending on me to amuse him?
- Am I allowing my child to add his personal touch to school work within my boundaries?

More Quotes on Personal Initiative

"It is wonderful how much may be done if we are always doing."—Thomas Jefferson

"You cannot build character and courage by taking away man's initiative and independence."—Abraham Lincoln

Reverence

Consideration for others;
respect for person and property

Dorothy sat at the dinner table aghast. Dessert had just been set out, and her

Notes

host's son was reaching across the table, sticking his fork into the cake before the host had an opportunity to serve it.

"I want a big piece," he whined.

Soothingly, the host gave his son the piece he desired. Without so much as a "thank you," the son picked it up and started to stuff it in his face.

"Please, use your fork, son," the host reminded him.

"I don't want to," retorted the son with a full mouth.

Dorothy grimaced inside. *It's too bad. That father is going to have many a struggle ahead because he has not taught his son to respect him or others.*

Respect doesn't come naturally to most children; it must be taught. Make sure you show respect toward your child by treating him in a considerate way, but don't overlook the importance of teaching him to respect you and others.

Charlotte's Thoughts on Reverence

1. Be prepared to exert a lot of zeal and persistence to cultivate within your child a respect for others.

Help your child recognize and reject the self-seeking attitudes in the world around him, especially in advertising and celebrities.

"As for reverence, consideration for others, respect for persons and property, I can only urge the importance of a sedulous cultivation of these moral qualities— the distinguishing marks of a refined nature—until they become the daily *habits* of the child's life; and the more, because a self-assertive, aggressive, self-seeking temper is but too characteristic of the times we live in" (Vol. 1, p. 166).

2. Help your child to form a sense of respect for historical events and people as well.

"Another notion that stands between us and any vital appreciation of the past is, that—'we are the people!' We are cocksure that we know all that is to be known, that we do all that is worth while; and we are able to regard the traditions and mementoes of the past with a sort of superior smirk, a notion that, if the book-writers have not made it all up, this story of the past is no such great thing after all: that 'a fellow I know' could do as much any day! There are few things more unpleasant than to see the superior air, and hear the cheap sneers, with which well-dressed people, not to say 'Arry and 'Arriet, disport themselves in the presence of any monument of antiquity they may make holiday to go and see. We have lost the habit of reverence" (Vol. 5, p. 313).

Make sure you show respect to your child. Try not to gossip about your child or embarrass him in front of others.

3. Use educational methods that respect your child as a person.

"The principles of authority on the one hand, and of obedience on the other, are natural, necessary and fundamental; but these principles are limited by the respect due to the personality of children, which must not be encroached upon, whether by the direct use of fear or love, suggestion or influence, or by undue play upon any one natural desire" (Vol. 6, p. xxix).

Questions to Ask about Reverence

- Am I working hard to cultivate in my child an attitude of respect for others?
- Is my child learning to recognize and reject self-assertive attitudes in the world around him?

"A self-assertive, aggressive, self-seeking temper is but too characteristic of the times we live in."

- Do I encourage my child to respect historical events and people?
- Am I careful to show respect to my child as a unique person?
- Am I trying to use educational methods that respect my child as a person?

More Quotes on Reverence

"It is never too late to give up our prejudices."—Henry David Thoreau

"Be kindly affectioned one to another with brotherly love; in honour preferring one another."—Romans 12:10

"There are two types of people—those who come into a room and say, 'Well, here I am!' and those who come in and say, 'Ah, there you are.' "—Frederick L. Collins

Self-Control
Keeping back the expression of our passions and emotions

"I'm a bit confused," Ann told Donna. "I hear everyone talking about my daughter as strong-willed, but you describe her as weak-willed. Why?"

"Let me give you an example," Donna replied. "Let's say you were on a diet, and a well-meaning neighbor brought over a delicious triple-layer chocolate cake. If you gave in and ate a piece of that cake, would you say, 'Oh, my will was just so strong, I had to have a piece'?"

"Of course not," Ann retorted. "I would say that I had been weak, that I needed more will-power to do what I should."

"Exactly," said Donna. "You need to strengthen your will so it can do what it's supposed to do instead of taking the easy way out and just doing what it wants to do."

"Right," confirmed Ann.

"And that's the same thing with your daughter," explained Donna. "Her will is weak. She needs your help to strengthen it to be able to do what she's supposed to do even when she doesn't want to."

A light dawned in Ann's eyes. Slowly she expressed her thoughts. "So it's not a matter of my fighting against her strong will; it's more like she and I need to work together to strengthen her will. She needs my help."

"You've got it," Donna said. "And I think if you explain this to your daughter, it will go a long way toward helping her learn self-control."

Charlotte's Thoughts on Self-Control

1. Teach your child by words and example that self-control brings joy.

"The bright eyes, the open regard, the springing step; the tones, clear as a bell;

Charlotte wrote at length about the "way of the will." You can read her comments on these pages: Volume 1, pages 7, 8, 324, 325; Volume 4, Book 2, pages 4, 126–155, 165–173; Volume 6, pages xxxi, 128–138.

"Habit is inevitable. If we fail to ease life by laying down habits of right thinking and right acting, habits of wrong thinking and wrong acting fix themselves of their own accord."

Notes

the agile, graceful movements that characterise the well-brought-up child, are the result, not of bodily well-being only, but of 'mind and soul according well,' of a quick, trained intelligence, and of a moral nature habituated to the 'joy of self-control' " (Vol. 1, p. 95).

2. View your child as weak-willed and your job as helping him strengthen his will to do what is right even when he doesn't feel like doing it.

"Supposing the parent take pains that the child shall be in a fit state to use his will, how is he to strengthen that will, so that by and by the child may employ it to control his own life by?" (Vol. 1, p. 327).

If your child has already formed a habit of throwing temper tantrums, see chapter 13 for suggestions on replacing that bad habit with a habit of self-control.

"But, all the time, nobody perceives that it is the mere want of will that is the matter with the child. He is in a state of absolute 'wilfulness,'—the rather unfortunate word we use to describe the state in which the will has no controlling power; willessness, if there were such a word, would describe this state more truly" (Vol. 1, pp. 320, 321).

"It is in him to be a little tyrant; 'he has a will of his own,' says his nurse, but she is mistaken in supposing that his stormy manifestations of greed, wilfulness, temper, are signs of will. It is when the little boy is able to stop all these and restrain himself with quivering lip that his will comes into play" (Vol. 6, p. 37).

3. Help your child understand that obedience is a stepping-stone to self-control.

"We have spoken already of the importance of training the child in the habit of obedience. Now, obedience is valuable only in so far as it helps the child towards making himself do that which he knows he ought to do" (Vol. 1, pp. 327, 328).

4. Encourage your child to feel a sense of conquest over his weak will whenever he exercises self-control.

"Every effort of obedience which does not give him a sense of *conquest* over his own inclinations, helps to enslave him, and he will resent the loss of his liberty by running into license when he can. That is the secret of the miscarrying of many strictly brought-up children" (Vol. 1, p. 328).

5. Invite your child's cooperation in developing this habit within himself.

"But invite his co-operation, let him heartily intend and purpose to do the thing he is bidden, and then it is his own will that is compelling him, and not yours; he has begun the greatest effort, the highest accomplishment of human life—the *making*, the compelling of himself" (Vol. 1, p. 328).

6. Watch for and applaud any efforts your child puts forth to control himself.

"Let him know what he is about, let him enjoy a sense of triumph, and of your congratulation, whenever he fetches his thoughts back to his tiresome sum, whenever he makes his hands finish what they have begun, whenever he throws

"It is when the little boy is able to stop all these and restrain himself with quivering lip that his will comes into play."

the black dog off his back, and produces a smile from a clouded face" (Vol. 1, p. 328).

7. Teach your child to think hard on good thoughts and actions will follow.

"Then, as was said before, let him know the secret of *willing*; let him know that, by an effort of will, he *can* turn his thoughts to the thing he wants to think of—his lessons, his prayers, his work, and away from the things he should not think of;—that, in fact, he can be such a brave, strong little fellow, he can *make* himself think of what he likes; and let him try little experiments—that if he once get his *thoughts* right, the rest will take care of itself, he will be sure to *do* right then; that if he feels cross, naughty thoughts coming upon him, the plan is, to think *hard* about something else, something nice—his next birthday, what he means to do when he is a man" (Vol. 1, p. 328).

8. Introduce and reinforce these principles little by little as opportunities arise.

"Not all this at once, of course; but line upon line, precept upon precept, here a little and there a little, as opportunity offers. Let him get into the *habit* of managing himself, controlling himself, and it is astonishing how much self-compelling power quite a young child will exhibit. 'Restrain yourself, Tommy,' I once heard a wise aunt say to a boy of four, and Tommy restrained himself, though he was making a terrible hullabaloo about some small trouble" (Vol. 1, pp. 328, 329).

Questions to Ask about Self-Control

- Am I trying to teach by word and example that self-control brings joy?
- Do I view my job as helping my child strengthen his weak will in order to make it do what is right?
- Does my child understand how obedience is a stepping-stone to self-control?
- Is my child beginning to feel a sense of conquest whenever he exhibits self-control?
- Am I gaining my child's cooperation in developing the habit of self-control?
- Am I watching for and careful to applaud my child's efforts toward self-control?
- Is my child learning to change his thoughts in order to change his actions?
- Am I introducing and reinforcing these principles little by little?

More Quotes on Self-Control

"Most powerful is he who has himself in his own power."—Seneca

"The happiness of a man in this life does not consist in the absence but in the mastery of his passions."—Alfred, Lord Tennyson

"That which we persist in doing becomes easier, not that the task itself has become easier, but that our ability to perform it has improved."—Ralph Waldo Emerson

"Let him know that, by an effort of will, he *can* turn his thoughts to the thing he wants to think of."

"We cannot always build the future for our youth, but we can build our youth for the future."—Franklin D. Roosevelt

Sweet, Even Temper
Making the best of things;
looking on the bright side

They had been married only a few months when Irene brought home several bags of groceries one evening. As she unloaded the food, it became increasingly apparent that their tiny apartment kitchen couldn't hold everything she had bought.

"Argh!" Irene exclaimed. "This is so frustrating! There isn't enough room in these little cupboards."

Irene's husband smiled and quietly replied, "I'm thankful we have so much food that it won't even fit in our kitchen."

That one comment made all the difference. Irene has never unloaded groceries since then without being thankful for all the food that is in the bags.

We can do the same for our children. It's amazing how furrowed brows and set jaws can disappear with a few well-spoken words.

Charlotte's Thoughts on Sweet, Even Temper

1. Don't excuse a sullen temperament on the basis of heredity or age.

"I am anxious, however, to a say a few words on the *habit* of sweet temper. It is very customary to regard temper as constitutional, that which is born in you and is neither to be helped nor hindered. 'Oh, she is a good-tempered little soul; nothing puts her out!' 'Oh, he has his father's temper; the least thing that goes contrary makes him fly into a passion,' are the sorts of remarks we hear constantly.

"It is no doubt true that children inherit a certain tendency to irascibility or to amiability, to fretfulness, discontentment, peevishness, sullenness, murmuring, and impatience; or to cheerfulness, trustfulness, good-humour, patience, and humility. It is also true that upon the preponderance of any of these qualities— upon *temper*, that is—the happiness or wretchedness of child and man depends, as well as the comfort or misery of the people who live with him. We all know people possessed of integrity and of many excellent virtues who make themselves intolerable to their belongings. The root of evil is, not that these people were *born* sullen, or peevish, or envious—that might have been mended; but that they were permitted to grow up in these dispositions. Here, if anywhere, the power of habit is invaluable: it rests with the parents to correct the original twist, all the more so if it is from them the child gets it, and to send their child into the world blest with an even, happy temper, inclined to make the best of things, to look on the bright side, to impute the best and kindest motives to others, and to make no extravagant claims on his own account—fertile source of ugly tempers" (Vol. 1, pp. 166, 167).

"To laugh at ugly tempers and let them pass because the child is small, is to sow the wind."

"To laugh at ugly tempers and let them pass because the child is small, is to sow the wind" (Vol. 1, p. 19).

2. *Correct your child's tendency before it becomes a temper.*

"The child is born with no more than certain *tendencies*.

"It is by force of habit that a tendency becomes a temper; and it rests with the mother to hinder the formation of ill tempers, to force that of good tempers. Nor is it difficult to do this while the child's countenance is as an open book to his mother, and she reads the thoughts of his heart before he is aware of them himself. Remembering that every envious, murmuring, discontented thought leaves a track in the very substance of the child's brain for such thoughts to run in again and again—that this track, this *rut*, so to speak, is ever widening and deepening with the traffic in ugly thoughts—the mother's care is to hinder at the outset the formation of any such track" (Vol. 1, p. 167).

If your child has already formed a sullen temper as a habit, see chapter 14 for suggestions on replacing that bad habit with the habit of a sweet, even temper.

3. *Watch for opportunities to redirect your child's thoughts along good lines.*

"She sees into her child's soul—sees the evil temper in the act of rising: now is her opportunity.

"Let her *change the child's thoughts* before ever the bad temper has had time to develop into conscious feeling, much less act: take him out of doors, send him to fetch or carry, tell him or show him something of interest,—in a word, give him something else to think about; but all in a natural way, and without letting the child perceive that he is being treated. As every fit of sullenness leaves place in the child's mind for another fit of sullenness to succeed it, so every such fit averted by the mother's tact tends to obliterate the evil traces of former sullen tempers. At the same time, the mother is careful to lay down a highway for the free course of all sweet and genial thoughts and feelings" (Vol. 1, pp. 167, 168).

"Take the child with an inherited tendency to a resentful temper: he has begun to think resentful thoughts; finds them easy and gratifying; he goes on; evermore the ugly traffic becomes more easy and natural, and resentfulness is rapidly becoming himself, that trait in his character which people couple with his name.

"But one custom overcomes another. The watchful mother sets up new tracks in other directions; and she sees to it, that while she is leading new thoughts through the new way, the old, deeply worn 'way of thinking' is quite disused" (Vol. 2, p. 89).

"Again, let us keep before the children that it is the manner of thoughts we think which matters; and, in the early days, when a child's face is an open book to his parents, the habit of sweet thoughts must be kept up, and every selfish, resentful, unamiable movement of children's minds observed in the countenance must be changed before consciousness sets in" (Vol. 3, pp. 135, 136).

Questions to Ask about Sweet, Even Temper

- Am I mistakenly excusing my child's sour disposition because other family members are like that or because he is young?
- Am I seeking to become such a good student of my child that I can read his thoughts on his face?

"Let her *change the child's thoughts* before ever the bad temper has had time to develop into conscious feeling, much less act."

• Am I helping my child learn to redirect his sullen thoughts along good lines?

More Quotes on Sweet, Even Temper

"Happiness is a thing to be practiced, like the violin."—John Lubbock

"Good thoughts bear good fruit, bad thoughts bear bad fruit—and man is his own gardener."—James Allen

"Cheerfulness and contentment are great beautifiers, and are famous preservers of good looks."—Charles Dickens

"A merry heart maketh a cheerful countenance: but by sorrow of the heart the spirit is broken."—Proverbs 15:13

"Finally, brethren, whatsoever things are true, whatsoever things are honest, whatsoever things are just, whatsoever things are pure, whatsoever things are lovely, whatsoever things are of good report; if there be any virtue, and if there be any praise, think on these things."—Philippians 4:8

Truthfulness
*Aligning words and actions
in accordance with fact*

"How are you coming with teaching Kenneth the difference between the truth and a lie?" Melody inquired.

"It's tough," replied Nancy. "With his special needs, we're never quite sure what he understands. But we're trying to use a combination of consequences and broken relationships, and it seems to be working. For example, he's been making a lot of messes in the bathroom lately. So we set the consequence that if he made a mess in the bathroom, we wouldn't be able to read his bedtime story."

Melody raised her eyebrows.

"Oh, don't worry. That's not the only time of day that we read to him!" Nancy read her thoughts. "Well, a couple of days ago he came in to tell me that he was done in the bathroom and ready for bed. I asked him if he had made a mess, and he said No. When I went to look, sure enough, there was a mess. I turned to Kenneth and with the saddest look I could muster, said sorrowfully, 'Yes, there is a mess. You must tell Mommy the truth. You made a mess and didn't tell Mommy the truth.' "

"What did he do?" asked Melody.

"His whole face changed from happy expectant to sad repentant, and he hugged my neck and said, 'I'm sorry,' " Nancy answered.

"Wow! That's something for a little guy with his limitations," responded Melody.

"I know!" Nancy replied. "So I explained that we wouldn't be able to read a

The habit of truthfulness is one of the "Top Three" habits that Charlotte talked about most. The other two are obedience (p. 96) and attention (p. 50).

"There is nothing which a mother cannot bring her child up to."

bedtime story since he had made a mess; I would have to use that time to clean it up—which he already knew. But then I told him that since he hadn't told Mommy the truth, we wouldn't be able to watch his favorite show that night. That almost broke his little heart. But I think it got through to him," continued Nancy, "because the next evening he came to me and said, 'I didn't make a mess, and I tell Mommy the truth.' And he was right!"

Charlotte's Thoughts on Truthfulness

1. Train your child to state facts carefully and exactly, without leaving anything out or exaggerating.

"And she is training her children in truthful habits, by making them careful to see the fact and to state it exactly, without omission or exaggeration" (Vol. 1, p. 47).

"At the same time the more imaginative the child, the more essential is it that the boundaries of the kingdom of make-believe should be clearly defined, and exact truthfulness insisted upon in all that concerns the narrower world where the grown-ups live. It is simply a matter of careful education; daily lessons in exact statement, without any horror or righteous indignation about misstatements, but warm, loving encouragement to the child who gives a long message quite accurately, who tells you just what Miss Brown said and no more, just what happened at Harry's party without any garnish. Every day affords scope for a dozen little lessons at least, and, gradually, the more severe beauty of truth will dawn upon the child whose soul is already possessed by the grace of fiction" (Vol. 2, p. 211).

2. Be scrupulous in requiring exact truth.

"It is unnecessary to say a word of the duty of Truthfulness; but the training of the child in the habit of strict veracity is another matter, and one which requires delicate care and scrupulosity on the part of the mother" (Vol. 1, p. 164).

"The girl who has been carefully trained to speak the exact truth simply does not think of a lie as a ready means of getting out of a scrape, coward as she may be" (Vol. 1, p. 111).

3. Lying can come through being careless in gathering the facts, careless in stating the facts, or through a deliberate intention to deceive. Teach your child to avoid all three causes, not just the third.

"The vice of lying causes: carelessness in *ascertaining* the truth, carelessness in *stating* the truth, and a deliberate intention to deceive. That all three are vicious, is evident from the fact that a man's character may be ruined by what is no more than a careless mis-statement on the part of another; the speaker repeats a damaging remark without taking the trouble to sift it; or he repeats what he has heard or seen with so little care to deliver the truth that his statement becomes no better than a lie.

"Now, of the three kinds of lying, it is only, as a matter of fact, the third which is severely visited upon the child; the first and the second he is allowed in. He tells you he has seen 'lots' of spotted dogs in the town—he has really seen two;

Charlotte wrote directly to young people about truthfulness in Volume 4, Book 1, pages 150–166.

"She is training her children in truthful habits, by making them careful to see the fact and to state it exactly, without omission or exaggeration."

If your child has already formed a habit of lying, see chapter 10 for suggestions on replacing that bad habit with a habit of truthfulness.

that 'all the boys' are collecting crests—he knows of three who are doing so; that 'everybody' says Jones is a 'sneak'—the fact is he has heard Brown say so. These departures from strict veracity are on matters of such slight importance that the mother is apt to let them pass as the 'children's chatter'; but, indeed, every such lapse is damaging to the child's sense of truth—a blade which easily loses its keenness of edge" (Vol. 1, pp. 164, 165).

4. *Require accuracy in both small and important matters.*

"The mother who trains her child to strict accuracy of statement about things small and great fortifies him against temptations to the grosser forms of lying; he will not readily colour a tale to his own advantage, suppress facts, equivocate, when the statement of the simple fact has become a binding habit, and when he has not been allowed to form the contrary vicious habit of playing fast and loose with words" (Vol. 1, p. 165).

5. *Don't excuse lying for the sake of humor.*

"Two forms of prevarication, very tempting to the child, will require great vigilance on the mother's part—that of exaggeration and that of clothing a story with ludicrous embellishments. However funny a circumstance may be as described by the child, the ruthless mother must strip the tale of everything over and above the naked truth: for, indeed, a reputation for facetiousness is dearly purchased by the loss of that dignity of character, in child or man, which accompanies the habit of strict veracity; it is possible, happily, to be humorous, without any sacrifice of truth" (Vol. 1, pp. 165, 166).

"Many persons are tempted to make a good story of a trifling incident. If a dog cock his tail at a whistle, they see enough fun in the situation to make you 'laugh consumedly.' All power to their elbow, as the Irishman would say. Humour, the power of seeing and describing the ludicrous side of things, is a gift that, like mercy, blesses him that gives and him that takes. It is a dangerous gift, all the same. The temptations to Irreverence, Discourtesy, even to a touch of Malice, for the embellishment of a story, are hard to be resisted; and, if these pitfalls be escaped, the incessant making of fun, perpetration of small jokes, becomes a weariness to the flesh of those who have to listen. The jocose person has need of self-restraint, or he becomes a bore; and his embellishments must be of the sort which no one is expected to believe, like the golden leg of Miss Kilmansegg, or his Veracity is at stake and he perils Truth to win a laugh" (Vol. 4, Book 1, pp. 159, 160).

6. *Treat deceit as a radical character defect that needs to be corrected rather than excused.*

"It is said that we English are no longer to be characterised as a truth-speaking people. This is a distressing charge, and yet we cannot put it away from us with a high hand. Possibly we are in a stage of civilisation which does not tend to produce the fine courage of absolute truthfulness. He who is without fear is commonly without falsehood; and a nation brought up amid the chivalries of war dares to be true. But we live in times of peace; we are no longer called on to defend the truth of our word by the strength of our hand. We speak with very

"It is possible, happily, to be humorous, without any sacrifice of truth."

little sense of responsibility, because no one calls us to account; and, so far as we are truth-tellers, we are so out of pure truth of heart and uprightness of life. That is, we may be, as a nation, losing the habit of truth to which the nation's childhood was trained, in ways however rough and ready; but we are growing up, and the truth that is among us is perhaps of a higher quality than the more general truthfulness of earlier days. Now, truth is indeed the white flower of a blameless life, and not the mere result of a fearless habit. The work before us is to bring up our children to this higher manner of truth. We no longer treat this or that particular lie or bit of deceit as a local ailment, for which we have only to apply the proper lotion or plaster; we treat it as symptomatic, as denoting a radical defect of character which we set ourselves to correct" (Vol. 2, pp. 204, 205).

7. Realize that it is better to cultivate the habit of truth from the outset rather than have to deal with the bad consequences of lying.

"It is well, however, to commend the subject to the attention of parents; for, though one child may have more aptitude than another, neither truthfulness nor the multiplication table come by nature. The child who appears to be perfectly truthful is so because he has been carefully trained to truthfulness, however indirectly and unconsciously. It is more important to cultivate the habit of truth than to deal with the accident of lying" (Vol. 2, p. 213).

8. Train your child to avoid qualifying his statements with "I think," or "I believe," or "perhaps," but to, instead, always speak accurately.

"First among the handmaidens of Truth, that is, spoken Truth, is Veracity—the habit of letting our words express the exact fact so far as we know it. Having spoken what we believe to be the fact, let us avoid qualifications. Do not let us say, 'At least I think so,' 'At least I believe so,' 'Perhaps it was not so,' 'All the girls were there, at least some of them,' 'We walked ten miles, at any rate six'; such qualifications imply a want of Veracity; we are self-convicted of a loose statement, and try to set ourselves right with our conscience by an excess of scrupulousness which has the effect of making our hearers doubt the Truth of what we have spoken" (Vol. 4, Book 1, p. 156).

9. Teach your child to think carefully and make sure he is certain before he speaks.

"But what are we to do, when, having said a thing, we begin to doubt if it is true? Words once spoken must be let alone: it is useless to unsay or qualify, explain or alter, or to appeal for confirmation or denial to another person. When we think how final words are, we shall be careful not to rush into statements without knowledge; we shall not come in with the cry, 'Mother! mother! there are a thousand cats in the garden.' 'Are there, George? Have you counted them?' 'Well, anyway, there's our cat and another!' We must be sure of our facts before we speak, and avoid speaking about matters concerning which we have only the vaguest knowledge. People are too apt to assume in conversation an intimate knowledge of matters of literature and art, for example, that they know very little about" (Vol. 4, Book 1, pp. 156, 157).

"The child who appears to be perfectly truthful is so because he has been carefully trained to truthfulness, however indirectly and unconsciously."

"They should know that truth, that is, justice in word, is their due and that of all other persons; there are few better equipments for a citizen than a mind capable of discerning the truth, and this just mind can be preserved only by those who take heed what they think" (Vol. 6, p. 61).

10. Don't allow your child, however, to constantly correct another person's comments in the name of truth.

"Another kind of Scrupulosity is very tiresome in talk. Somebody says, 'I saw seven men in the lane,' and the scrupulous person corrects him with, 'Excuse me, I think it was six men and a youth.' 'I met Mr Jones on Tuesday,' and the correction is, 'I think, if you recollect, it was on Wednesday.' 'It has been fine all the week': correction, 'No, I think not; there was a shower on Thursday'; and so on, to distraction; for there are few habits which more successfully put an end to conversation than the distinctly priggish one of looking after the Veracity of other people in matters of not the smallest moment. Common politeness requires us to assume the good faith of the speaker; and, that being assumed, it is not of the least consequence whether there were ten or twelve people in the hayfield, whether a flock of sheep, passed on the road, numbered eighty or a hundred. Veracity requires us to speak the fact so far as we know it, to take pains not to talk about what we do not know; but it by no means requires us to keep watch over the conversation of others and correct their information by means of our own, probably even less accurate" (Vol. 4, Book 1, pp. 157, 158).

11. Do not allow your child to get away with exaggerations intended to manipulate.

"Another more or less casual departure from Veracity comes of the habit of Exaggeration. We have 'a thousand things to do': perhaps we have four; 'everyone says so,' which means that our friends Mrs Simpson and Mary Carter have said so, or perhaps only Mrs Simpson. Few heads of a household do not know the tiresome tyranny of—'We *always* do so-and-so': probably we have done it once" (Vol. 4, Book 1, p. 158).

12. Teach your child not to spread rumors, but to carefully sift what he hears and reads.

"In the case of sickness, war, calamity, people are eager to make the most and the worst of what has happened, and the headlines of the newspaper showing the biggest number of casualties are most often quoted and most readily believed, though to-morrow may show how false they are. We cannot keep a delicate sense of Truth if we let ourselves listen to and carry rumours. Let us use our Common Sense to sift what we hear, and still more what we read, and wait for facts to be ascertained before we help to spread reports. Men have been ruined, the good name of a family destroyed, through the thoughtless carrying on of an idle rumour" (Vol. 4, Book 1, p. 158).

13. Encourage your child not to use excessive language for common situations.

"Exaggeration in speech, even when it is more foolish than mischievous, is a failure in Veracity. One cannot be 'awfully sorry' not to go for a walk and 'awfully

"We cannot keep a delicate sense of Truth if we let ourselves listen to and carry rumours."

glad' to get a letter, and leave anything to say when we have lost our best friend or gained a great happiness" (Vol. 4, Book 1, p. 158).

14. Do not allow your child to generalize; it gives the false impression that he has more knowledge or experience than he actually has.

"The habit of generalising, of stating something about a whole class of persons or things which we have noticed in only one or two cases, is one to be carefully guarded against by a person who would fain be, like our King Alfred, a truth-teller. 'All the cups are cracked,' when one is so. 'All the streets are up': perhaps two are. 'Oh, no, I can't bear Rossetti's pictures': the critic has seen but one. 'I love Schumann's songs': again, the critic has heard one. Let us stop generalisations of this kind before they escape our lips. They are not truthful, because they give the idea of a wider knowledge or experience than we possess; and, by the indulgence of this manner of loose statement, we incapacitate ourselves for the scientific habit of mind—accurate observation and exact record" (Vol. 4, Book 1, p. 159).

15. Emphasize simplicity, sincerity, and fidelity.

"Let us take courage: Truth, the handmaid of Justice, is a beautiful presence in every Mansoul, and with her are her attendant group, Veracity; Simplicity, whose part it is to secure that every spoken word means just what it appears to mean, and nothing more and nothing less: Sincerity, which secures that word of mouth tallies exactly with thought of heart, that we say exactly what we think: Fidelity, which makes us faithful to every promise at any cost—always excepting such promises as should never have been made; the only honourable thing that we can do is to break a promise which is wrong in itself. It is true that the Dæmons of the qualities are there also—Duplicity, with hints and innuendoes and double meanings; Deceit, trying to trip up Sincerity and pour out words of congratulation, sympathy, kindness, from the teeth outwards; Perfidiousness, which breaks through faith and makes promises of none effect. But, again, let us take courage; these are the aliens to be routed by every valiant Mansoul: *Magna est Veritas et Prævalebit*" (Vol. 4, pp. 165, 166).

"A bare enumeration of the duties which truthfulness comprehends, of the vices which are different forms of lying, is helpful and instructive. The heart rises and resolves upon the mere hearing that *veracity* is that truthfulness in common talk which is careful to state the least important fact as it is; that *simplicity* tells its tale without regard to self, without any thought of showing self to advantage in the telling; that *sincerity* tells the whole truth purely, however much it might be to the speaker's advantage to keep any part back; that *frankness* is the habit of speaking of our own affairs openly and freely—a duty we owe to the people we live amongst; that *fidelity*, the keeping of our trusts, in great things and small, belongs to the truthful character" (Vol. 5, p. 245).

Questions to Ask about Truthfulness

- Is my child progressing in stating facts carefully and exactly, without omissions or exaggerations?
- Am I trying to be scrupulous in requiring exact truth from my child?
- Am I teaching my child to be careful in gathering and stating facts, as well as

Magna est Veritas et Prævalebit *means "Truth is great and will prevail."*

"Anything may be accomplished by training, that is, the cultivation of persistent habits."

not deliberately intending to deceive?
- Do I require accuracy in both small and important matters?
- Do I tend to excuse lying for humor's sake?
- Am I treating deceit as a radical character defect that must be corrected?
- Am I putting forth effort now to cultivate the habit of truth in my child so I don't have to deal with the bad consequences of lying?
- Is my child learning to speak accurately and not to qualify his statements with "I think" or "perhaps"?
- Is my child taking steps toward thinking carefully and making sure he is certain before he speaks?
- Am I allowing my child to constantly correct another person's comments?
- Do I allow my child to get away with exaggerations that are intended to manipulate?
- Is my child learning to carefully sift what he hears and reads, and not to spread rumors?
- Is my child making progress in not using excessive language for common situations?
- Am I allowing my child to generalize, thus giving a false impression that he knows more than he actually does?
- Am I trying to emphasize simplicity, sincerity, and fidelity?

More Quotes on Truthfulness

"The elegance of honesty needs no adornment."—Merry Browne

"When regard for truth has been broken down or even slightly weakened, all things will remain doubtful."—St. Augustine

"The most dangerous untruths are truths moderately distorted."—Georg Christoph Lichtenberg

"A lie stands on one leg, the truth on two."—Benjamin Franklin

"I hope I shall always possess firmness and virtue enough to maintain what I consider the most enviable of all titles, the character of an honest man."—George Washington

"For my mouth shall speak truth; and wickedness is an abomination to my lips."—Proverbs 8:7

"Lying lips are abomination to the Lord: but they that deal truly are his delight."—Proverbs 12:22

"Wherefore putting away lying, speak every man truth with his neighbour."—Ephesians 4:25

"Every day, every hour, the parents are either passively or actively forming those habits in their children upon which, more than upon anything else, future character and conduct depend."

Usefulness
Offering valuable or productive service

Debbie emerged from the bedroom to hear the clinking of dishes in the kitchen. *That's funny*, she thought. *It's my turn to do dishes today.*

As she rounded the corner, she saw her daughter unloading the dishwasher full of clean dishes. "Good morning," her daughter smiled.

"Good morning," Debbie replied. "You don't have to do that today. Remember?"

"I know," said her daughter. "I just thought it might help you."

Being a useful member of the family is such an important habit to learn! And what a great way to show love to the other family members!

Charlotte's Thoughts on Usefulness

1. Help your child carry out his good intentions to actions.

" 'Hell is paved with good intentions' is a dreadful saying with which we are all familiar. I suppose it means that nothing is so easy to form as a good intention, and nothing so easy to break, and that lost and ruined souls have, no doubt, formed many good intentions. Therefore we must face the fact that the intention to be of use is not enough. We must get the habit, the trick, of usefulness" (Vol. 4, Book 1, p. 207).

2. Encourage and allow your older child to make himself useful in caring for younger siblings, running errands, and helping with school work.

"In most families there is the brother who cuts whistles and makes paper boats for the little ones, who gallops like a war-horse with Billy on his back, whom his mother trusts with messages and his father with commissions of importance; or, there is the sister to whose skirts the babies cling, who has learnt Latin enough to help her young brothers in their tasks, who can cut a garment or trim a hat for one of the maids; who writes notes for her mother and helps to nurse the baby through measles" (Vol. 4, Book 1, p. 207).

"Nobody can do well what he has not had a good deal of practice in doing; and you may depend upon it that the useful members of a family have had much practice in being of use, that is, they have looked out for their chances.

"Each of us has in his possession an exceedingly good servant or a very bad master, known as Habit. The heedless, listless person is a servant of habit; the useful, alert person is the master of a valuable habit" (Vol. 4, Book 1, p. 208).

3. Teach your child that love is shown by acts of service.

"Another point to be borne in mind is, that love grows, not by what it gets, but by what it gives. Therefore, the young people must not get out of the habit of rendering services of love. There is danger of confounding mere affection, a more or less animal emotion, showing itself in coaxing and fondling, in 'Mother, darling,' 'Father, dear,' and—no more, with love, which, however affectionate it

See also Alertness to Seize Opportunities on page 122.

"We must face the fact that the intention to be of use is not enough. We must get the habit, the trick, of usefulness."

Gaucherie *means "awkwardness."*

"The worth of any calling depends upon its being of *use*; and no day need go by without giving us practice in usefulness."

be in word and gesture, does not rest in these, but must exhibit itself in service" (Vol. 5, p. 205).

4. Assure your child that as he grows older and may be less inclined to demonstrate his love for parents physically, in hugs and kisses, acts of service can still exhibit love.

"The little children are demonstrative, ready to give and take caresses, 'loving' in their ways; but the boys and girls have, partly out of *gaucherie*, partly from a growing instinct of reticence, changed all that. They want at this awkward stage of life a great deal of tact and tenderness at the hands of their parents, and the channels of service, friendliness, and obedience must be kept visibly open for the love which will no longer flow in endearments" (Vol. 5, p. 205).

5. Teach your child that working hard to be useful now will prepare him to fulfill his calling in the future.

"The boy knows he must go out into the world and do something definite. For a girl, too, there are many careers, as they are called, opened in these days; and, if a girl is only called to the sweet place of a home daughter, all she need ask for herself is 'to be of use,' and, perhaps, no calling will offer her more chances of usefulness.

"Some boys know, at an early age, that they are being brought up for the navy, for example. For others, both boys and girls, their calling does not come until, perhaps, they have left college.

"All callings have one thing in common—they are of use; and, therefore, a person may prepare for his calling years before he knows what it is. What sort of person is of use in the world? You think of the most brilliant and handsome of your friends, and say to yourself, 'So-and-so, anyway, is a person the world could not do without'; but you may be quite wrong. The good looks, wit and cleverness, which give boy or girl the first place in school, often enough lead to a back seat in the world; because the person with these attractive qualities may be like a vessel without ballast, at the mercy of winds and waves. None need think small things of himself and of his chances of being serviceable because he is without the attractive qualities he admires in another. Everyone has immense 'chances,' as they are called; but the business of each is to be ready for his chance. The boy who got a medal from the Royal Humane Society for saving life, was ready for his chance; he had learned to swim; and, also, he had practised himself in the alert mind and generous temper which made him see the right thing to do and do it on the instant, without thought of the labour or danger of his action; without any thought, indeed, but of the struggling, sinking creature in the water.

"This illustrates what I mean; boys and girls who would be ready for their chances in life must have well-trained, active bodies; alert, intelligent, and well-informed minds; and generous hearts, ready to dare and do all for any who may need their help. It is such persons as these the world wants, persons who have worked over every acre of that vast estate of theirs which we have called Mansoul; men and women ordered in nerve and trained in muscle, self-controlled and capable; with well-stored imagination, well-practised reason; loving, just, and true.

"There is nothing in the wide world so precious, so necessary for the world's uses, as a boy or girl prepared on these lines for the calling that may come; and that is why I have tried to lay before you some of the great possibilities of the Kingdom of Mansoul. These possibilities belong to each of us; and the more we realise what we can be and what we can do, the more we shall labour to answer to our call when it comes. The boy who works only that he may pass, or be the head of his class, may get what he works for; but perhaps no one is of use unless he means to be of use. This is not a thing that comes to us casually, because it is the very best thing in life; and that fellow who means to have a good time, or to be first in any race, even the race for riches, may get the thing he aims at; but do not let him deceive himself; he does not also get the honour of being of use" (Vol. 4, Book 1, pp. 205–207).

"Each one is wanted for the special bit of work he is fit for; and, of each, it is true that —
" 'Thou cam'st not to thy place by accident:
  It is the very place God meant for thee' " (Vol. 4, Book 1, p. 210).

Questions to Ask about Usefulness

- Is my child learning to carry out his good intentions to actions?
- Does my child try to make himself useful in our family?
- Does my child understand that love is shown by acts of service?
- Is my older child growing less comfortable with hugs and kisses from a parent? Is he still comfortable showing his love through useful service?
- Is my child beginning to understand how usefulness now will help prepare him for his future callings?

More Quotes on Usefulness

"Enough, if something from our hands have power,
To live and act and serve the future hour."—Wordsworth

"Do all the good you can
By all the means you can
In all the ways you can
To all the people you can
As long as ever you can."—John Wesley

"By love serve one another."—Galatians 5:13

"It rests with parents and teachers to lay down lines of habit on which the life of the child may run henceforth with little jolting or miscarriage, and may advance in the right direction with the minimum of effort."

Chapter 6
Physical Habits

In Volume 3, *School Education*, Charlotte set forth certain aspects of physical training that she believed should be cultivated within the children. And consistent as she was, she approached that training from the standpoint of habits. She also mentioned some physical habits in her other writings. So they have all been collected here to turn our thoughts toward those habits that we should encourage our children to develop with their bodies.

Keep in mind that Charlotte's goal for physical fitness was a body that is serviceable to perform one's duty and calling in this world. These physical habits fall in line with that goal.

Alertness to Seize Opportunities

Fortitude

Health

Managing One's Own Body

Music

Outdoor Life

Quick Perception of Senses

Self-Control in Emergencies

Self-Discipline in Habits

Self-Restraint in Indulgences

Training the Ear and Voice

"Parents would do well to see to it that they turn out their children fit for service, not only by observing the necessary hygienic conditions, but by bringing their bodies under rule, training them in habits and inspiring them with the ideas of knightly service."

Notes

See also Usefulness on page 117.

Alertness to Seize Opportunities
*Being aware of ways to serve
in your surroundings
and taking the initiative to do them*

"Can I help, Mommy?"

"May I help . . . "

"May I help, Mommy?"

"Of course you may!"

"What can . . . may I do?"

"Look around you, dear, and see if you can find the clues that tell you how you may help."

"What do you mean, Mommy?"

"What do you see happening here in the kitchen?"

"You are taking off your apron and the food is on the table, ready for eating."

"That's right. Now what hasn't been done yet that you might help me do?"

"Oh! May I go tell Daddy that supper is ready?"

"Very good, dear! Yes, please do."

Soon the family was sitting around the table, but one chair was empty.

"I'm coming, Mommy! I found another clue! As I went to my chair I noticed that the napkin holder was empty, so here are more napkins to put in it."

"Well done! You are getting to be an expert clue finder!"

Charlotte's Thoughts on Alertness to Seize Opportunities

1. Encourage your child to watch for and not miss opportunities to help, such as delivering a message or opening a door.

"Many a good man and woman thinks regretfully of the opportunities in life they have let slip through a certain physical inertness. They missed the chance of doing some little service, or some piece of courtesy, because they did not see in time. It is well to bring up children to think it is rather a sad failure if they miss a chance of going a message, opening a door, carrying a parcel, any small act of service that presents itself" (Vol. 3, p. 108).

2. Encourage your child to watch just as diligently for opportunities to learn.

"They should be taught to be equally alert to seize opportunities of getting knowledge; it is the nature of children to regard each grown-up person they meet as a fount of knowledge on some particular subject; let their training keep up the habit of eager inquiry" (Vol. 3, p. 108).

3. Equip your child for success by cultivating this habit early in life.

"Success in life depends largely upon the cultivation of alertness to seize opportunities, and this is largely a physical habit" (Vol. 3, p. 108).

"It is well to bring up children to think it is rather a sad failure if they miss a chance of going a message, opening a door, carrying a parcel, any small act of service that presents itself."

Questions to Ask about Alertness to Seize Opportunities

- Is my child learning to watch for opportunities to help and taking the initiative to do so?
- Is my child beginning to watch for opportunities to learn?
- Am I seeking to cultivate this habit early in my child's life?

More Quotes on Alertness to Seize Opportunities

"Human felicity is produced not so much by great pieces of good fortune that seldom happen, as by little advantages that occur every day."—Benjamin Franklin

"Opportunity is missed by most people because it is dressed in overalls and looks like work."—Thomas Edison

"I was seldom able to see an opportunity until it had ceased to be one."—Mark Twain

Fortitude
Bearing hardship or discomfort with courage

As Cathy watched the mothers and children at the park, she began to notice a definite connection between how the mothers reacted and how the children acted.

And I do mean "act." Some of these kids should get an award for Best Actor! Especially that one in the blue sweatshirt. Of course, his mother is his best audience. When he tripped and fell, I thought she was going to call an ambulance. And his performance matched her panic. That poor child is going to lose many a fun moment worrying about his scraped knees.

On the other hand, that woman with the little girl in pink seems to have the right idea. When the girl landed in the dirt, that mom was quick to catch that split second of indecision—that little window of opportunity when the child was trying to decide whether she should create a scene. That mother calmly looked at the girl and said with a smile, "You're okay." And I really think she was sure about that; she must have done a quick mental assessment of the situation and figured out that it didn't look like anything really harmful or serious had happened. Now the little girl is continuing to play happily, while the little boy is still sitting beside his mother whining.

Charlotte's Thoughts on Fortitude

1. Learning fortitude in dealing with physical sensations can help develop mental fortitude.

"Perhaps parents are less fully awake to the importance of regulating a child's sensations. We still kiss the place to make it well, make an *obvious* fuss if a string is uncomfortable or a crumpled rose-leaf is irritating the child's tender skin. We

"Service is another knightly quality which a child should be nerved for by heroic examples until he grudges to let slip an opportunity."

have forgotten the seven Christian virtues and the seven deadly sins of earlier ages, and do not much consider in the bringing up of our children whether the grace of fortitude is developing under our training. Now fortitude has its higher and its lower offices. It concerns itself with things of the mind and with things of the body, and, perhaps, it is safe to argue that fortitude on the higher plane is only possible when it has become the habit of the nature on the lower" (Vol. 2, p. 286).

2. Encourage your child to bear discomfort courageously.

"A baby may be trained in fortitude, and is much the happier for such training. A child should be taught that it is beneath him to take any notice of cold or heat, pain or discomfort" (Vol. 2, p. 286).

"Few of us are likely to be tried in a field of battle; but the battle-field has an advantage over the thousand battles we each have to fight in our lives, because the sympathy of numbers carries men forward. The Courage required to lose a leg at home through a fall or an injury on the cricket field is, perhaps, greater than that displayed by the soldier on the field; and the form of Courage which meets pain and misfortune with calm endurance is needed by us all. No one escapes the call for Fortitude, if it be only in the dentist's chair" (Vol. 4, Book 1, p. 113).

3. Teach your child to concentrate on other things rather than the discomfort.

"We do not perceive the sensations to which we do not attend, and it is quite possible to forget even a bad toothache in some new and vivid interest" (Vol. 2, p. 286).

"Never let us reflect upon small annoyances, and we shall be able to bear great ones sweetly. Never let us think over our small pains, and our great pains will be easily endurable" (Vol. 4, Book 1, p. 90).

4. A child who concentrates on physical discomfort is likely to grow up into an adult who obsesses about physical sensations and misses out on the joy of living.

"Health and happiness depend largely upon the disregard of sensations, and the child who is encouraged to say, 'I am so cold,' 'I am so tired,' 'My vest pricks me,' and so on, is likely to develop into the hysterical girl or the hypochondriac man; for it is an immutable law, that, as with our appetites, so with our sensations, in proportion as we attend to them will they dominate us until a single sensation of slight pain or discomfort may occupy our whole field of vision, making us unaware that there is any joy in living, any beauty in the earth" (Vol. 2, pp. 286, 287).

5. A child who focuses on his comfort level is learning to concentrate on self instead of others.

"But these are the least of the reasons why a child should be trained to put up with little discomforts and take no notice. The child who has been allowed to become self-regardful in the matter of sensations, as of appetites, has lost his

Charlotte wrote directly to young people about fortitude in Volume 4, Book 2, pages 41–48.

"No one escapes the call for Fortitude, if it be only in the dentist's chair."

child's estate, he is no longer humble; he is in the condition of thinking about himself; instead of that infinitely blessed condition of not being aware of himself at all" (Vol. 2, p. 287).

6. Children with physical ailments should not be excluded and can benefit most from this training.

"Nor must we permit ourselves to make an exception to this rule in the case of the poor little invalid. For him, far more than for the healthy child, it is important that he should be trained to take no account of his sensations; and many a brave little hero suffers anguish without conscious thought, and therefore, of course, suffers infinitely less than if he had been induced to dwell upon his pains" (Vol. 2, p. 287).

7. Be careful not to turn your child's thoughts to his physical ailments.

"We say, induced, because, though a child may cry with sudden distress, he does not really think about his aches and pains unless his thoughts be turned to his ailments by those about him" (Vol. 2, p. 287).

8. Don't intentionally inflict hardness on your child in order to "train him in fortitude"; simply redirect his thoughts away from physical discomfort when it occurs.

"I am not advising any Spartan regimen. It is not permitted to us to inflict hardness in order that the children may learn to endure. Our care is simply to direct their consciousness from their own sensations. The well-known anecdote of the man who, before the days of chloroform, had his leg cut off without any conscious sensations of pain, because he determinedly kept his mind occupied with other things, is an extreme but instructive instance of what may be done in this direction" (Vol. 2, pp. 287, 288).

9. Be watchful for anything that might actually be dangerous or harmful to your child and deal with it in a calm manner.

"At the same time, though the child himself be taught to disregard them, his sensations should be carefully watched by his elders, for they must consider and act upon the danger signals which the child himself must be taught to disregard. But it is usually possible to attend to a child's sensations without letting him know they have been observed" (Vol. 2, p. 288).

10. Encourage your child to concentrate on his own duties and other people's rights, rather than his rights and other people's duties.

"He may be taught to occupy himself with *his own rights and other people's duties*, and, if he is, his state of mind is easily discernible by the catchwords often on his lips, 'It's a shame!' 'It's not fair!' or he may, on the other hand, be so filled with the notion of *his own duties and other people's rights*, that the claims of self slip quietly into the background" (Vol. 2, p. 289).

11. Pray for your child to have a servant's heart, then encourage that attitude with your actions.

"This kind cometh forth only by prayer, but it is well to clear our thoughts

"It is sad to pray, and frustrate the answer by our own action; but this is, alas, too possible."

Notes

"When we think how little power we have to do the tiresome things we set ourselves to do every day, we appreciate the self-compelling power a child can use, given a strong enough impulse."

and know definitely what we desire for our children, because only so can we work intelligently towards the fulfilment of our desire. It is sad to pray, and frustrate the answer by our own action; but this is, alas, too possible" (Vol. 2, p. 289).

12. Use stirring stories and examples of fortitude to motivate your child's determination in the right direction.

"Touch the right spring and children are capable of an amazing amount of steady effort. I know a little boy of ten who set himself the task of a solitary race of three miles every day in the hot summer holidays because he was to compete in a race when he went back to school; and this, not because he cared much about sports, but because his eldest brother had always distinguished himself in them, and he must do the same. When we think how little power we have to do the tiresome things we set ourselves to do every day, we appreciate the self-compelling power a child can use, given a strong enough impulse. The long name, Fortitude, would have its effect on the little boy in the dentist's hands. It is good to know that it is a manly and knightly virtue to be strong to bear pain and inconvenience without making any sign. The story of the Spartan boy and the fox will still wake an echo; and the girl who finds it a fine thing to endure hardness will not make a fuss about her physical sensations. She will be pained for the want of fortitude which called the reproof, 'Could ye not watch with me one hour?' and will brace herself to bear, that she may able to serve" (Vol. 3, pp. 110, 111).

Questions to Ask about Fortitude

- Do I understand how physical fortitude can develop into mental fortitude?
- Is my child learning to bear discomfort courageously?
- Is my child learning how to concentrate on other things rather than the discomfort?
- Am I looking toward my child's future and training him in fortitude so he won't grow up obsessed with physical sensations and miss the joy of living?
- Is my child progressing in thinking of others instead of himself and his comfort?
- Am I cultivating fortitude in my child who has physical ailments, or do I excuse him?
- Am I trying not to turn my child's thoughts toward his physical ailments?
- Am I careful not to intentionally inflict hardness on my child?
- Am I learning to redirect my child's thoughts away from physical discomfort when it occurs?
- Do I keep watch for any physical danger or harm that may occur to my child and deal with it calmly?
- Am I encouraging my child to concentrate on his duties and other people's rights, rather than his rights and other people's duties?
- Do I pray for my child to have a servant's heart?
- Do I model what it means to have a servant's heart by my actions?
- Am I seeking to use stirring stories and examples of fortitude to motivate my child in that direction?

More Quotes on Fortitude

"We could never learn to be brave and patient, if there were only joy in the world."—Helen Keller

"Although the world is full of suffering, it is full also of the overcoming of it."—Helen Keller

"Character cannot be developed in ease and quiet. Only through experience of trial and suffering can the soul be strengthened, ambition inspired, and success achieved."—Helen Keller

"Patience serves as a protection against wrongs as clothes do against cold. For if you put on more clothes as the cold increases, it will have no power to hurt you. So in like manner you must grow in patience when you meet with great wrongs, and they will then be powerless to vex your mind."—Leonardo da Vinci

"I think a hero is an ordinary individual who finds strength to persevere and endure in spite of overwhelming obstacles."—Christopher Reeve

"Courage and perseverance have a magical talisman, before which difficulties disappear and obstacles vanish into air."—John Quincy Adams

Health
Taking good care of your body, through nutrition, hygiene, exercise, and rest

"OK, sweetie, I think you're ready to take over your own tooth-brushing from here," Violet announced.

"What do you mean?" asked her son David.

"You're doing a fine job each night. You're remembering to brush just like we taught you, and I don't think you need me here watching you every night. You're ready to brush solo!" responded Violet with a grin.

"Really?"

"Yes, really. But remember, it's your responsibility now. So if you get a cavity, you have no one to blame but yourself."

David's face fell. "Oh."

"But if you keep brushing like you have been, I'm sure you have nothing to worry about, dear," Violet reassured him. "You can do it!"

Charlotte's Thoughts on Health

1. Family meals are a great time to teach good nutrition and encourage good eating habits.

"No pains should be spared to make the hours of meeting round the family table the brightest hours of the day. This is supposing that the children are

"No pains should be spared to make the hours of meeting round the family table the brightest hours of the day."

See also Self-Restraint in Indulgences on page 144.

Charlotte wrote directly to young people about health in Volume 4, Book 1, pages 11–20.

"Good health is not only a blessing, but a *duty."*

Notes

allowed to sit at the same table with their parents; and, if it is possible to let them do so at every meal excepting a late dinner, the advantage to the little people is incalculable. Here is the parents' opportunity to train them in manners and morals, to cement family love, and to accustom the children to habits, such as that of thorough mastication, for instance, as important on the score of health as on that of propriety" (Vol. 1, p. 27).

2. Don't allow your child unhealthy indulgences.

"Authority is neither harsh nor indulgent. She is gentle and easy to be entreated in all matters immaterial, just because she is immovable in matters of real importance; for these, there is always a fixed principle. It does not, for example, rest with parents and teachers to dally with questions affecting either the health or the duty of their children. They have no authority to allow children in indulgences—in too many sweetmeats, for example—or in habits which are prejudicial to health; nor to let them off from any plain duty of obedience, courtesy, reverence, or work" (Vol. 3, p. 17).

3. Teach your older child that his health is his responsibility.

"The care of her own health is another responsibility which should be made over to the young maiden. She cannot learn too soon that good health is not only a blessing, but a *duty*; that we may all take means to secure more or less vigorous health, and that we are criminal in so far as we fail to make use of these means. Any little book on the laws of health will put her in possession of the few simple principles of hygiene: the daily bath, attended with much friction of the skin; regular and sufficient exercise in the open air; the vigorous use of all the limbs; exercise of moderation in diet and in sleep; the free admission of fresh air to the bedroom; the due airing of the underclothing taken off at night; the necessity for active habits, for regular and hard, but not excessive brain-work; the resolute repression of ugly tempers and unbecoming thoughts,—all of these are conditions of a sound mind in a sound body" (Vol. 5, p. 246).

"How many know that health is a duty, and not merely an advantage; that a serviceable body, strong and capable, is a debt we owe to ourselves, our kin, and our kind?" (Vol. 5, p. 386).

4. Emphasize that poor health habits now will reap a failing body in future years.

"And for keeping ourselves in this delightful state of existence we are all more or less responsible. The girl who eats too much, or eats what does not suit her, and is laid up with a bilious attack; the girl who sits for hours poring over a novel, to the damage of her eyes, her brain, and her general nervous system, is guilty of a lesser fault of the nature of suicide. We are all apt, especially in youth, to overlook our accountability in the matter of health, and to think we may do what we like with our own; but, indeed, no offences are more inevitably and severely punished by the action of natural law than the neglect of the common principles of hygiene" (Vol. 5, pp. 246, 247).

Questions to Ask about Health

• Are we making progress toward having nutritious family meals?

- Are we trying to take advantage of family meals for teaching good eating habits?
- Am I allowing my child an unhealthy indulgence—whether candy or a bad habit?
- Is my older child making progress toward taking responsibility for his good health?
- Does my child understand that poor health habits now will result in a failing body in future years?

More Quotes on Health

"Our bodies are our gardens—our wills are our gardeners."—William Shakespeare

"The greatest wealth is health."—Virgil

"Lack of activity destroys the good condition of every human being, while movement and methodical physical exercise save it and preserve it."—Plato

"Sleep that knits up the ravelled sleeve of care,
The death of each day's life, sore labour's bath,
Balm of hurt minds, great nature's second course,
Chief nourisher in life's feast."—William Shakespeare

Managing One's Own Body
Knowing where one's body parts are in space and being able to use them to best advantage

Toni fell breathlessly into the armchair, laughing. "That was fun!" she gasped. "It's too bad we get to square dance only once a year."

"I was just thinking the same thing," panted her older brother.

"We could change that," suggested their mother.

Toni sat up. "What do you mean?"

"Maybe we could get some of your friends together once a week for a homeschool square dance club," Mom replied.

"Oh, wouldn't that be fun!" Toni's grin spread across her face. "But who would do the calling?"

"You forget. I grew up watching my parents square dance every Friday night," Mom reminded her. "I can holler out 'Ring the Dishrag and Promenade' just as well as the next guy!"

Regular physical exercise is helpful in so many ways, yet it is so often neglected in homeschooling circles. Exercise doesn't have to be tedious and boring. Make it enjoyable and mentally stimulating as well, and it will become a favorite habit.

"The more we are prodded the lazier we get."

Charlotte's students learned folk dancing as part of their generous curriculum.

See page 131 for a description of Swedish Drill.

Charlotte's Thoughts on Managing One's Own Body

1. Dancing, calisthenics, and daily physical exercise will help your child become familiar with his body's movements and place in the space around him.

"To give the child pleasure in light and easy motion—the sort of delight in the management of his own body that a good rider finds in managing his horse—dancing, drill, calisthenics, some sort of judicious physical exercise, should make part of every day's routine" (Vol. 1, p. 132).

"It is not possible to do more than mention two more important subjects—the Handicrafts and Drills—which should form a regular part of a child's daily life. For physical training nothing is so good as Ling's Swedish Drill, and a few of the early exercises are within the reach of children under nine. Dancing, and the various musical drills, lend themselves to grace of movement, and give more pleasure, if less scientific training, to the little people" (Vol. 1, p. 315).

2. Swedish drill can be adapted for all ages.

"Swedish drill is especially valuable, and many of the exercises are quite suitable for the nursery" (Vol. 1, p. 132).

3. Physical training can help support moral training.

"Certain moral qualities come into play in alert movements, eye-to-eye attention, prompt and intelligent replies; but it often happens that good children fail in these points for want of physical training" (Vol. 1, p. 132).

4. Just as our bodies adjust to repeated physical actions, so our minds respond to repeated actions or thoughts and form habits. Use this illustration to teach your child about forming habits.

"It is well that a child should be taught to keep under his body and bring it into subjection, first, to the authority of his parents and, later, to the authority of his own will; and always, because no less than this is due, to the divine Authority in whom he has his being. But to bring ourselves under authority at all times would require a constantly repeated effort of thought and will which would make life too laborious. Authority must be sustained by habit. We all know something of the genesis of a habit, and most of us recognise its physical basis, *i.e.* that frequently-repeated thoughts or acts leave some sort of register in the brain tissue which tends to make the repetition of such thoughts, at first easy, and at last automatic. In all matters of physical exercise it is obvious to us that—do a thing a hundred times and it becomes easy, do a thing a thousand times and it becomes mechanical, as easy to do as not. This principle is abundantly applied in cricket, boating, golf, cycling, all the labours we delight in. But there is an outfit of half-physical, half-moral habits of life which the playing-field tends to form, but which are apt to be put on and off with the flannels if they are not steadily and regularly practised in the home life also. These are the habitudes which it is the part of parents to give their children, and, indeed, they do form part of the training of all well brought-up young people; but it is well not to lose sight of this part of our work" (Vol. 3, pp. 104, 105).

"It is well that a child should be taught to keep under his body and bring it into subjection, first, to the authority of his parents and, later, to the authority of his own will."

Questions to Ask about Managing One's Own Body

- Do I encourage my child toward some kind of daily exercise, like walking, dancing, or calisthenics?
- Am I trying to encourage Swedish Drill or some other exercise that requires full attention, balance, and strength?
- Do I understand how physical exercise can support moral training?
- Does my child understand the similarity between training muscles by repeated physical movements and training the mind by repeated thoughts or actions until it becomes a habit?

More Quotes on Managing One's Own Body

"Walking is the best possible exercise. Habituate yourself to walk very far."—Thomas Jefferson

Swedish Drill (Drilling)

So many times as a homeschool parent I find it easy to ignore or at least minimize the importance of PE (Physical Education, or "gym class," as we called it when I went to school). Somehow I can't envision Charlotte Mason teaching the children how to play kick ball or dodge ball. (Not to mention that those games are a little difficult to do at home when you have only three or four children involved!) And I couldn't reconcile her beautiful educational philosophy with the notion of compelling children to do mindless repetitions, like twenty-five jumping jacks and fifty sit-ups.

Therefore, this whole idea of "drilling" (i.e., Swedish drill) that was used in her schools intrigued me, and I went on a hunt for more information. Well, the wonderful inter-library loan lady at my local library found me a gem: *The Swedish Drill Teacher* by M. H. Spalding, copyright 1910. This little 72-page book (which sold for six shillings in London) details the principles behind and methods of Swedish drill; and as I read about it, I was struck with how neatly it falls into step with Charlotte's philosophy of education.

For example, the exercises and movements were used with a view to improving "the general health of the body rather than towards muscular development." The drills were done outside whenever possible to allow for fresh air and deep breathing. The movements were done to command so the "pupils learn the power of quick and correct response to the command, and this involves concentration and quickness of thought, alertness of action, and effort of will. Since fresh commands for new and more complicated movements are continually being learnt, these qualities are always being more and more highly and acutely developed."

Those comments dovetail wonderfully with Charlotte's emphasis of a "serviceable body" as the goal of physical training (*School Education*, pp. 102, 103), her encouragement to spend lots of time outdoors (*Home Education*, p. 42), and the prominence she gave to the habits of full attention and mental alertness (*Home Education*, pp. 156, 185).

So what exactly is Swedish drill, you ask?

"A great function of the educator is to secure that acts shall be so regularly, purposefully, and methodically sown that the child shall reap the habits of the good life, in thinking and doing, with the minimum of conscious effort."

Swedish drill was a series of movements the students performed in response to the teacher's vocal instructions. The movements were performed slowly and gently (for the most part), with an emphasis on balance and complete muscle control. As students grew more proficient, the instructions progressed to more complicated postures or movements.

Movements centered around the arms bending and stretching, the arm and shoulder muscles, abdominal muscles, and legs muscles. Some jumping, marching, and running were also included, along with breathing exercises when needed to regulate after a strenuous exercise. Each drill session began with "introductory movements," similar to what we call "warming up."

The teachers would start with various fundamental positions in different combinations. For example, here are some

• Fundamental Arm positions: hands on hips, hands on shoulders, hands behind head with fingers lightly interlocked, arms extended (either up, down, out, or forward);

• Fundamental Foot positions: astride (legs parallel with shoulders but wider than shoulders), walk (a comfortable step in the direction indicated), lunge (a long step in the direction indicated);

• Fundamental Body positions: standing, sitting, lying, kneeling.

The instruction would be spoken once, with a pause for students to get a mental image of the position and how to move; then the "execution command" would be given (like "firm!" or "place!"), at which time the students would move. So the instruction "With feet astride, hands on hips (—pause—), firm!" would tell the students to place their hands on their hips while standing (with good posture, of course).

Simple arm instructions might be "Arms forward, sideways, and downward—stretch: 1, 2, 3" (with a change of position on each number).

After the students found those fundamental positions no longer a challenge, the teacher would start to mix things up a bit with variations. For example, our first instruction used above could be expanded from "with feet astride, hands on hips—firm!" to "Hips—firm! Feet astride—place: 1, 2! (Student would move one foot on each number spoken.) Feet together—place: 1, 2! Left foot forward—place! Feet change: 1, 2!" (On "1" the left foot is brought back; on "2" the right foot is moved forward.)

Or they could increase the complexity of arm movement instructions by having each arm do a different position. "Left arm upward, right arm forward—stretch!"

Next, they could combine arm and leg positions, such as "With left foot forward, right hand neck rest, left hand hips—firm! Feet and arms—change: 1, 2! (On "1" students come back to neutral position, and on "2" the positions of feet and arms are reversed.)

The possibilities for combinations are endless when you throw in heel raising, facing different sides of the room, toe standing, knee bending, "half" positions (doing the movement with one side of the body only, such as half kneel), knee raising, leg raising, bending or twisting at the waist, controlled jumping, and marching in patterns. If you'll pardon the comparison, the whole thing almost reminds me of a very advanced game of Simon Says.

The teacher was also encouraged to come up with some fun games and names

"Habit begins as a cobweb, and ends as a cable."

for certain movements for the younger children (ages 6 to 8). For example, the "Do as I say, not as I do" game expected the children to listen carefully to the instructions and follow them even if the teacher took a different position. She might tell the children "Hips—firm!" but put her own hands behind her head. Or a fun balance movement would be "Taking off the shoe," for which each student would bend the knee up and stand on one foot while taking off his or her shoe and putting it on again. Small children would also get to do "giant marching" or "dwarf marching" and "bunny jumps."

There you have it: a quick overview of Swedish drill. I hope the explanation wasn't too confusing. It's hard to condense a 72-page book of instructions and physical movements.

Judging from the sample schedules, Charlotte's schools did drill for about 30 minutes at a time. You can be sure the drill teacher had thought through the combinations and sequence before attempting to lead the children for that length of time. Some of us would be challenged just to think up enough variations to occupy ten minutes if we were operating off the top of our heads! But as a quick diversion in the midst of lessons, it might prove to be an enjoyable spontaneous exercise.

Music
Singing in tune

"Hey, Mom, may we listen to that patriotic songs CD again?" came the request from the back of the van.

"Sure," Mom replied.

The music filled the van, and the children's voices joined in. Mom smiled. *They'll be ready to learn how to sing in harmony soon,* she thought.

Many children learn to sing in tune simply by hearing music in their surroundings. They pick it up like they pick up the tones in their natural language. Other children may need a little more guidance to learn how to hear the proper notes. But the great part about music is that no matter how much a child knows, there is always more he can learn. He can delve into musical instruction as far as he wants to go.

Charlotte's Thoughts on Music

1. Surround your child with good music so he constantly hears musical sounds.

"As for a musical training, it would be hard to say how much that passes for inherited musical taste and ability is the result of the constant hearing and producing of musical sounds, the *habit* of music, that the child of musical people grows up with" (Vol. 1, p. 133).

"Many great men have put their beautiful thoughts, not into books, or pictures, or buildings, but into musical score, to be sung with the voice or played

> "It would be hard to say how much that passes for inherited musical taste and ability is the result of the constant hearing and producing of musical sounds, the *habit* of music."

Notes

on instruments, and so full are these musical compositions of the minds of their makers, that people who care for music can always tell who has composed the music they hear, even if they have never heard the particular movement before. Thus, in a manner, the composer speaks to them, and they are perfectly happy in listening to what he has to say. Quite little children can sometimes get a good deal of this power; indeed, I knew a boy of three years old who knew when his mother was playing 'Wagner,' for example. She played to him a great deal, and he listened. Some people have more power in this way than others, but we might all have far more than we possess if we listened.

"Use every chance you get of hearing music (I do not mean only tunes, though these are very nice), and ask whose music has been played, and, by degrees, you will find out that one composer has one sort of thing to say to you, and another speaks other things; these messages of the musicians cannot be put into words, so there is no way of hearing them if we do not train our ear to listen" (Vol. 4, Book 1, p. 31).

"A great deal of time and a good deal of money is commonly spent to secure to the young people the power of performing indifferently upon an instrument; nor is even an indifferent performance to be despised: but it is not always borne in mind that to listen with discriminating delight is as educative and as "happy-making" as to produce; and that this power might, probably, be developed in everybody, if only as much pains were spent in the cultivation of the musical sense as upon that of musical facility. Let the young people hear good music as often as possible, and that under instruction. It is a pity we like our music, as our pictures and our poetry, mixed, so that there are few opportunities of going through, as a listener, a course of the works of a single composer. But this is to be aimed at for the young people; let them study occasionally the works of a single great master until they have received some of his teaching, and know his style" (Vol. 5, p. 235).

Charlotte's students learned singing with the Sol-fa method. To learn more about that method, visit the Bonus Features page for this book at http://simplycharlottemason. com/books/layingdowntherails/

2. Some children may take to singing quite naturally, while others may require more training in music.

"Mr Hullah maintained that the art of singing is entirely a trained habit—that every child may be, and should be, trained to sing. Of course, *transmitted* habit must be taken into account" (Vol. 1, p. 133).

3. Provide carefully graduated exercises or lessons that teach musical tones and intervals.

"It is a pity that the musical training most children get is of a random character; that they are not trained, for instance, by carefully graduated ear and voice exercises, to produce and distinguish musical tones and intervals" (Vol. 1, pp. 133, 134).

"A great help towards learning to hear music is to know the notes, to be able to tell with one's eyes shut any note or chord that is struck on the piano or sung with the voice. This is as entertaining as a puzzle, and if we find that we are rather dull of hearing at first we need not be discouraged. The hearing ear comes, like good batting, with much practice" (Vol. 4, Book 1, p. 31).

"Let the young people hear good music as often as possible."

Questions to Ask about Music

- Am I surrounding my child with good music?
- Does my child take to singing naturally or need more help?
- Am I providing my child with graduated music lessons that teach musical tones and intervals in singing?

More Quotes on Music

"Take a music bath once or twice a week for a few seasons. You will find it is to the soul what a water bath is to the body."—Oliver Wendell Holmes

"And the night shall be filled with music,
And the cares, that infest the day,
Shall fold their tents, like the Arabs,
And as silently steal away."—Henry Wadsworth Longfellow

"Alas for those that never sing,
But die with all their music in them!"—Oliver Wendell Holmes

Outdoor Life
Regularly enjoying and studying God's creation outdoors

"Do I have to go today? I really need to finish this Algebra, and I haven't even gotten started on my History reading yet," Dan appealed.

"Yes, let's lay aside the school work for a little while and get outside," replied Mom. "We won't be gone too long, and the Algebra will be here when you get back."

"All right." Dan closed his book and grabbed his jacket.

The family spent an hour near the lake, soaking up the sunshine and sketching the ducks. Both Dan and his mom could feel the tension roll off their shoulders and their neck muscles relax as they stood under the big trees.

"Hey, Mom," Dan said quietly, without taking his eyes from the water. "Thanks for making me come today."

Charlotte's Thoughts on Outdoor Life

1. Regular time outdoors can affect your attitude and your health.

"Here is where most Continental nations have the advantage over us; they keep up the habit of out-of-door life; and as a consequence, the average Frenchman, German, Italian, Bulgarian, is more joyous, more simple, and more hardy than the average Englishman" (Vol. 1, p. 29).

2. Nature study can be a source of delight no matter your age.

"Let them once get touch with Nature, and a habit is formed which will be a

"Let them once get touch with Nature, and a habit is formed which will be a source of delight through life."

source of delight through life" (Vol. 1, p. 61).

"Two or three hours of the afternoon should be given to vigorous out-of-door exercise, to a long country walk, if not to tennis, cricket, etc. The walk is interesting in proportion as it has an object, and here the student of botany has a great advantage. At almost every season there is something to be seen in some out-of-the-way spot, to make up the list of specimens illustrating an order. The girl who is neither a botanist nor an artist may find an object for her walk in the catching of some aspect of nature, some bit of landscape, to describe in writing. The little literary effort should be both profitable and pleasant, and such a record should be a dear possession in after days" (Vol. 5, pp. 260, 261).

3. Not everyone needs to be an expert, but each person should marvel over and care for God's creation.

"We were all meant to be naturalists, each in his degree, and it is inexcusable to live in a world so full of the marvels of plant and animal life and to care for none of these things" (Vol. 1, p. 61).

Questions to Ask about Outdoor Life

- Am I remembering how regular time outdoors can affect attitudes and health?
- Do I try to encourage nature study as a source of delight to people of all ages?
- Does my child understand that he doesn't need to be an expert, but that he should marvel over and care for God's creation?

More Quotes on Outdoor Life

"I love to think of nature as an unlimited broadcasting station, through which God speaks to us every hour, if we will only tune in."—George Washington Carver

"In wilderness I sense the miracle of life, and behind it our scientific accomplishments fade to trivia."—Charles A. Lindbergh

"The sun, with all those planets revolving around it and dependent on it, can still ripen a bunch of grapes as if it had nothing else in the universe to do."—Galileo

"To sit in the shade on a fine day and look upon verdure is the most perfect refreshment."—Jane Austen

"Great things are done when men and mountains meet. This is not done by jostling in the street."—William Blake

"To me a lush carpet of pine needles or spongy grass is more welcome than the most luxurious Persian rug."—Helen Keller

"We were all meant to be naturalists, each in his degree."

"To one who has been long in city pent,
'Tis very sweet to look into the fair
And open face of heaven,—to breathe a prayer
Full in the smile of the blue firmament."—John Keats

"Look deep into nature, and then you will understand everything better."—Albert Einstein

Quick Perception of Senses
Being aware of things around you that you can see, hear, feel, taste, or smell

Ted plucked the feather off the ground and held it up. "Look what I found!"

"Want to play a little game with it?" asked Mom.

The other children gathered around. The word "game" always attracted a crowd in this family.

"Ted, you start. I want you to tell me all that you can discover about this feather by using only your sense of smell."

"Smell?" Ted was curious.

"Yes, smell."

The other children laughed at Ted's expression. "And Margaret, you will tell me all you can discover with your sense of hearing. Philip will use his sense of seeing, and Mark will use his sense of touching. Ready?"

Four heads nodded vigorously and turned to see what Ted could discover first.

Charlotte's Thoughts on Quick Perception of Senses

1. Challenge your child to use all his senses and observe all that he can about objects around him: shades of color; relative temperature; degrees of hardness, texture, and size.

"We have barely touched on the sorts of object-lessons, appealing now to one sense and now to another, which should come incidentally every day in the family. We are apt to regard an American Indian as a quite uneducated person; he is, on the contrary, highly educated in so far as that he is able to discriminate sensory impressions, and to take action upon these, in a way which is bewildering to the book-learned European. It would be well for parents to educate a child, for the first half-dozen years of his life, at any rate, on 'Red Indian' lines. Besides the few points we have mentioned, he should be able to discriminate colours and shades of colour; relative degrees of heat in woollen, wood, iron, marble, ice; should learn the use of the thermometer; should discriminate objects according to their degrees of hardness; should have a cultivated eye and touch for texture; should, in fact, be able to get as much information about an object from a few minutes' study as to its form, colour, texture, size, weight, qualities, parts, characteristics, as he could learn out of many pages of a printed book" (Vol. 2, p. 188).

Charlotte called this exercise "Sensory Gymnastics."

"A habit is so easily formed, so strong to compel."

Notes

2. Daily sensory gymnastics are not the same as nature study but can supplement and support nature study.

"We approach the subject by the avenue of the child's senses rather than by that of the objects to be studied, because just now we have in view the occasional test exercises, the purpose of which is to give thorough culture to the several senses. An acquaintance with Nature and natural objects is another thing, and is to be approached in a slightly different way. A boy who is observing a beetle does not consciously apply his several senses to the beetle, but lets the beetle take the initiative, which the boy reverently follows: but the boy who is in the habit of doing sensory daily gymnastics will learn a great deal more about the beetle than he who is not so trained" (Vol. 2, pp. 188, 189).

3. Occasionally give your child an object and ask him to tell all that he can discover about it by using only one of his senses; for example, touch.

"Definite object-lessons differ from these incidental exercises in that an object is in a manner exhausted by each of the senses in turn, and every atom of information it will yield got out of it. A good plan is to make this sort of a lesson a game. Pass your object round—a piece of bread, for example—and let each child tell some fact that he discovers by touch; another round, by smell; again, taste; and again, by sight. Children are most ingenious in this kind of game, and it affords opportunities to give them new words, as friable, elastic, when they really ask to be helped to express in a word some discovery they have made. Children learn in this way to think with exactitude, to distinguish between friable and brittle; and any common information that is offered to them in the course of these exercises becomes a possession for ever" (Vol. 2, p. 189).

4. Play a game of "What Can You Remember?" to cultivate this habit.

"A good game in the nature of an object-lesson, suitable for a birthday party, is to have a hundred objects arranged on a table, unknown to the children; then lead the little party into the room, allow them three minutes to walk round the table; afterwards, when they have left the room, let them write or tell in a corner, the names of all the objects they recollect. Some children will easily get fifty or sixty" (Vol. 2, pp. 189, 190).

5. The best way to cultivate the senses is by getting to know the world of nature.

"No doubt the best and happiest exercise of the senses springs out of a loving familiarity with the world of nature, but the sorts of gymnastics we have indicated render the perceptions more acute, and are greatly enjoyed by children. That the sensations should not be permitted to minister unduly to the subjective consciousness of the child is the great point to be borne in mind" (Vol. 2, p. 190).

6. Encourage your child to observe his surroundings by randomly asking whether he noticed accurately a particular thing that you noticed.

"Closely connected with that alertness is the habit of quick perception as to all that is to be seen, heard, felt, tasted, smelt in a world gives illimitable information through our five gateways of knowledge. Mr Grant, in his most interesting studies of Neapolitan character, describes the training of a young Camorrist (the

"Every habit has its beginning. The beginning is the *idea* which comes with a stir and takes possession of us."

Camorra is a dangerous political faction; and, ill as we may think of the ends of such training, the means are well worth recording). 'The great object of this part of his training was to teach him to observe habitually with minuteness and accuracy, and it was conducted in something like the following manner. When walking through the city the Camorrist would suddenly pause and ask, "How was the woman dressed who sat at the door of the fourth house in the last street?" or, "What were the two men talking about whom we met at the corner of the last street but three?" or, "Where was cab 234 ordered to drive to?" or perhaps it would be, "What is the height of that house and the breadth of its upper window?" or "Where does that man live?" ' This habit, again largely a physical habit, of quick perception has been dwelt upon in other aspects" (Vol. 3, p. 109).

7. Young children are naturally observant, but the habit of observation will help your child continue the skill even as he grows older.

"All that now need be urged is that the quickness of observation natural to a child should not be relied upon; in time, and especially as school studies press upon him, his early quickness deserts the boy, but the trained habit of seeing all that is to be seen, hearing all that is to be heard, remains through life" (Vol. 3, p. 109).

See also Observation on page 70.

Questions to Ask about Quick Perception of Senses

- Am I challenging my child to use all his senses to observe objects around him?
- Am I seeking to use daily sensory gymnastics to supplement and support nature study?
- Do I occasionally give my child an object and ask him to tell all that he can discover about it using only one of his senses?
- Do I play "What Can You Remember?" with my child?
- Do I try to encourage my child to cultivate his senses by getting to know nature?
- Am I randomly asking my child whether he noticed accurately a particular aspect of a situation he shared with me?
- Am I encouraging my child to continue cultivating the habit of observation as he grows older?

More Quotes on Quick Perception of Senses

"How use doth breed a habit in a man!"—William Shakespeare

Self-Control in Emergencies
*Thinking clearly and
keeping emotions in check
no matter the circumstances*

"The food will be ready in five minutes," called Mom. "Everyone get on your

"If we wish children to be able, when they grow up, to keep under their bodies and bring them into subjection we must do this *for* them in their earlier years."

socks and shoes so we can take it over to the Brownings' house. We're supposed to deliver it by 5:30."

In five minutes Mom carefully gave each child something to carry out to the van. Judy, the oldest, received the large casserole dish. As Mom buckled little Joey into his car seat, she heard a loud crash and turned to see Judy at the bottom of the stairs, her eyes starting to fill with tears. Beside her, on the sidewalk, lay the casserole dish's contents.

Mom could feel the panic starting to rise within her, but she pushed it back down and tried to walk slowly to where Judy lay.

"I'm sorry, Mom," Judy whispered, the tears starting to flow.

First things first, thought Mom. "Are you all right?" she asked, trying to use a calm voice.

"Yes, I'm all right," replied Judy. "But what about the casserole?" The tears were slowing down as Judy sensed her mother's calmness.

Mom did some quick thinking, *OK, we need a clean-up and a main course for the Brownings*. "Don't worry about it, dear. I know it was an accident," she reassured Judy. "Let's scoop this food off the sidewalk, so we don't leave a mess. We'll just put the dish on the kitchen counter for now. Then we can stop at the deli and pick up some fried chicken to take over instead."

Little emergencies happen throughout any family's week. If we can train ourselves to respond to those little, incidental emergencies in a calm manner, we will be laying the foundation for responding to larger, possibly life-threatening emergencies in the same way.

Charlotte's Thoughts on Self-Control in Emergencies

1. A person who can keep presence of mind can be of great service to others.

"Self-control in emergencies is another habit of the disciplined life in which a child should be trained from the first; it is the outcome of a general habit of self-control. We all see how ice accidents, boat accidents, disasters by fire (like a late melancholy event in Paris), might be minimised in their effects if only one person present were under perfect self-control, which implies the power of organising and controlling others" (Vol. 3, p. 106).

See also Self-Control on page 105.

"And here is the line which divides the effective from the non-effective people, the great from the small, the good from the well-intentioned and respectable; it is in proportion as a man has self-controlling, self-compelling power that he his able to do, even of his own pleasure; that he can depend upon himself, and be sure of his own action in emergencies" (Vol. 1, p. 323).

2. Keep a calm spirit and encourage your child to do the same no matter what happens around him.

"But the habit of holding oneself well in hand, the being impervious to small annoyances, cheerful under small inconveniences, ready for action with what is called 'presence of mind' in all the little casualties of the hour—this is a habit which should be trained in the nursery. If children were sent into the world with this part of their panoply complete, we should no longer have the spectacle of the choleric Briton and of the nervous and fussy British lady at every foreign *doûane*;

A doûane is a border check or customs stop.

"Self-control in emergencies is another habit of the disciplined life in which a child should be trained from the first."

people would not jostle for the best places at a public function; the mistresses of houses would not be fretted and worn out by the misdoings of their maids; the thousand little sorenesses of social life would be soothed, if children were trained to bear little hurts to body and mind without sign. 'If you are vexed, don't show it,' is usually quite safe teaching, because every kind of fretfulness, impatience, resentfulness, nervous irritability generally, grows with expression and passes away under self-control" (Vol. 3, pp. 106, 107).

"It is well to be sure of ourselves, to know for certain that we have Courage for everything that may come, not because we are more plucky than others, but because all persons are born with this Lord and Captain of the Heart. Assured of our Courage, we must not let this courage sleep and allow ourselves to be betrayed into panic by a carriage accident or a wasp or a rat. It is unseemly, unbecoming, for any of us, even the youngest, to lose our presence of mind when we are hurt or in danger. We not only lose the chance of being of use to others, but we make ourselves a burden and a spectacle. Anxious fuss in the small emergencies of life, such as travelling, household mischances, pressure of work, is a form of panic fear, the fear that all may not go well, or that something may be forgotten and left undone. Let us possess ourselves and say: 'What does it matter? All undue concern about things and arrangements is unworthy of us.' It is only persons that matter; and the best thing we can do is to see that one person keeps a serene mind in unusual or fretting circumstances; then we shall be sure that one person is ready to be of use" (Vol. 4, Book 1, pp. 113, 114).

3. Remember that physical calmness can promote mental calmness, just as mental calmness can result in physical calmness.

"It is worth while to remember that the physical signs promote the mental state just as much as the mental state causes the physical signs" (Vol. 3, p. 107).

Questions to Ask about Self-Control in Emergencies

- Does my child understand that a person who can keep presence of mind can be of great service to others?
- Am I striving to keep a calm spirit no matter what happens around me?
- Is my child taking steps toward keeping a calm spirit no matter what happens around him?
- Do I encourage my child toward physical calmness, as well as mental calmness?

More Quotes on Self-Control in Emergencies

"Nothing gives one person so much advantage over another as to remain always cool and unruffled under all circumstances."—Thomas Jefferson

"A hero is no braver than an ordinary man, but he is braver five minutes longer."—Ralph Waldo Emerson

"Character is the result not merely of the great ideas which are given to us, but of the habits which we labour to form *upon those ideas*."

Self-Discipline in Habits
*Regulating oneself to continue
doing the good habits learned*

It was one of those days when Jenny had little to no energy left. She felt like all she did was pick up toys, clean up messes, change diapers, and settle conflicts. She was sick and tired of getting up out of her comfortable chair to enforce her instructions to her little one. Jenny wished her son would just do what she told him to do so she could sit for longer than two minutes.

Once more Jenny gave the firm but gentle command, "Leave the books on the shelf." She saw that little hand reach out, and she knew that little boy was going to pull every last book off if she let him. And at that point, Jenny was ready to let him "just this time." She argued with herself that she was too tired to do what she knew she should do. She wanted to do what *she* wanted to do this time! That's when the ah-ha! moment struck.

A little voice inside said, "Don't expect your child to be more disciplined than you are. If you cannot make yourself respond properly each time he requires help from you, don't expect him to respond properly each time you require something from him."

It requires self-discipline to consistently shape our children's characters. We call that shaping "discipline" for a good reason. Our ultimate goal is that our children will embrace the discipline we impose from outside until it becomes a part of them on the inside. In other words, we want them to become self-disciplined. We want them to be strong enough to do what they know is right even when they don't feel like doing it.

Sound familiar? At that moment in Jenny's parenting, she was struggling with self-discipline. She didn't want to do what she knew was right because she didn't feel like doing it. Jenny was modeling the exact character flaw that she was trying to train out of her son.

It takes self-discipline to teach self-discipline. Your child will learn the most about discipline by watching how disciplined you are. Don't expect more from your child than you're ready to put forth yourself. It's not just a matter of your enforcing a set of standards; it's a matter of your modeling by example the character you're trying to teach.

Charlotte's Thoughts on Self-Discipline in Habits

1. Training in good habits is not complete until your child continues doing them by himself.

"The discipline of habit is never complete until it becomes self-discipline in habits. It is not a trifle that even the nursery child messes his feeder, spills his milk, breaks his playthings, dawdles about his small efforts. The well-trained child delights to bring himself into good habits in these respects. He knows that to be cleanly, neat, prompt, orderly, is so much towards making a man of him, and man and hero are in his thought synonymous terms" (Vol. 3, p. 107).

2. Consistency is a key to forming and continuing good habits—no matter

"The discipline of habit is never complete until it becomes self-discipline in habits."

the season or the location.

"Supposing that good habits have not been set up at home, parents look to school life to supply the omission; but the habits practised in school and relaxed at home, because 'it's holidays now, you know,' do not really become habits of the life.

"The fact that habits have a tendency to become local, that in one house a child will be neat, prompt, diligent; in another untidy, dawdling, and idle, points to the necessity for self-discipline on the part of even a young child.

"Self-reverence, self-knowledge, self-control,
These three alone lead life to sovereign power" (Vol. 3, p. 107).

3. Make the transition from supervised habits to self-disciplined habits in small steps.

"This subject of training in becoming habits is so well understood amongst us that I need only add that such habits are not fully formed so long as supervision is necessary. At first, a child wants the support of constant supervision, but, by degrees, he is left to do the thing he ought of his own accord" (Vol. 3, p. 108).

4. Aim toward good habits of action, body language, and words.

"Habits of behaviour, habits of deportment, habits of address, tones of voice, etc., all the habits of a gentleman-like bearing and a kind and courteous manner, fall under this head of self-discipline in bodily habits" (Vol. 3, p. 108).

Questions to Ask about Self-Discipline in Habits

- Is my child making progress toward continuing good habits by himself?
- Do I try to require my child to maintain his good habits consistently, no matter the season or location?
- Am I making the transition from supervised habits to self-disciplined habits in small steps?
- Is my goal good habits of action, body language, and words?

More Quotes on Self-Discipline in Habits

"Some people regard discipline as a chore. For me, it is a kind of order that sets me free to fly."—Julie Andrews

"A bad habit never disappears miraculously; it's an undo-it-yourself project."—Abigail Van Buren

"What you do when you don't have to, determines what you will be when you can no longer help it."—Rudyard Kipling

"The more self-disciplined you are, the more you will progress."—Thomas a Kempis

"Habits are not fully formed so long as supervision is necessary."

See also Temperance on page 47.

If you expect your child to keep his hands busy and industrious, be sure to provide plenty of appropriate materials for him to use.

"Self-restraint in indulgences is a habit which most educated mothers form with care."

Self-Restraint in Indulgences
Enjoying pleasure in moderation;
not being controlled by desire

"No school today," announced Mom at breakfast.

The children glanced at each other, then back at Mom.

"So what do you intend to do with your day, Evan?" Mom asked her oldest.

Evan thought a moment as he finished chewing his toast. "I think I would like to get some more work done on that bookcase. Dad says we can stain it just as soon as I'm done sanding. I'd like to finish the sanding and surprise him. Then there's that new book I got from the library yesterday. I'd like to read it."

"Will you play catch with Joey and me, Evan?" little Jamie wanted to know.

Evan gave his brother a grin. "Sure, Jamie, I think I can squeeze that in."

A whole day in which to do as you please. Wouldn't that be an unexpected treat? How would you use it? Self-restraint in indulgences can apply to leisure time, what you eat, shopping sprees—lots of things. Read on to learn some practical ideas for developing this habit in your child.

Charlotte's Thoughts on Self-Restraint in Indulgences

1. Provide your child's basic needs and comforts in life so he won't be as apt to grasp at indulgences when opportunity presents itself.

"Self-restraint in indulgences is a habit which most educated mothers form with care. Children are well and agreeably fed, and they do not hanker after a bit of this and a taste of the other. Whether one or two sweetmeats a day are allowed, or whether they go without any, well brought-up children do not seem to mind. It is the children of cottage homes who, even when they are comfortably fed and clothed, keep the animal instinct of basking in the heat of the fire" (Vol. 3, p. 105).

2. Encourage your older child to be industrious in his free time.

"But there is perhaps danger lest the habits of the nursery and schoolroom should lapse in the case of older boys and girls. It is easy to get into the way of lounging in an arm-chair with a novel in the intervals between engagements which are, in fact, amusements. This sort of thing was a matter of conscience with an older generation; lethargic, self-indulgent intervals were not allowed. When people were not amusing themselves healthfully, they were occupying themselves profitably; and, little as we may think of the crewel-work our grandmothers have left behind, it was better for them morally and physically than the relaxed muscles and mind of the novel and the lounge" (Vol. 3, pp. 105, 106).

3. Be sure your child is getting enough rest. Be cautious about participating in so many activities that your child becomes fatigued.

"No doubt the bodily fatigue which follows our more active exercises has something to say in the matter, but it is a grave question whether bodily exercises of any kind should be so frequent and so excessive as to leave us without mental and moral vigour in the intervals" (Vol. 3, p. 106).

Questions to Ask about Self-Restraint in Indulgences

- Am I careful to provide my child's basic needs and comforts in life?
- Is my child progressing in being industrious in his free time?
- Am I sure my child is getting enough rest, or is he participating in so many activities that he is getting fatigued?

More Quotes on Self-Restraint in Indulgences

"We never repent of having eaten too little."—Thomas Jefferson

"It is the great curse of Gluttony that it ends by destroying all sense of the precious, the unique, the irreplaceable."—Dorothy Sayers

"How long will you lie there, you sluggard? When will you get up from your sleep? A little sleep, a little slumber, a little folding of the hands to rest and poverty will come on you like a bandit and scarcity like an armed man."—Proverbs 6:9–11

Training the Ear and Voice
Hearing and pronouncing words accurately

"You do have an unusual name," Wanda commented.

Daneen nodded. "Yes, I don't meet too many other Daneens. But I must say that I appreciate your pronouncing it correctly."

Wanda was surprised. "Is that uncommon?"

"Oh, yes," replied Daneen. "You would be surprised how often I have to repeat it for people and then how many different ways they mispronounce it. I try not to make a big deal about it, but I do notice those rare people who hear it once and pronounce it correctly right from the start. You're one of those rare people. Thank you."

Wanda smiled. "You can thank my mother. She invented this little game when we were growing up. Whenever she came across an unusual word, she would call us all together, say the word once, and see who could pronounce it correctly after only that one hearing. After a while, it got easier for all of us, and I guess it's become a habit."

Charlotte's Thoughts on Training the Ear and Voice

1. Require your child to pronounce vowel sounds correctly, and don't allow him to leave off final consonants of words.

"The training of the ear and voice is an exceedingly important part of physical culture. Drill the children in pure vowel sounds, in the enunciation of final consonants; do not let them speak of 'walkin'' and 'talkin',' of a 'fi-ine da-ay,' 'ni-

Charlotte wrote directly to young people about indulgences and self-restraint in Volume 4, Book 1, pages 191–203.

Notes

"No other part of the world's work is of such supreme difficulty, delicacy and importance, as that of parents in the right bringing up of their children."

Notes

ice boy-oys' " (Vol. 1, p. 133).

"The little people will probably have to be pulled up on the score of pronunciation. They must render 'high,' 'sky,' 'like,' 'world,' with delicate precision; 'diamond,' they will no doubt wish to hurry over, and say as 'di'mond,' just as they will reduce 'history' to 'hist'ry.' But here is another advantage of slow and steady progress—the *saying* of each word receives due attention, and the child is trained in the habit of careful enunciation" (Vol. 1, p. 206).

2. Make a game of pronouncing difficult words precisely after a single hearing.

"Drill them in pronouncing difficult words—'imperturbability,' 'ipecacuanha,' 'Antananarivo,'—with sharp precision after a single hearing; in producing the several sounds of each vowel; and the sounds of the consonants *without* attendant vowels" (Vol. 1, p. 133).

3. Use oral foreign language study as a way to reinforce ear and voice training.

"French, taught orally, is exceedingly valuable as affording training for both ear and voice" (Vol. 1, p. 133).

Questions to Ask about Training the Ear and Voice

- Do I require my child to pronounce vowel sounds correctly?
- Do I allow my child to leave off final consonant sounds in words?
- Am I learning how to make a game of pronouncing difficult words precisely after a single hearing?
- Am I trying to use oral foreign language study to reinforce this habit?

More Quotes on Training the Ear and Voice

"Speak properly, and in as few words as you can, but always plainly; for the end of speech is not ostentation, but to be understood."—William Penn

"The discipline of habit is at least a third part of the great whole which we call education."

Chapter 7
Religious Habits

Charlotte spent a great deal of thought and ink outlining some wonderful "Habits of the Religious Life" in Volume 3. Her additional comments on these religious habits, that can be found in the other volumes, are compiled here as well to give you a full picture of these important concepts.

Regularity in Devotions (including)

    Prayer

    Reading the Bible

    Praise

Reverent Attitude

Sunday-Keeping

Thanksgiving

Thought of God

Notes

Charlotte wrote directly to young people about knowledge of God, prayer, thanksgiving, praise, and faith in Volume 4, Book 2, pages 174–202.

"Above all, 'watch unto prayer' and teach your child dependence upon divine aid in this warfare of the spirit; but, also, the absolute necessity for his own efforts."

Regularity in Devotions
*Having a personal time of
prayer, praise, and Bible reading*

"Where do you find good devotional books for your children?" Lori asked.

"They're not easy to find," replied Susan. "There are a lot of devotional books available, but not many that are really good."

"So what do your children do for their devotions?" came Lori's next question.

"Read the Bible directly," Susan explained. "The younger children can read the great stories of the Bible. As the children get older, I tell them that they might begin looking for four things in their reading: a command to obey, a promise to claim, a temptation to avoid, or a principle to live by. It's simple, but it seems to help them to have a little guideline. Then I just give them a devotional book once in a while when I can find a really good one."

"Do you require them to keep a prayer journal or anything?" Lori wanted to know.

"No, I don't require one or discourage one," answered Susan. "It's strictly up to them to determine what works best for their personalities. Yes, I encourage them to pray and praise God, but I try not to make them adhere to someone else's personal preferences, like journals or lists."

Lori had one more question. "And do you make them have daily devotions?"

"I haven't had to enforce it as a rule, no. They, of course, participate in family devotions from the time they're little. Then once they learn to read, we give them their own Bibles. They hear about the importance of personal devotions at church and in our small group meetings, and I usually leave my door open when I'm having my devotions so they can see that it's an important activity in my own life," Susan finished up. "I'm thankful they are forming the habit for themselves."

Charlotte's Thoughts on Regularity in Devotions

1. Communicate the importance of daily devotions by word and example.

"The habit of regularity in children's devotions is very important. The mother cannot always be present, but I have known children far more punctual in their devotions when away from their mother, because they know it to be her wish, than if she were there to remind them" (Vol. 3, p. 142).

2. Establish a set time and place for daily devotions.

"They may say, like a little friend of mine, aged four, 'Mother, I always worship idols.' 'Do you indeed, Margaret? when?' 'Why, when I say my prayers to the chair.' But it is a great thing for all of us to get the habit of 'saying our prayers' at a given time and in a given place, which comes to be to us as a holy place. The chair, or the bedside, or the little prayer-table, or, best of all, the mother's knee, plays no small part in framing the soul to a habit of devotion" (Vol. 3, p. 142).

3. Be sure to schedule an unhurried time for devotions when your child is fully awake and alert.

"In this connection it is worth while to remark that the evening prayers of

"The habit of regularity in children's devotions is very important."

children and of school girls and boys should not be left until the children are tired and drop asleep over their evening exercises. After tea is a very good set time for prayers when it can be managed" (Vol. 3, p. 142).

"In the first place, 'every word of God' is the food of the spiritual life; and these words come to us most freely in the moments we set apart in which to recollect ourselves, read, say our prayers. Such moments in the lives of young people are apt to be furtive and hurried; it is well to secure for them the necessary leisure—a quiet twenty minutes, say—and that, early in the evening; for the fag end of the day is not the best time for its most serious affairs. I have known happy results where it is the habit of the young people to retire for a little while, when their wits are fresh, and before the work or play of the evening has begun" (Vol. 5, p. 209).

4. A well-chosen devotional book can be a good supplement to your child's devotional time.

"Again, the Christian life should be a *progressive* life. The boy should not be allowed to feel himself like a door on its hinges, always swinging over the same ground. New and definite aims, thoughts, subjects of prayer should be set before him week by week, that 'something attempted, something done,' may give him courage; and that, suppose he is harassed by failure, he may try in a new direction with new hope. Even those who do not belong to the Church of England would find her Sunday Collects, Epistles, and Gospels helpful, as giving the young people something definite to think about, week by week. We can hardly hope in this life to grow up to all there is in those weekly portions, but the youngest Christian finds enough to go on with, and has the reposing sense of being led, step by step, in his heavenward progress. I am not suggesting this as a substitute for wider reading of the Bible, only as a definite thought, purpose, and prayer for every week as it comes, in addition to whatever other prayers general or special needs may call for. The bringing of the thought of the collect and its accompanying scriptures home will afford occasion for a few earnest words, week by week, not to be readily forgotten. And this in itself is a gain, for we all experience some difficulty in speaking of the best things to the people we live amongst, especially to the young people" (Vol. 5, pp. 209, 210).

5. Encourage both spontaneous prayer and set times of purposeful prayer.

"But, though there is this continual commerce between God and the Soul, the habit of prayer must be strengthened by set seasons, places, and purposes. We must give ourselves time to pray and times of prayer; rising early in the morning, we must seek our God and lay our day before Him, with its fears, hopes, and desires, in reverent attitude and with attentive mind. We must bring those who are dear to us for the blessing of our Father, and those in sorrow, need, sickness, or any other adversity, for His help. As the habit of prayer becomes confirmed, we shall be constrained to go abroad and help, while yet upon our knees" (Vol. 4, Book 2, p. 189).

"Let us consider what is commonly done in the nursery in this respect. No sooner can the little being lisp than he is taught to kneel up in his mother's lap, and say 'God bless . . .' and then follows a list of the near and dear, and 'God

"As the habit of prayer becomes confirmed, we shall be constrained to go abroad and help, while yet upon our knees."

bless . . . and make him a good boy, for Jesus' sake. Amen.' It is very touching and beautiful. I once peeped in at an open cottage door in a moorland village, and saw a little child in its nightgown kneeling in its mother's lap and saying its evening prayer. The spot has ever since remained to me a sort of shrine. There is no sight more touching and tender. By-and-by, so soon as he can speak the words,

'Gentle Jesus, meek and mild,'

is added to the little one's prayer, and later, 'Our Father.' Nothing could be more suitable and more beautiful than these morning and evening approaches to God, the little children brought to Him by their mothers. And most of us can 'think back' to the hallowing influence of these early prayers. But might not more be done? How many times a day does a mother lift up her heart to God as she goes in and out amongst her children, and they never know! 'Today I talked to them' (a boy and girl of four and five) 'about Rebekah at the well. They were very much interested, especially about Eliezer praying in his heart and the answer coming at once. They said, "How did he pray?" I said, "I often pray in my heart when you know nothing about it. Sometimes you begin to show a naughty spirit, and I pray for you in my heart, and almost directly I find the good spirit comes, and your faces show my prayer is answered." O. stroked my hand and said, "Dear mother, I shall think of that!" Boy looked thoughtful, but didn't speak; but when they were in bed I knelt down to pray for them before leaving them, and when I got up, Boy said, "Mother, God filled my heart with goodness while you prayed for us; and, mother, I will try to-morrow." '

"Is it possible that the mother could, when alone with her children, occasionally hold this communing out loud, so that the children might grow up in the sense of the presence of God? It would probably be difficult for many mothers to break down the barrier of spiritual reserve in the presence of even their own children. But, could it be done, would it not lead to glad and natural living in the recognised presence of God?

"A mother, who remembered a little penny scent-bottle as an early joy of her own, took three such small bottles home to her three little girls. They got them next morning at the family breakfast, and enjoyed them all through the meal. Before it ended the mother was called away, and little M. was sitting rather solitary with her scent-bottle and the remains of her breakfast. And out of the pure well of the little girl's heart came this, intended for nobody's ear, 'Dear mother, you are too good!' Think of the joy of the mother who should overhear her little child murmuring over the first primrose of the year, 'Dear God, you are too good!' Children are so imitative, that if they hear their parents speak out continually their joys and fears, their thanks and wishes, they, too, will have many things to say" (Vol. 2, pp. 54–56).

6. Give your child plenty of direct contact with the Bible itself, not watered down re-tellings, and select those passages that are appropriate for children.

"The habit of hearing, and later, of reading the Bible, is one to establish at an early age. We are met with a difficulty—that the Bible is, in fact, a library containing passages and, indeed, whole books which are not for the edification of children; and many parents fall back upon little collections of texts for morning and evening use. But I doubt the wisdom of this plan. We may believe that the narrative teaching of the Scriptures is far more helpful to children, anyway, than the stimulating moral and spiritual texts picked out for them in little devotional

"The habit of hearing, and later, of reading the Bible, is one to establish at an early age."

books. The twopenny single books of the Bible, published by the Bible Society, should be a resource for parents. A child old enough to take pleasure in reading for himself would greatly enjoy reading through the Gospel of St Mark, bit by bit, for example, in a nice little book, as part of his morning's devotions" (Vol. 3, pp. 142, 143).

"Let all the circumstances of the daily Bible reading—the consecutive reading, from the first chapter of Genesis onwards, with necessary omissions—be delightful to the child; let him be in his mother's room, in his mother's arms; let that quarter of an hour be one of sweet leisure and sober gladness, the child's whole interest being allowed to go to the story without distracting moral considerations; and then, the less talk the better; the story will sink in, and bring its own teaching, a little now, and more every year as he is able to bear it" (Vol. 1, p. 337).

"A word about the reading of the Bible. I think we make a mistake in burying the text under our endless comments and applications. Also, I doubt if the picking out of individual verses, and grinding these into the child until they cease to have any meaning for him, is anything but a hindrance to the spiritual life. The Word is full of vital force, capable of applying itself. A seed, light as thistledown, wafted into the child's soul, will take root downwards and bear fruit upwards. What is required of us is, that we should implant a love of the Word; that the most delightful moments of the child's day should be those in which his mother reads for him, with sweet sympathy and holy gladness in voice and eyes, the beautiful stories of the Bible; and now and then in the reading will occur one of those convictions, passing from the soul of the mother to the soul of the child, in which is the life of the Spirit. Let the child grow, so that,

'New thoughts of God, new hopes of heaven,'

are a joy to him, too; things to be counted first amongst the blessings of a day. Above all, do not read the Bible at the child: do not let any words of the Scriptures be occasions for gibbeting his faults. It is the office of the Holy Ghost to convince of sin; and He is able to use the Word for this purpose, without risk of that hardening of the heart in which our clumsy dealings too often result" (Vol. 1, pp. 348, 349).

Before children can read independently, you can train them in this habit with set family devotions. After they learn to read well, help them make the transition to personal devotions.

7. Teach your child that, though devotions are very helpful to us, his having devotions does not earn him merit with God.

"But while pressing the importance of habits of prayer and devotional reading, it should be remembered that children are little formalists by nature, and that they should not be encouraged in long readings or long prayers with a notion of any merit in such exercises" (Vol. 3, p. 143).

8. Encourage your child to make praise an integral part of his daily devotions.

"Perhaps we do not attach enough importance to the habit of praise in our children's devotions. Praise and thanksgiving come freely from the young heart; gladness is natural and holy, and music is a delight" (Vol. 3, p. 143).

9. Teach your child to sing hymns and other worship songs reverently, offering his best praise.

"Perhaps we do not attach enough importance to the habit of praise."

Notes

"The singing of hymns at home and of the hymns and canticles in church should be a special delight."

"The singing of hymns at home and of the hymns and canticles in church should be a special delight; and the habit of soft and reverent singing, of offering our very best in praise, should be carefully formed" (Vol. 3, p. 143).

10. Teach your young child hymns that have a story in the lyrics.

"Hymns with a story, such as: 'A little ship was on the sea,' 'I think when I read that sweet story of old,' 'Hushed was the evening hymn,' are perhaps the best for little children" (Vol. 3, p. 143).

Questions to Ask about Regularity in Devotions

- Am I seeking to communicate the importance of daily devotions by my word and example?
- Am I helping my child establish a set time and place for devotions?
- Is that scheduled time unhurried and set when my child is fully awake and alert?
- Am I carefully selecting devotional books to supplement my child's devotional times?
- Am I trying to encourage my child to have both spontaneous prayer and set times of purposeful prayer?
- Is my child getting plenty of direct contact with Scripture that is appropriate for his age?
- Does my child understand that devotions are helpful but do not earn him favor with God?
- Is my child incorporating praise in his daily devotions?
- Is my child learning to sing reverently, offering his best praise?
- Am I teaching my child hymns, especially those that have a story in the lyrics?

More Quotes on Regularity in Devotions

Prayer

"There is nothing that makes us love someone so much as praying for them."—William Law

"Prayer . . . the key of the day and the lock of the night."—Thomas Fuller

Reading the Bible

"The Bible will keep you from sin, or sin will keep you from the Bible."—D. L. Moody

"Unless we form the habit of going to the Bible in bright moments as well as in trouble, we cannot fully respond to its consolations because we lack equilibrium between light and darkness."—Helen Keller

Praise

"God is to be praised with the voice, and the heart should go therewith in holy exultation."—Charles H. Spurgeon

Reverent Attitude

Expressing worship in one's demeanor and actions

Janet picked up the phone and recognized Cheryl's voice on the other end. "Hi, Janet. Do you have time for a quick question?"

"Yes, I do," replied Janet. In the background she could hear Cheryl's toddlers chattering noisily.

"We want to train our Jennifer to sit quietly in church, but we're not quite sure how to do that," Cheryl came right to the point. "How can I teach her to be quiet and not cause a disturbance?"

"Good question," Janet responded. "I'd recommend that you train her to sit on your lap in short increments at home. Practicing during family devotions is one good way to train this habit."

"Yes, we're starting to do that," Cheryl said. "But a church meeting is so much longer!"

"Yes, it is. So when you're sitting in church, give her a boundary in the chair row or pew: mom's knees to dad's knees a few seats apart. Let her play with quiet toys within that boundary. Start with fifteen minutes in that setting, then take her out and give her a short break to run. Come back in to the service for fifteen minutes, then take her out for another short break. Are you with me so far?" asked Janet.

Cheryl agreed, "That's making sense."

"Then just increase the time she stays in the service a little at a time. For instance, after a few weeks of fifteen minutes, go to seventeen minutes in the service before giving a break. A couple of weeks later, go to twenty minutes before a break, and so on," Janet explained.

"I see!" Cheryl sounded relieved. "Thanks so much, Janet." A squeal sounded in the background. "Gotta run!"

Sitting quietly in a church service is a good start to teaching your child to show reverence. Once he is old enough to understand what is happening around him, he will be able to build on that habit and begin to participate in worship with the other believers around him as he is able.

Charlotte's Thoughts on Reverent Attitude

1. Don't insist on mere outward conformity, but realize that reverent actions can awaken reverent feelings.

"The importance of reverent attitudes is a little apt to be overlooked in these days. We are, before all things, sincere, and are afraid to insist upon 'mere forms,' feeling it best to leave the child to the natural expression of his own emotions. Here perhaps we are wrong, as it is just as true to say that the form gives birth to the feeling as that the feeling should give birth to the form" (Vol. 3, p. 141).

2. Teach your child to demonstrate a worshipful demeanor during prayer, whether at meals, at family worship, at personal prayers, or in church.

"The importance of reverent attitudes is a little apt to be overlooked in these days."

Notes

"Children should be taught to take time, to be reverent at grace before meals, at family prayers, at their own prayers, in church, when they are old enough to attend. Perhaps some of us may remember standing daily by our mother's knee in reverent attitude to recite the Apostles' Creed, and the recollection of the reverence expressed in that early act remains with one through a lifetime" (Vol. 3, p. 141).

3. Exhort your child to show as much respect for God as the angels do.

" 'Because of the angels' should be a thought to repress unbecoming behaviour in children" (Vol. 3, p. 141).

"It is not well to allow the children in a careless familiarity with the Name of Jesus, or in the use of hymns whose tone is not reverent" (Vol. 1, p. 352).

4. Don't assume that actions or postures that demonstrate reverence are tiresome to your child.

"It is a mistake to suppose that the forms of reverence need be tiresome to them. They love little ceremonies, and to be taught to kneel nicely while saying their short prayers would help them to a feeling of reverence in after life" (Vol. 3, p. 141).

5. Allow your young child a quiet and appropriate book or toy to keep his hands busy during the church service, and encourage children of all ages to participate in the parts of the service that they can.

"In connection with children's behaviour in church, the sentiment and forms of reverence cannot be expected if they are taken to church too young, or to too long services, or are expected to maintain their attention throughout. If children must be taken to long services, they should be allowed the resource of a Sunday picture-book, and told that the hymns and the 'Our Father,' for example, are the parts of the service for them. But in these days of bright short services especially adapted for children the difficulty need not arise" (Vol. 3, pp. 141, 142).

"Children should be trained in the habits of attention and real devotion during short services or parts of services. The habit of finding their places in the prayer-book and following the service is interesting and aids attention, but perhaps it would be well to tell children, of even ten or eleven, that during the litany, for example, they might occupy themselves by saying over silently hymns that they know" (Vol. 3, pp. 143, 144).

Questions to Ask about Reverent Attitude

- Am I trying to use reverent actions to encourage reverent feelings in myself and my child?
- Is my child learning to demonstrate a worshipful demeanor during prayer times?
- Does my child desire to show as much respect for God as the angels do?
- Am I mistakenly assuming that reverent actions or postures are tiresome to my child?
- Is my child making progress in sitting quietly during church services and participating as he is able?

"Children should be trained in the habits of attention and real devotion during short services or parts of services."

More Quotes on Reverent Attitude

"Fear God and keep his commandments: for this is the whole duty of man."—Ecclesiastes 12:13

Sunday-Keeping
*Setting aside Sunday
to focus especially on God
and to rest from everyday pursuits*

I do enjoy a vacation every once in a while, thought Tina. *It helps me come back to my everyday tasks refreshed and ready to jump in again with new energy. And Sunday is beginning to feel like a little mini vacation—one that we get to enjoy every week! I'm so glad we started setting Sunday aside as a special day to rest and focus on God!*

Just as a vacation doesn't feel like a vacation when someone forces you to go and tells you over and over what you may not do while you are at your destination, so the idea of a day of rest doesn't convey God's good intention when presented as a rigid list of do's and don'ts. God's plan for resting one day in seven is for our good—physically, mentally, emotionally, spiritually. Let's accurately represent God's good plan to our children, and give them this valuable habit of a special day every week to rest and focus on God.

Charlotte's Thoughts on Sunday-Keeping

1. Sunday activities should be special to the day—not rigid or dull, but quiet and glad.

"The habit of Sunday observances, not rigid, not dull, and yet peculiar to the day, is especially important. Sunday stories, Sunday hymns, Sunday walks, Sunday talks, Sunday painting, Sunday knitting even, Sunday card-games, should all be special to the day,—quiet, glad, serene" (Vol. 3, p. 144).

2. A change of pace on Sunday is helpful physically and mentally.

"The people who clamour for a Sunday that shall be as other days little know how healing to the jaded brain is the change of thought and occupation the seventh day brings with it" (Vol. 3, p. 144).

3. Sunday activities should promote communion with nature and with God.

"There is hardly a more precious inheritance to be handed on than that of the traditional English Sunday, stripped of its austerities, we hope, but keeping its character of quiet gladness and communion with Nature as well as with God" (Vol. 3, p. 144).

4. Communicate to your child the pleasure of Sunday activities as enjoyable

"Put anxious cares aside on Sunday, for the children's sake."

See A Family Habit of Reading Aloud in chapter 8 for more thoughts on this activity.

"The point in the Sunday readings and occupations, is, to keep the heart at peace and the mind alive and receptive."

Notes

and helpful to our bodies and minds, rather than emphasizing restrictions.

"Only one point more—a word as to the manner of keeping Sunday in the family. Do not let the young people feel themselves straitened by narrow views: give them freely the broad principle that what is right on Saturday is right on Sunday—right, but not in all things convenient; the Sunday has pursuits of its own; and we are no more willing to give up any part of it to the grind of the common business or the common pleasures of life, than the schoolboy is to give up a holiday to the grind of school-work. Even for selfish reasons of health and comfort we cannot afford to give up the repose to body, mind, and spirit which we owe to the change of thought and occupations the day brings" (Vol. 5, pp. 210, 211).

5. Make Sundays pleasant in attitude and conversation.

"Having made the principle of Sunday-keeping plain, make the practice pleasant. Let it be a joyous day—everybody in his best temper and gentlest manners. Put anxious cares aside on Sunday, for the children's sake; and if there be no 'vain deluding mirth,' let there be gaiety of heart and talk" (Vol. 5, p. 211).

6. Keep a special book that your family reads aloud and shares together only on Sundays; well-chosen poetry would also be appropriate.

"Let the day be full of its own special interests and amusements. An hour's reading aloud, from Sunday to Sunday, of a work of real power and interest, might add to the interest of Sunday afternoon; and this family reading should supply a pleasant *intellectual* stimulus.

"A little poetry may well be got in: there is time to digest it on Sunday; not only George Herbert, Vaughan, Keble, and the like, but any poet who feeds the heart with wise thoughts, and does not too much disturb the peace of the day with the stir of life and passion" (Vol. 5, p. 211).

7. Sunday activities should leave room for awareness and contemplation of any thoughts God impresses on our minds.

"The point in the Sunday readings and occupations, is, to keep the heart at peace and the mind alive and receptive, open to any holy impression which may come from above, it may be in the fields or by the fireside. It is not that we are to be seeking, making efforts all day long, in church and out of it. We may rest altogether, in body and spirit; on condition that we do not become *engrossed*, that we keep ourselves open to the influences which fall in unexpected ways. This thought determines the choice of the Sunday story-book. Any pure, thoughtful study of character, earnest picture of life, will do to carry our thoughts upward, though the Divine Name be not mentioned; but tales full of affairs and society, or tales of passion, are hardly to be chosen" (Vol. 5, p. 211).

8. Use appropriate music to help make Sundays pleasant.

"Music in the family is the greatest help towards making Sunday pleasant; but here, again, it is, perhaps, well to avoid music which carries associations of passion and unrest. There can, however, be little difficulty in making a suitable choice, when it is hardly too much to say that the greatest works of the greatest masters are consecrated to the service of religion" (Vol. 5, p. 212).

Questions to Ask about Sunday-Keeping

- Am I trying to make Sunday activities special—not rigid or dull, but quiet and glad?
- Is my child learning that a change of pace on Sunday is helpful physically and mentally?
- Do my Sunday activities promote communion with God and with nature?
- Am I emphasizing the pleasure of Sunday activities as enjoyable and helpful to our bodies and minds, rather than emphasizing restrictions?
- Am I seeking to make Sundays pleasant in attitude and conversation?
- Does our family have a special book or well-chosen poetry to read aloud only on Sundays?
- Does our Sunday schedule leave room for awareness and contemplation of any thoughts God impresses on our minds?
- Do I use appropriate music to help make Sundays pleasant?

More Quotes on Sunday-Keeping

"In the name of Jesus Christ, who was never in a hurry, we pray, O God, that You will slow us down, for we know that we live too fast. With all of eternity before us, make us take time to live—time to get acquainted with You, time to enjoy You, time to enjoy Your blessings, and time to know each other."—Peter Marshall

"Sunday is the core of our civilization, dedicated to thought and reverence."—Ralph Waldo Emerson

"A Sunday well-spent brings a week of content."—Proverb

Thanksgiving
Being grateful to God for all His blessings

"Let's make a Thankful Calendar," Natalie told her two girls. "We'll hang this calendar here by your closet door. See, it has big spaces for the days so we can write down each day before you go to bed what you thank God for on that day."

The girls were excited about their Thankful Calendar, and the next night after they had put on their nightgowns, they all gathered around the calendar to record its first entries.

"Ashley, you go first," instructed Natalie. "What happened today that you want to thank God for?"

Ashley beamed as she answered, "We got to play at the park!"

So Natalie wrote "Play at park" in the space for that day.

"Now you, Brigette."

"I'm thankful that Daddy was able to fix my doll Emily," replied Brigette solemnly.

"Music in the family is the greatest help towards making Sunday pleasant."

Notes

"Yes," Natalie nodded and wrote, "Daddy fixed Emily."

And so the Thankful Calendar had its beginning. Over the months the girls learned to thank God for many things, both little and big. They also learned the important lesson of thanking God "in everything."

Charlotte's Thoughts on Thanksgiving

1. Teach your child to give thanks for answered prayer.

"Perhaps most of us fall on our knees and give thanks for special mercies that we have begged of our Father's providing care—the restored health of one beloved, the removal of some cause of anxiety, the opening up of some opportunity that we have longed for. For such graces as these we give ungrudging thanks, and we do well" (Vol. 4, Book 2, p. 193).

2. Cultivate a thankful heart all throughout the day as well.

"But the continual habit of thanksgiving is more;—
  "Not thankful when it pleaseth me,
  As if Thy blessings had spare days,
  But such a heart whose pulse may be,
  Thy praise"
    HERBERT (Vol. 4, Book 2, p. 193).

Questions to Ask about Thanksgiving

• Is my child learning to thank God for answered prayer?
• Is my child developing a thankful heart for all God's blessings throughout the day?

More Quotes on Thanksgiving

"Swift gratitude is the sweetest."—Greek proverb

"In everything give thanks, for this is the will of God in Christ Jesus concerning you."—1 Thessalonians 5:18

"A thankful heart is not only the greatest virtue, but the parent of all other virtues."—Cicero

"Pride slays thanksgiving, but an humble mind is the soil out of which thanks naturally grow. A proud man is seldom a grateful man, for he never thinks he gets as much as he deserves."—Henry Ward Beecher

"The worship most acceptable to God comes from a thankful and cheerful heart."—Plutarch

"Sow an act, reap a habit; sow a habit, reap a character; sow a character, reap a destiny."

Thought of God
Thinking rightly about God throughout each day's events

"Oh, my!" Lynn exclaimed as they turned the corner into the access road. Cars were lined up all the way out of the new store's parking lot. "Well, we can't go backward, so I guess we'll stay in line and see what it looks like as we get closer."

Lynn and the children had made a special trip to the store to get one item that they needed—an item they couldn't get anywhere else. When they had reached their destination, they had found a deserted building with a sign on the door directing them to the store's new location. So they had embarked on the adventure of finding this new place, and now they were facing quite the traffic backup.

As they inched their way forward, Lynn told the children, "We'll just go to the end of this row and then turn back up the next row toward the exit. If the Lord wants us to get inside, He'll have to find us a parking space. If there aren't any parking spaces, we'll know that He didn't want us to shop here today."

Just as they rounded the end of the row and started into the next, a car on their right put on its reverse lights and started to back out of its parking place. No other cars were in sight as Lynn maneuvered their van into the empty slot.

"OK," she said as she turned off the engine. "Looks like the Lord wants us to go on in."

Praying without ceasing and walking in the Spirit are possible only to the extent that we keep our minds focused on God. What a blessing to help your child learn the habit of keeping God in all his thoughts!

Charlotte's Thoughts on Thought of God

1. Direct your child's thoughts to God whether he is happy, resting, working, or giving.

"It is said of the wicked that 'God is not in all their thoughts.' Of the child it should be said that God is in all his thoughts; happy-making, joyous thoughts, restful and dutiful thoughts, thoughts of loving and giving and serving, the wealth of beautiful thoughts with which every child's heart overflows" (Vol. 3, p. 140).

"There is one thing the mother will allow herself to do as interpreter between Nature and the child, but that not oftener than once a week or once a month, and with look and gesture of delight rather than with flow of improving words— she will point out to the child some touch of especial loveliness in colouring or grouping in the landscape or in the heavens. One other thing she will do, but very rarely, and with tender filial reverence (most likely she will say her prayers, and speak out of her prayer, for to touch on this ground with hard words is to wound the soul of the child): she will point to some lovely flower or gracious tree, not only as a beautiful work, but a beautiful thought of God, in which we may believe He finds continual pleasure, and which He is pleased to see his human children rejoice in. Such a seed of sympathy with the Divine thought sown in the heart of

"Of all the knowledge which a child should get, the knowledge of God is first in importance."

the child is worth many of the sermons the man may listen to hereafter, much of the 'divinity' he may read" (Vol. 1, pp. 79, 80).

"The parent must not make blundering, witless efforts: as this is the highest duty imposed upon him, it is also the most delicate; and he will have infinite need of faith and prayer, tact and discretion, humility, gentleness, love, and sound judgment, if he would present his child to God, and the thought of God to the soul of his child" (Vol. 1, p. 345).

2. Answer your child's questions about things divine by guiding him into true, happy thinking about God.

"We are inclined to think that a child is a little morbid and precocious when he asks questions and has imaginings about things divine, and we do our best to divert him. What he needs is to be guided into true, happy thinking; every day should bring him 'new thoughts of God, new hopes of heaven.' He understands things divine better than we do, because his ideas have not been shaped to a conventional standard; and thoughts of God are to him an escape into the infinite from the worrying limitations, the perception of the prison bars, which are among the bitter pangs of childhood" (Vol. 3, pp. 140, 141).

"It is probable that parents as a class feel more than ever before the responsibility of their prophetic office. It is as revealers of God to their children that parents touch their highest limitations; perhaps it is only as they succeed in this part of their work that they fulfil the Divine intention in giving them children to bring up—in the nurture and admonition of the Lord" (Vol. 2, p. 41).

"Think what the vision of God should be to the little child already peering wistfully through the bars of his prison-house. Not a far-off God, a cold abstraction, but a warm, breathing, spiritual Presence about his path and about his bed—a Presence in which he recognises protection and tenderness in darkness and danger, towards which he rushes as the timid child to hide his face in his mother's skirts" (Vol. 2, p. 47).

"The knowledge of God ranks first in importance, is indispensable, and most happy-making. Mothers are on the whole more successful in communicating this knowledge than are teachers who know the children less well and have a narrower, poorer standard of measurement for their minds" (Vol. 6, p. 158).

3. Emphasize an ongoing relationship of love and personal service to God as Heavenly Father and King, rather than just a duty to "be good."

"One caution I should like to offer. A child's whole notion of religion is 'being good.' It is well that he should know that being good is not his whole duty to God, although it is so much of it; that the relationship of love and personal service, which he owes as a child to his Father, as a subject to his King, is even more than the 'being good' which gives our Almighty Father such pleasure in His children" (Vol. 3, p. 136).

"A mother knows how to speak of God as she would of an absent father with all the evidences of his care and love about her and his children. She knows how to make a child's heart beat high in joy and thankfulness as she thrills him with the thought, 'my Father made them all,' while his eye delights in flowery meadow, great tree, flowing river" (Vol. 6, p. 159).

4. Encouraging this habit of thought of God now will help your child practice the presence of God as an adult.

"To keep a child in this habit of the thought of God—so that to lose it, for even a little while, is like coming home after an absence and finding his mother out—is a very delicate part of a parent's work" (Vol. 3, p. 141).

Questions to Ask about Thought of God

- Is my child learning to think rightly about God in all that is happening during the day?
- Am I trying to answer my child's questions about God by guiding him into true, happy thinking about God?
- Is my child growing to view God as a loving Father and sovereign King, rather than just Someone Who requires him to "be good"?
- Are both my child and I learning to practice the presence of God?

More Quotes on Thought of God

"Lord, make me see thy glory in every place."—Michelangelo

"Lord, purge our eyes to see
Within the seed a tree
Within the glowing egg a bird,
Within the shroud a butterfly.
Till, taught by such we see
Beyond all creatures, Thee . . ."—Christina Rossetti

"Let us not be Christians as to the few great things of our lives, and atheists as to the many small things which fill up a far greater space of them. God is in both, waiting for the glory we can give Him in them."—Dwight L. Moody

Notes

"A mother knows how to speak of God as she would of an absent father with all the evidences of his care and love about her and his children."

Chapter 8
A Family Habit of Reading Aloud

Charlotte gave some wonderful suggestions for making the habit of a family read-aloud an enjoyable time as well as a learning experience.

1. Reading a book together as a family strengthens family bonds and provides many occasions for discussion.

"There are few stronger family bonds than this habit of devoting an occasional hour to reading aloud, on winter evenings, at any rate. The practice is pleasant at the time, and pleasant in the retrospect, it gives occasion for much bright talk, merry and wise, and quickens family affection by means of intellectual sympathy. Indeed, the wonder is that any family should neglect such a simple means of pure enjoyment, and of moral, as well as intellectual culture" (Vol. 5, p. 220).

2. Be sure to make reading aloud a consistent habit that everyone looks forward to.

"But this, of reading aloud, is not a practice to be taken tip and laid down at pleasure. Let the habit drop, and it is difficult to take it up again, because every one has in the meantime struck a vein of intellectual entertainment for himself—trashy stuff, it may be,—which makes him an unwilling listener to the family 'book.' No; let an hour's reading aloud be a part of the winter evening at home—on one or two evenings a week, at any rate—and everybody will look forward to it as a hungry boy looks for his dinner" (Vol. 5, p. 220).

3. The family read-aloud time gives parents opportunity to correct in the reader the three faults that make listening unpleasant: careless enunciation, stumbling, and gasping or yawning.

"If reading is to be pleasant to the listeners, the reading itself must be distinct, easy, and sympathetic. And here is something more which parents must do for their children themselves, for nobody else will get them into the habit of reading for the pleasure of other people from the moment when they can read fluently at all. After indistinct and careless enunciation, perhaps the two most trying faults in a reader are, the slowness which does not see what is coming next, and stumbles over the new clause, and the habit of gasping, like a fish out of water, several times in the course of a sentence" (Vol. 5, pp. 220, 221).

4. To prevent gasping or yawning, breathe through the nose not the mouth.

"The last fault is easy of cure: 'Never breathe through the lips, but always through the nostrils, in reading,' is a safe rule: if the lips be closed in the act of taking breath, enough air is inhaled to inflate the lungs, and supply 'breath' to the reader: if an undue supply is taken in by mouth and nostrils both, the

> "If reading is to be pleasant to the listeners, the reading itself must be distinct, easy, and sympathetic."

Notes

inconvenience is caused which relieves itself in gasps" (Vol. 5, p. 221).

5. To prevent stumbling, learn to look a line ahead.

"The stumbling reader spoils his book from sheer want of attention. He should train himself to look on, to be always a line in advance, so that he may be ready for what is coming" (Vol. 5, p. 221).

6. To prevent careless enunciation, deal with only one fault per reading and only if it occurs.

"Faults in enunciation should be dealt with one by one. For instance, one week the reader takes pains to secure the 'd' in 'and'; the other letters will take care of themselves, and the less they are heard the better. Indeed, if the final consonants are secured, *d*, *t*, and *ng* especially, the reading will be distinct and finished.

"Another advantage of the family *lecture* is, that it enables parents to detect and correct provincialisms; and, however anxious we may be, on historical grounds, to preserve *dialect*, few people desire to preserve it in the persons of their own children. For the rest, practice makes perfect. Let everybody take his night or his week for reading, with the certainty that the pleasure of the whole family depends on his reading well" (Vol. 5, p. 221).

"Let everybody take his night or his week for reading, with the certainty that the pleasure of the whole family depends on his reading well."

Part 3

Repairing
the Rails

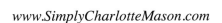

Chapter 9
Breaking a Bad Habit

Charlotte gave ten definite steps to eliminating a bad habit and replacing it with a good one. Read her comments here, then find more specific suggestions and examples in the following chapters for dealing with lying, dawdling, mean behavior, temper tantrums, and sulking.

Ten Steps to Dealing with a Bad Habit

"Let me offer a few definite practical counsels to a parent who wishes to deal seriously with a bad habit" (Vol. 2, p. 175).

1. Realize that your child probably does this habit somewhat automatically by now, without conscious thought.

"Let us remember that this bad habit has made its record in the brain" (Vol. 2, p. 175).

2. Devote four to eight weeks of making sure your child does not do the bad habit.

"There is only one way of obliterating such record; the absolute cessation of the habit for a considerable space of time, say some six or eight weeks" (Vol. 2, p. 175).

"How long may it take to cure a bad habit, and form the contrary good one?
"Perhaps a month or six weeks of careful incessant treatment may be enough" (Vol. 2, p. 238).

3. Understand that it will take several weeks for the old bad habit to be erased.

"During this interval new growth, new cell connections, are somehow or other taking place, and the physical seat of the evil is undergoing a natural healing" (Vol. 2, p. 175).

4. You must replace the bad habit with a good one that seems just as attractive to your child.

"But the only way to secure this pause is to introduce some new habit as attractive to the child as is the wrong habit you set yourself to cure" (Vol. 2, p. 175).

5. Identify the core trait of the defect and take it in the opposite direction mentally; figure out what that trait would look like if it were used for good.

"As the bad habit usually arises from the defect of some quality in the child it should not be difficult for the parent who knows his child's character to introduce

"Education as we understand it, deals entirely with individuals; not with children, but with the child; the faulty habit is supplanted, observe the word, the desirable habit produced, within a definite period, say one month or six, and then the parents' easy work is to keep the child upon the lines of habit thus produced."

the contrary good habit" (Vol. 2, p. 175).

"Susie is an inquisitive little girl. Her mother is surprised and not always delighted to find that the little maid is constantly on voyages of discovery, of which the servants speak to each other as prying and poking. Is her mother engaged in talk with a visitor or the nurse—behold, Susie is at her side, sprung from nobody knows where. Is a confidential letter being read aloud—Susie is within earshot. Does the mother think she has put away a certain book where the children cannot find it—Susie volunteers to produce it. Does she tell her husband that cook has asked for two days' leave of absence—up jumps Susie, with all the ins and outs of the case. 'I really don't know what to do with the child. It is difficult to put down one's foot and say you ought not to know this or that or the other. Each thing in itself is harmless enough; but it is a little distressing to have a child who is always peering about for gossipy information.' Yes it is tiresome, but is not a case for despair, nor for thinking hard things of Susie, certainly not for accepting the inevitable.

"Regarding this tiresome curiosity as the defect of its quality, the mother casts about for the quality, and, behold, Susie is reinstated. What ails the child is an inordinate desire for knowledge, run to seed, and allowed to spend itself on unworthy objects. When the right moment comes, introduce Susie to some delightful study, of Nature, for example, which will employ all her prying proclivities. Once the new idea has taken possession of the little girl, a little talk should follow about the unworthiness of filling one's thoughts with trifling matters so that nothing really interesting can get in. For weeks together see that Susie's mind is too full of large matters to entertain the small ones; and, once the inquisitive habit has been checked, encourage the child's active mind to definite progressive work on things worth while. Susie's unworthy curiosity will soon cease to be a trial to her parents" (Vol. 2, p. 177).

6. Enlist your child's will by motivating him with the idea of what the new good habit can do for him. Use a story, if possible.

"Take a moment of happy confidence between parent and child; introduce, by tale or example, the stimulating idea; get the child's will with you" (Vol. 2, p. 175).

7. Coach and cheer your child on during the next few weeks, but try not to tell him directly what to do (no nagging or bribing!); make him do the conscious thinking and choosing. Yes, it will take energy and effort on your part, but think of it as nursing your child through a serious illness.

"Do not tell him to do the new thing, but quietly and cheerfully *see that he does it* on all possible occasions, for weeks if need be, all the time stimulating the new idea, until it takes great hold of the child's imagination" (Vol. 2, p. 175).

"Now here is a point all parents are not enough awake to—that serious mental and moral ailments require prompt, purposeful, curative treatment, to which the parents must devote themselves for a short time, just as they would to a sick child. Neither punishing him nor letting him alone—the two lines of treatment most in favour—ever cured a child of any moral evil. If parents recognised the efficacy and the immediate effect of treatment, they would never allow the spread of ill weeds.

"Get the child's will with you."

For let this be borne in mind, whatever ugly quality disfigures the child, he is but as a garden overgrown with weeds: the more prolific the weeds, the more fertile the soil; he has within him every possibility of beauty of life and character. Get rid of the weeds and foster the flowers. It is hardly too much to say that most of the failures in life or character made by man or woman are due to the happy-go-lucky philosophy of the parents. They say, 'The child is so young; he does not know any better; but all that will come right as he grows up.' Now, a fault of character left to itself can do no other than strengthen" (Vol. 2, p. 87).

"In another way, more within our present control, we do not let children alone enough in their work. We prod them continually and do not let them stand or fall by their own efforts. One of the features, and one of the disastrous features, of modern society, is that, in our laziness, we depend upon prodders and encourage a vast system of prodding. We are prodded to our social duties, to our charitable duties, and to our religious duties. If we pay a subscription to a charity, we expect the secretary to prod us when it becomes due. If we attend a meeting, do we often do so of our own spontaneous will, or because somebody asks us to go and reminds us half a dozen times of the day and the hour? Perhaps it is a result of the hurry of the age that there is a curious division of labour, and society falls into those who prod and those who are prodded. Not that anybody prods in all directions, nor that anybody else offers himself entirely as a pincushion. It is more true, perhaps, to say that we all prod, and that we are all prodded. Now, an occasional prick is stimulating and wholesome, but the *vis inertiae* of human nature is such that we would rather lean up against a wall of spikes than not lean at all. What we must guard against in the training of children is the danger of their getting into the habit of being prodded to every duty and every effort. Our whole system of school policy is largely a system of prods. Marks, prizes, exhibitions, are all prods; and a system of prodding is apt to obscure the meaning of *must* and *ought* for the boy or girl who gets into the habit of mental and moral lolling up against his prods" (Vol. 3, pp. 38, 39).

Vis inertiae *means "the tendency to remain at rest."*

8. *Be extra careful to watch for any relapses or performing of the old bad habit.*

"Watch most carefully against any recurrence of the bad habit" (Vol. 2, p. 175).

9. *Demonstrate your sorrow if your child slips back into the old habit.*

"Should the old fault recur, do not condone it. Let the punishment, chiefly the sense of your estrangement, be acutely felt. Let the child feel the shame not only of having done wrong, but of having done wrong when it was perfectly easy to avoid the wrong and do the right" (Vol. 2, p. 175, 176).

10. *Pray for your child during this time, and encourage him to rely on God's help while also working hard himself.*

"Above all, 'watch unto prayer' and teach your child dependence upon divine aid in this warfare of the spirit; but, also, the absolute necessity for his own efforts" (Vol. 2, p. 176).

"Watch most carefully against any recurrence of the bad habit."

Chapter 10
Dealing with Lying

Along with these specific suggestions directed toward the habit of lying, take into consideration the general principles in chapter 9, "Breaking a Bad Habit."

1. Our goal should be not just punishment but repentance and a change in habits of thinking.

"If punishment were necessarily reformative, and able to cure us all of those 'sins we have a mind to,' why, the world would be a very good world; for no manner of sin escapes its present punishment. The fact is, not that punishment is unnecessary or that it is useless, but that it is inadequate and barely touches our aim; which is, not visitation for the offence, but the correction of that fault of character of which the offence is the outcome. Jemmy tells lies and we punish him; and by so doing we mark our sense of the offence; but, probably, no punishment could be invented drastic enough to cure Jemmy of telling lies in the future; and this is the thing to be aimed at. No, we must look deeper; we must find out what weak place in character, what false habit of thinking, leads Jemmy to tell lies, and we must deal with this false habit in the only possible way, by forming the contrary habit of true thinking, which will make Jemmy grow up a true man. 'I think I have never told a lie since,' said a lady, describing the single conversation in which her father cured her, when she was a child, of lying by setting up an altogether new train of thought" (Vol. 2, pp. 172, 173).

2. Recognize that lying is often a result of selfishness and treat the selfishness.

"Lies inspired by Selfishness.—This is a form of lying for which superficial treatment is quite idle. The lie and the vice of which it is the instrument are so allied that those two cannot be put asunder. Professor Stanley Hall well points out that school is a fertile field for this kind of lying. But it is the selfishness and not the lying that must be dealt with. Cure the first, and the second disappears, having no further occasion. How? This is a hard question. Nothing but a strong impulse to the heroism of unselfishness, initiated and sustained by the grace of God, will deliver boy or girl from the vice of selfishness of which lying is the ready handmaid. But let us not despair; every boy and girl is open to such impulse, is capable of heroic effort. Prayer and patience, and watchfulness for opportunities to convey the stimulating idea—these will not be in vain. Every boy and girl is a hero *in posse*. There is no worse infidelity than that which gives up the hope of mending any flaw of character, however bad, in a young creature. All the same, happy those parents who have not allowed selfishness and virtue (whether in the form of truthfulness, or under some other name) to come to hand to hand conflict. It is easy to give direction to the tendencies of a child; it is agonisingly difficult to alter the set of character in a man" (Vol. 2, p. 209).

In posse means "in potential."

"We must deal with this false habit in the only possible way, by forming the contrary habit of true thinking."

Notes

> "We know that to form in his child right habits of thinking and behaving is a parent's chief duty, and that this can be done for every child definitely and within given limits of time."

3. It might be helpful to make your older child aware of these instances when he could be tempted not to tell the exact truth.

"**Malicious Lies.**—Scrupulosity, rash generalisation, exaggeration, amusing representation, are, as it were, the light skirmishers which assault the defences of the fortress of Truth as chance offers; but there are also the sappers and miners who dig under its foundations, and these ask for our more serious attention. There are, as we have seen, Malice and Envy, which lead to Calumny; and of all lies none are more hateful than those told to lower another in the esteem of his friends. The law of the land steps in to save our reputation from hurt, as it does to save us from bodily harm, but many hurtful words may be lightly spoken without fear of the law against libel.

"**Cowardly Lies.**—Cowardice, again, makes for Falsehood. We have done or said a thing that we are made ashamed of, and our first impulse is to deny it. We didn't drop the match which caused the fire, or forget to write the note which politeness required, or say the thing which offended Mrs Foster. The lie is the refuge of the coward when he is found out in a fault. But let us rally our forces and own up; our friends love us the better, in spite of our fault, if we will only say we have done it; they like our courage and honour us for remembering that 'all liars are an abomination unto the Lord.'

" 'Dare to be true. Nothing can need a lie;
   A fault which needs it most grows two thereby.'

"**The Falsehood of Reserve.**—Akin to the lie of Concealment is the habit of Reserve, which, though it does not tell a lie, fails to tell the truth. 'Where have you been to-day?' 'Oh! I went for a walk in the direction of Milton.' We have really been to the town and bought chocolate or shopped, let us say. Frank speech would have made all plain, and to be frank about our little affairs is of the nature of Truth, and is a duty we owe to the people we live with. As a matter of fact, most people know when a lie is being told them, or when something is being held back.

"**Boasting Lies.**—Vain persons tell boasting lies; they think their friends will value them the more for what they have got or for the things they have seen or done, or for the fine people they know. Like all lying, this is foolish as well as wicked. If we gain, by boastful lies, the friendship of the foolish and the vain; that very friendship is an injury to our own character, and it is only the vain and foolish that we can deceive; good and sensible people are quite up to us, and the more we boast the less they think of us.

"**Romancing Lies.**—There are people who live so constantly in castles in Spain of their own building that they romance in their talk. They will tell you they have been here and there, have talked with this and that grand person, or perhaps that they have been kidnapped and left on a desert island, or that they are not really the children of their parents, but changelings, the sons and daughters of a duke or of a rag-picker. This manner of lying comes of a very dangerous habit of mind. When people cannot discern between fact and fancy, and mix the two in their talk, they are gradually losing the use of their Reason, and are qualifying themselves to end in a madhouse. We may not allow ourselves to say things of which Reason and Conscience do not approve.

"**Lies for Friendship's Sake.**—It is not easy to speak the truth when to do so will get a friend into trouble. 'Did you leave the gate open?' 'No.' 'Did Tom?' You know that Tom did, and that it is his fault that the sheep have eaten the carnations. What are you to say? No decent boy could own up another's fault, but neither may he tell a lie to screen his friend at his own expense. But if you say, 'Tom is my friend, I cannot tell of what he does or does not do,' most likely no more questions will be asked. One more caution: 'All's fair in love and war' is made to cover many lies. People think they must speak the truth on their own side, but a lie is good enough for their opponents. They forget that a lie is a two-edged sword, injuring those who speak more than those who hear, and that no one can wear 'the white flower of a blameless life' who is not known to friend and foe alike as one whose word is to be trusted" (Vol. 4, Book 1, pp. 163–165).

4. Deal with your older child on the basis of conscience and simple sincere teaching.

"The mother's task in dealing with her growing daughter is one of extreme delicacy. It is only as her daughter's ally and confidante she can be of use to her now. She will keep herself in the background, declining to take the task of self-direction out of her daughter's hands. She will watch for opportunities to give word or look of encouragement to every growing grace. She will deal with failings with a gentle hand, remembering that even failures in veracity or integrity, distressing as they are, arise usually from the very moral weakness which she is setting herself to strengthen.

"On discovering such fault, the mother will not cover her daughter with shame; the distress she feels she will show, but so that the girl perceives her mother is sharing her sorrow, and sorrowing for her sake. What is the root of the error? No due sense of the sanctity of truth, an undue fear of consequences, chiefly of loss of esteem. The girl is betrayed into a deliberate lie; she has not, she says, written such and such a letter, said such and such words, you knowing all the time that she has done this thing. Deal gently with her: she is no longer a child to be punished or "disgraced" at her parents' pleasure; it is before her own conscience she must stand or fall now. But do not let her alone with the hopeless sense that there is no more to be done for her. Remember that conscience and intellect are still immature, that will is feeble. Give her simple sincere teaching in the nature of truth. Let her know what truth is—the simple statement of facts as they are; that all our spoken words deal with facts, and that, therefore, the obligation of truth is laid upon them all; we should never open our lips without speaking the truth. That even a jest which misleads another is a lie; that perfect truthfulness, in thought, speech, and act, is an obligation laid upon us by God. That the duty is binding, not only with regard to our friends, but towards every one with whom we hold speech.

"The Christian mother will add deeper teaching about the Truth from Whom all truth proceeds. She will caution her daughter as to the need of self-recollectedness in speech. She says she is "quite well, thank you," when she has a headache; that she "will be done in a minute," when the minute means half an hour; these departures from fact slip out without thought—therefore, think first, and speak after. But such trifles surely do not matter? if so, who may cast a stone? Most of us might mend our ways in this matter; but every guard she can place upon herself is of real value to the girl with an inadequate sense of truth, as a means of training herself in the truthful habits which go to form a truthful character. Then, train her by trusting her. Believe her always; give her opportunities to condemn herself in speaking the truth, and her courage will

"Give her simple sincere teaching in the nature of truth."

answer the demand upon it" (Vol. 5, pp. 243–245).

Mrs. Sedley's Tale

In "Mrs Sedley's Tale" (Vol. 5, pp. 77–88), Charlotte wrote a living story to help us understand how to correct the bad habit of lying. The story, given here in its entirety, is written as if the mother were recording her thoughts and subsequent conversation with her husband and sister. A summary of the main points is given at the end.

It is strange how a moral weakness in her child gives a mother the same sense of yearning pity that she has for a bad bodily infirmity. I wonder if that is how God feels for us when we go on year by year doing the thing we hate? I think a mother gets to understand many things about the dealings of God that are not plain to others. For instance, how it helps me to say, "I believe in the forgiveness of sins," when I think of my poor little Fanny's ugly fault. Though there is some return of it nearly every day, what could I do but forgive?

But forgiveness that does not heal is like the wretched ointments with which poor people dress their wounds. In one thing I know I have not done well; I have hardly said a word to John about the poor little girl's failing, though it has troubled me constantly for nearly a year. But I think he suspects there is something wrong; we never talk quite freely about our shy, pretty Fanny. Perhaps that is one reason for it. She is such a nervous, timid little being, and looks so bewitching when the long lashes droop, the tender mouth quivers, and the colour comes and goes in her soft cheek, that we are shy of exposing, even to each other, the faults we see in our graceful, fragile little girl. Perhaps neither of us quite trusts the other to deal with Fanny and to use the knife sparingly.

But this state of things must not go on: it is a miserable thing to write down, but I cannot believe a word the child says! And the evil is increasing. Only now and then used Fanny to be detected in what we called a fib, but now the doubt lest that little mouth may be at any moment uttering a lie takes the delight out of life, and accounts for the pale looks which give my husband much concern.

For example, only within the last day or two I have noticed the following and other such examples:—

"Fanny, did you remember to give my message to cook?"

"Yes, mother."

"And what did she say?"

"That she wouldn't be able to make any jam to-day, because the fruit had not come."

I went into the kitchen shortly after, and found cook stirring the contents of a brass pan, and, sad to say, I asked no questions. It was one of Fanny's circumstantial statements of the kind I have had most reason to doubt. Did she lie because she was afraid to own that she had forgotten? Hardly so: knowing the child's sensitive nature, we have always been careful not to visit her small misdemeanours with any punishment whenever she "owned up." And then, cowardice would hardly cause her to invent so reasonable an answer for cook. Again:—

"No other part of the world's work is of such supreme difficulty, delicacy and importance, as that of parents in the right bringing up of their children."

"Did you meet Mrs Fleming's children?"

"Oh yes, mother! and Berty was so rude! He pushed Dotty off the curb-stone!"

Nurse, who was sitting by the fire with baby, raised her eyebrows in surprise, and I saw the whole thing was an invention. Another more extraordinary instance:—

"Mother, when we were in the park we met Miss Butler, just by the fountain, you know; and she kissed me, and asked me how my mother was";—said *apropos* of nothing, in the most quiet, easy way.

I met Miss Butler this morning, and thanked her for the kind inquiries she had been making through my little girl; and—"Do you think Fanny grown?"

Miss Butler looked perplexed; Fanny was a great favourite of hers, perhaps because of the loveliness of which her parents cannot pretend to be unaware.

Apropos *means "further comment on the present topic."*

"It is more than a month since I have seen the little maid, but I shall look in soon, and gladden her mother's heart with all the praises my sweet Fan deserves!"

Little she knew that shame, and not pride, dyed my cheek; but I could not disclose my Fanny's sad secret to even so near a friend.

But to talk it out with John is a different matter. He ought to know. There had I been thinking for months in a desultory kind of way as to the why and wherefore of this ingrained want of truthfulness in the child, and yet I was no nearer the solution, when a new departure in the way of lying made me at last break the ice with John; indeed, this was the only subject about which we had ever had reserves.

"Mother, Hugh was so naughty at lessons this morning! He went close up to Miss Clare while she was writing, nudged her elbow on purpose, and made her spill the ink all over the table-cloth."

I chanced to meet Miss Clare in the hall, and remarked that I heard she had found Hugh troublesome this morning.

"Troublesome? Not at all; he was quite industrious and obedient."

I said nothing about the ink, but went straight to the schoolroom, to find the table neat, as Miss Clare always leaves it, and no sign of even a fresh ink-spot. What possessed the child? This inveterate and inventive untruthfulness was like a form of mania. I sat in dismay for an hour or more, not thinking, but stunned by this new idea—that the child was not responsible for her words; and yet, could it be so? Not one of our children was so merry at play, so intelligent at lessons. Well, I would talk it over with her father without the loss of another day.

*   *   *   *   *

"John, I am miserable about Fanny. Do you know the child tells fibs constantly?"

"Call them lies; an ugly thing deserves an ugly name. What sort of lies? What tempts her to lie?"

John did not seem surprised. Perhaps he knew more of this misery than I supposed.

"That's the thing! Her fi— lies are so uncalled-for, so unreasonable, that I do not know how to trust her."

"Unreasonable? You mean her tales don't hang together; that's a common case with liars. You know the saying—"Liars should have good memories'?"

"Don't call the poor child a liar, John; I believe she is more to be pitied than

"The habits of the child are, as it were, so many little hammers beating out by slow degrees the character of the man."

Notes

"The point of view it seems well to take is, that all beautiful and noble possibilities are present in varying degree in everyone, but that each person is subject to assault and hindrance in various ways of which he should be aware."

blamed. What I mean is, you can't find rhyme or reason for the lies she tells." And I gave my husband a few instances like those I have written above.

"Very extraordinary! There's a hint of malice in the Hugh and the ink-bottle tale, and a hint of cowardice in that about the jam; but for the rest, they are inventions pure and simple, with neither rhyme nor reason, as you say."

"I don't believe a bit in the malice. I was going to correct her for telling an unkind tale about Hugh, but you know how she hangs on her brother; and she told her tale with the most innocent face. I am convinced there was no thought of harming him."

"Are you equally sure that she never says what is false to cover a fault; in fact, out of cowardice?"

"No; I think I have found her out more than once in ingenious subterfuges; you know what a painfully nervous child she is. For instance, I found the other day a blue cup off that cabinet, with handle gone, hidden behind the woodwork. Fanny happened to come in at the moment, and I asked her if she knew who had broken it.

" 'No, mother, I don't know, but I think it was Mary, when she was dusting the cabinet; indeed, I'm nearly sure I heard a crash.'

"But the child could not meet my eye, and there was a sort of blenching as of fear about her."

"But, as a rule, you do not notice these symptoms?"

"As a rule, poor Fanny's tarradiddles come out in the most quiet, easy way, with all the boldness of innocence; and even when she is found out, and the lie brought home to her, she looks bewildered rather than convicted."

"I wish you would banish the whole tribe of foolish and harmful expressions whose tendency is to make light of sin. Call a spade a spade. A 'tarradiddle' is a thing to make merry over; a fib you smile and wink at; but a *lie*—why, the soul is very far gone from original righteousness that can endure the name, even while guilty of the thing."

"That's just it; I cannot endure to apply so black a name to the failings of our child; for, do you know, I begin to suspect that poor little Fanny does it unawares—does not know in the least that she has departed from the fact. I have had a horrible dread upon me from time to time that her defect is a mental, and not a moral one: that she has not the clear perception of true and false with which most of us are blessed."

"Whe—ew!" from John; but his surprise was feigned. I could see now that he had known what was going on all the time, and had said nothing, because he had nothing to say; in his heart he agreed with me about our pretty child. The defect arose from a clouded intelligence, which showed itself in this way only, now; but how dare we look forward? Now I saw why poor John was so anxious to have the offence called by the blackest moral name. He wished to save us from the suspicion of an evil—worse, because less open to cure. We looked blankly at each other, he trying to carry the matter off with a light air, but his attempt failed.

I forgot to say that my sister Emma was staying with us, the 'clever woman of the family,' who was "going in" for all sorts of things, to come out, we believed, at the top of her profession as a lady doctor. She had taken no part in the talk about Fanny—which was rather tiresome of her, as I wanted to know what she thought; but now, while we were vainly trying to hide our dismay, she broke out into a long laugh, which seemed a little unfeeling.

"Oh, you absurd parents! You are too good and earnest, and altogether too droll! Why in the world, instead of sitting there with blank eyes—conjuring up bogeys to frighten each other—why don't you look the thing in the face, and find out by the light of modern thought what really ails Fan? Poor pet! 'Save me from my parents!' is a rendering which might be forgiven her."

"Then you don't think there's any mental trouble?" we cried in a breath, feeling already as if a burden were lifted, and we could straighten our backs and walk abroad.

" 'Mental trouble?' What nonsense! But there, I believe all you parents are alike. Each pair thinks their own experiences entirely new; their own children the first of the kind born into the world. Now, a mind that had had any scientific training would see at once that poor Fanny's lies—if I must use John's terrible bad word—inventions, I should have called them, are symptomatic, as you rightly guessed, Annie, of certain brain conditions; but of brain disease—oh, no! Why, foolish people, don't you see you are entertaining an angel unawares? This vice of 'lying' you are mourning over is the very quality that goes to the making of poets!"

"Poets and angels are well in their places," said John, rather crossly, "but my child must speak the truth. What she states for a fact, I must know to be a fact, according to the poor common-sense view of benighted parents."

"And there is your work as parents. Teach her truth, as you would teach her French or sums—a little to-day, a little more to-morrow, and every day a lesson. Only as you teach her the nature of truth will the gift she has be effectual. But I really should like to know what is your notion about truth—are we born with it, or educated up to it?"

"I am not sure that we care to be experimented upon, and held up to the world as blundering parents," said I; "perhaps we had better keep our crude notions to ourselves." I spoke rather tartly, I know, for I was more vexed for John than for myself. That he should be held up to ridicule in his own house—by a sister of mine, too!

"Now I have vexed you both. How horrid I am! And all the time, as I watch you with the children, I don't feel good enough to tie your shoes. Don't I say to myself twenty times a day, 'After all, the insight and love parents get from above is worth a thousandfold more than all science has to teach'?"

"Nay, Emma, it is we who have to apologise for being jealous of science—that's the fact—and quick to take offence. Make it up, there's a good girl! and let Annie and me have the benefit of your advice about our little girl, for truly we are in a fog."

"Well, I think you were both right in considering that her failing had two sources: moral cowardice the first; she does something wrong, or wrong in her eyes, and does not tell—why?"

"Aye, there's the difficulty; why is she afraid to tell the truth? I may say that we have never punished her, or ever looked coldly on her for any fault but this of prevarication. The child is so timid that we feared severe measures might make truth-telling the more difficult."

"There I think you are right. And we have our finger on one of the weak places: Fanny tells lies out of sheer fear—moral weakness; causeless it may be, but there it is. And I'm not so sure that it is causeless; she is always in favour for good behaviour, gentleness, obedience, and that kind of thing; indeed, this want

"Teach her truth, as you would teach her French or sums—a little to-day, a little more to-morrow, and every day a lesson."

Notes

of veracity seems to me her one fault. Now, don't you think the fear of having her parents look coldly on her and think less well of her may be, to such a timid, clinging child, a great temptation to hide a fault?"

"Very likely; but one does not see how to act. Would you pass over her faults altogether without inquiry or notice?"

"I'm afraid you must use the knife there boldly, for that is the tenderest way in the end. Show little Fan your love—that there is *no* fault you cannot forgive in her, but that the one fault which hurts you most is, not to hear the exact truth."

"I see. Suppose she has broken a valuable vase and hides the fact, I am to unearth her secret—not, as I am very much inclined to do, let it lie buried for fear of involving her in worse falsehood, but show her the vase and tax her with hiding it."

"And her immediate impulse will be to say, 'I didn't.' No; make sure of your ground, then show her the pieces; say the vase was precious, but you do not mind about that; the thing that hurts you is that she could not trust her mother. I can imagine one of the lovely scenes you mothers have with your children, too good for outsiders to look in upon."

The tears came into my eyes, for I could imagine the scene too. I could see the way to draw my child closer and closer by *always* forgiving, always comprehending and loving her, and always protesting against the falsehood which *would* rise between us. I was lost in a happy reverie—how I might sometime come to show her that her mother's ever-ready forgiveness was but a faint picture of what someone calls the "all-forgiving gentleness of God," when I heard John break in:—

"Yes, I can see that if we both make a point of free and tender forgiveness of every fault, on condition that she owns up, we may in time cure her of lying out of sheer fear. But I don't see that she gets the principle of truth any more. The purely inventive lies go on as before, and the child is not to be trusted."

" 'Purely inventive,' there you have it. Don't you see? The child is full of imagination, and figures to herself endless scenes, evolved like the German student's camel. The thousand and one things which *might* happen are so real to her that the child is, as you said, bewildered; hardly able to distinguish the one which has happened. Now, it's perfect nonsense to lament over this as a moral failing—it is a want of mental balance; not that any quality is deficient, but that her conceptive power runs away with her perceptive; she sees the many things that might be more readily than the thing that is. Doesn't she delight in fairy tales? "

"Well, to tell the truth, I have thought them likely to foster her failing, and have kept her a good deal on a diet of facts."

"I shouldn't wonder if you are wrong there. An imperious imagination like Fanny's demands its proper nourishment. Let her have her daily meal: 'The Babes in the Wood,' 'The Little Match-Girl,' 'The Snow-Maiden,' tales and legends half-historic; above all, the lovely stories of the Bible; whatever she can figure to herself and live over and over; but *not* twaddling tales of the daily doings of children like herself, whether funny or serious. The child wants an opening into the larger world where all things are possible and where beautiful things are always happening. Give her in some form this necessary food, and her mind will be so full of delightful imaginings that she will be under no temptation to invent about the commonplaces of everyday life."

My husband laughed:—"My dear Emma, you must let us do our best with the

"Diligently cultivate the knowledge and the love of the truth."

disease; the cure is too wild! 'Behold, this dreamer cometh!'—think of sending the child through life with that label."

"Your quotation is unfortunate, and you have not heard me out. I do believe that to starve her imagination would be to do real wrong to the child. But, at the same time, you must diligently cultivate the knowledge and the love of the truth. Now, the truth is no more than the fact as it is; and it is my belief that Fanny's falsehoods come entirely from want of perception of the fact through pre-occupation of mind."

"Well, what must we do?"

"Why, give her daily, or half-a-dozen times a day, lessons in truth. Send her to the window: 'Look out, Fanny, and tell me what you see.' She comes back, having seen a cow where there is a horse. She looks again and brings a true report, and you teach her that it is not true to say the thing which is not. You send a long message to the cook, requiring the latter to write it down as she receives it and send you up the slate; if it is all right, the kiss Fanny gets is for speaking the truth: gradually, she comes to revere truth, and distinguishes between the facts of life where truth is all in all, and the wide realms of make-believe, where fancy may have free play."

"I do believe you are right, Emma; most of Fanny's falsehoods seem to be told in such pure innocence, I should not wonder if they do come out of the kingdom of make-believe. At any rate, we'll try Emma's specific—shall we, John?"

"Indeed, yes; and carefully, too. It seems to me to be reasonable, the more so, as we don't find any trace of malice in Fanny's misleading statements."

"Oh, if there were, the treatment would be less simple; first, you should deal with the malice, and then *teach* the love of truth in daily lessons. That is the mistake so many people make. They think their children are capable of loving and understanding *truth* by nature, which they are not. The best parents have to be on the watch to hinder all opportunities of misstatement."

"And now, that you may see how much we owe you, let me tell you of the painful example always before our eyes, which has done more than anything to make me dread Fanny's failing. It is an open secret, I fear, but do not let it go further out of this house. You know Mrs Casterton, our neighbour's wife? It is a miserable thing to say, but you cannot trust a word she utters. She tells you, Miss So-and-So has a bad kind of scarlet fever, and even while she is speaking you know it to be false; husband, children, servants, neighbours, none can be blind to the distressing fact, and she has acquired the sort of simpering manner a woman gets when she loses respect and self-respect. What if Fanny had grown up like her?"

"Poor woman! and this shame might have been spared her, had her parents been alive to their duty."

Some Practical Suggestions from "Mrs Sedley's Tale"

1. Confront your child when you can prove he lied to cover up a misdeed. Emphasize how much the lie has come between you two. Assure him of your forgiveness and love for him, but communicate your disappointment in his obvious lack of trust in you.

2. If your child consistently tells purely inventive lies, read fairy tales to nourish his active imagination and keep it occupied.

"The best parents have to be on the watch to hinder all opportunities of misstatement."

Notes

See also Truthfulness on page 110.

3. Help your child practice accurate reporting with daily lessons in truth. Send him to the window with, "Tell me what you see," and make sure his narration is complete truth. Also send him with a message to tell someone and have the recipient write down what was told so you can compare the child's words to the original message you gave him.

"Every day, every hour, the parents are either passively or actively forming those habits in their children upon which, more than upon anything else, future character and conduct depend."

Chapter 11
Dealing with Dawdling

Along with these specific suggestions directed toward the habit of dawdling, take into consideration the general principles in chapter 9, "Breaking a Bad Habit."

1. Realize that time and rewards will not cure the bad habit of dawdling; it must be replaced with the good habit of attending to the task at hand.

"The effort of decision, we have seen, is the greatest effort of life; not the doing of the thing, but the making up of one's mind as to which thing to do first. It is commonly this sort of mental indolence, born of indecision, which leads to dawdling habits. How is the dilatory child to be cured? Time? She will know better as she grows older? Not a bit of it: "And the next, *more* dilatory" will be the story of her days, except for occasional spurts. Punishments? No; your dilatory person is a fatalist. 'What can't be cured must be endured,' he says, but he will endure without any effort to cure. Rewards? No; to him a reward is a punishment presented under another aspect: the possible reward he realises as actual; there it is, within his grasp, so to say; in foregoing the reward he is punished; and he bears the punishment. What remains to be tried when neither time, reward, nor punishment is effectual? That panacea of the educationist: 'One custom overcometh another.' This inveterate dawdling is a habit to be supplanted only by the contrary habit, and the mother must devote herself for a few weeks to this cure as steadily and untiringly as she would to the nursing of her child through measles" (Vol. 1, pp. 119, 120).

2. During a neutral time, explain briefly the miseries that must come from dawdling and the child's duty to overcome it. Seek to enlist your child's will for overcoming the bad habit.

"Having in a few—the fewer the better—earnest words pointed out the miseries that must arise from this fault, and the duty of overcoming it, and having so got the (sadly feeble) will of the child on the side of right-doing, she simply sees that for weeks together the fault does not recur" (Vol. 1, p. 120).

3. Devote yourself for several weeks to coaching your child with constant, expectant, and minimal nonverbal reminders to attend to the task at hand.

"The child goes to dress for a walk; she dreams over the lacing of her boots—the tag in her fingers poised in mid air—but her conscience is awake; she is constrained to look up, and her mother's eye is upon her, *hopeful* and *expectant*. She answers to the rein and goes on; midway, in the lacing of the second boot, there is another pause, shorter this time; again she looks up, and again she goes on. The pauses become fewer day by day, the efforts steadier, the immature young will is being strengthened, the habit of prompt action acquired. After that first talk, the mother would do well to refrain from one more word on the subject; the

> "The effort of decision, we have seen, is the greatest effort of life."

Notes

eye (expectant, not reproachful), and, where the child is far gone in a dream, the lightest possible touch, are the only effectual instruments" (Vol. 1, p. 120).

4. Gradually phase out your presence but replace it with definite time-tables.

"By-and-by, 'Do you think you can get ready in five minutes to-day without me?' 'Oh yes, mother.' 'Do not say "yes" unless you are quite sure.' 'I *will* try.' And she tries, and succeeds" (Vol. 1, p. 120).

5. Guard carefully against relaxing your efforts and allowing any relapse into dawdling.

"Now, the mother will be tempted to relax her efforts—to overlook a little dawdling because the dear child has been trying so hard. This is absolutely fatal. The fact is, that the dawdling habit has made an appreciable record in the very substance of the child's brain. During the weeks of cure new growth has been obliterating the old track, and the track of a new habit is being formed. To permit any reversion to the old bad habit is to let go all this gain. To form a good habit is the work of a few weeks; to guard it is a work of incessant, but by no means anxious care" (Vol. 1, pp. 120, 121).

6. Reward attention and prompt completion of a task with the natural consequence of leisure time.

"One word more,—prompt action on the child's part should have the reward of absolute leisure, time in which to do exactly as she pleases, not granted as a favour, but accruing (without any words) as a right" (Vol. 1, p. 121).

7. Give a definite time-table in which any homework should be completed, allowing for a pleasant evening afterwards. (Keep in mind that students using Charlotte Mason's methods should rarely have homework.)

"In the matter of home work, the parents may still be of great use to their boys and girls after they begin to go to day-school; not in helping them, that should not be necessary; but let us suppose a case:—'Poor Annie does not finish her lessons till half-past nine, she really has so much to do'; 'Poor Tom is at his books till ten o'clock; we never see anything of the children in the evening,' say the distressed parents; and they let their children go on in a course which is absolutely ruinous both to bodily health and brain power.

"Now, the fault is very seldom in the lessons, but in the children; they *moon* over their books, and a little wholesome home treatment should cure them of that ailment. Allow them, at the utmost, an hour and a half for their home-work; treat them tacitly as defaulters if they do not appear at the end of that time; do not be betrayed into word or look of sympathy; and the moment the time for lessons is over, let some delightful game or story-book be begun in the drawing-room. By-and-by they will find that it *is* possible to finish lessons in time to secure a pleasant evening afterwards, and the lessons will be much the better done for the fact that concentrated attention has been bestowed upon them. At the same time the custom of giving home-work, at any rate to children under fourteen, is greatly to be deprecated. The gain of a combination of home and school life is lost to the children; and a very full scheme of school work may be carried through in the

"To permit any reversion to the old bad habit is to let go all this gain."

morning hours" (Vol. 1, pp. 147, 148).

8. Use natural consequences that relate to the child's conduct as rewards and punishments as much as possible.

"In considering the means of securing attention, it has been necessary to refer to discipline—the dealing out of rewards and punishments,—a subject which every tyro of a nurse-maid or nursery governess feels herself very competent to handle. But this, too, has its scientific aspect: there is a *law* by which all rewards and punishments should be regulated: they should be the *natural*, or, at any rate, the *relative consequences* of conduct; should imitate, as nearly as may be without injury to the child, the treatment which such and such conduct deserves and receives in after life. Miss Edgeworth, in her story of *Rosamond and the Purple Jar*, hits the right principle, though the incident is rather extravagant. Little girls do not often pine for purple jars in chemists' windows; but that we should suffer for our wilfulness in getting what is unnecessary by doing without what is necessary, is precisely one of the lessons of life we all have to learn, and therefore is the right sort of lesson to teach a child" (Vol. 1, p. 148).

9. Consider carefully to make sure those natural consequences will help correct the fault.

"It is evident that to administer rewards and punishments on this principle requires patient consideration and steady determination on the mother's part. She must consider with herself what fault of disposition the child's misbehaviour springs from; she must aim her punishment at that fault, and must brace herself to see her child suffer present loss for his lasting gain. Indeed, exceedingly little actual punishment is necessary where children are brought up with care. But this happens continually—the child who has done well gains some natural reward (like that ten minutes in the garden), which the child forfeits who has done less well; and the mother must brace herself and her child to bear this loss; if she equalise the two children she commits a serious wrong, not against the child who has done well, but against the defaulter, whom she deliberately encourages to repeat his shortcoming. In placing her child under the discipline of consequences, the mother must use much tact and discretion. In many cases, the *natural consequence* of the child's fault is precisely that which it is her business to avert, while, at the same time, she looks about for some consequence related to the fault which shall have an *educative* bearing on the child: for instance, if a boy neglects his studies, the *natural* consequence is that he remains ignorant; but to allow him to do so would be criminal neglect on the part of the parent" (Vol. 1, pp. 148, 149).

Inconstant Kitty

In "Inconstant Kitty" (Vol. 5, pp. 24–32), Charlotte wrote a living story to help us understand how to correct the bad habit of dawdling and wandering thoughts. The story, given here in its entirety, is written as if the mother were writing a letter to her aunt, asking for advice. A summary of the main points is given at the end. First, we pick up the mother's letter

---

Notes

In Miss Edgeworth's story, Rosamond and her mother go out to buy a new pair of shoes for Rosamond, since her old ones are wearing out. On the way Rosamond sees a purple jar in a shop window and desperately wants it. Her mother gives her a choice between buying the jar or buying the new shoes, with the stipulation that if she buys the jar she will have to wait until next month to get the shoes. Rosamond chooses the jar, is disappointed in it when she finally has an opportunity to look at it closely, and then must bear the natural consequence of wearing her old, dilapidated shoes during the coming weeks.

"To form a good habit is the work of a few weeks; to guard it is a work of incessant, but by no means anxious care."

somewhere in the middle of the correspondence.

"But now for the real object of this letter—does it take your breath away to get four sheets? We want you to help us about Kitty. My husband and I are at our wits' end, and would most thankfully take your wise head and kind heart into counsel. I fear we have been laying up trouble for ourselves and for our little girl. The ways of nature are, there is no denying it, very attractive in all young creatures, and it is so delightful to see a child do as ' 'tis its nature to,' that you forget that Nature, left to herself, produces a waste, be it never so lovely. Our little Kitty's might so easily become a wasted life.

"But not to prose any more, let me tell you the history of Kitty's yesterday—one of her days is like the rest, and you will be able to see where we want your help.

"Figure to yourself the three little heads bent over 'copy-books' in our cheery schoolroom. Before a line is done, up starts Kitty.

" 'Oh, mother, may I write the next copy—s h e l l ? "Shell" is so much nicer than—k n o w, and I'm so tired of it.'

" 'How much have you done?'

" 'I have written it three whole times, mother, and I really *can't* do it any more! I think I could do—s h e l l. "Shell" is so pretty!'

"By-and-by we read; but Kitty cannot read—can't even spell the words (don't scold us, we know it is quite wrong to spell in a reading lesson), because all the time her eyes are on a smutty sparrow on the topmost twig of the poplar; so she reads, 'W i t h, birdie!' We do sums; a short line of addition is to poor Kitty a hopeless and an endless task. 'Five and three make—nineteen,' is her last effort, though she knows quite well how to add up figures. Half a scale on the piano, and then—eyes and ears for everybody's business but her own. Three stitches of hemming, and idle fingers plait up the hem or fold the duster in a dozen shapes. I am in the midst of a thrilling history talk: 'So the Black Prince—' 'Oh, mother, do you think we shall go to the sea this year? My pail is quite ready, all but the handle, but I can't find my spade *anywhere*!'

"And thus we go on, pulling Kitty through her lessons somehow; but it is a weariness to herself and to all of us, and I doubt if the child learns anything except by bright flashes. But you have no notion how quick the little monkey is. After idling through a lesson she will overtake us at a bound at the last moment, and thus escape the wholesome shame of being shown up as the dunce of our little party.

"Kitty's dawdling ways, her restless desire for change of occupation, her always wandering thoughts, lead to a good deal of friction, and spoil our school-room party, which is a pity, for I want the children to enjoy their lessons from the very first. What do you think the child said to me yesterday in the most coaxing pretty way? 'There are so many things nicer than lessons! Don't you think so, mother?' Yes, dear aunt, I see you put your finger on those unlucky words 'coaxing pretty way,' and you look, if you do not say, that awful sentence of yours about sin being bred of allowance. Isn't that it? It is quite true; we are in fault. Those butterfly ways of Kitty's were delicious to behold until we thought it time to set her to work, and then we found that we should have been training her from babyhood. Well,

" 'If you break your plaything yourself, dear,

"The mother who takes pains to endow her children with good habits secures for herself smooth and easy days; while she who lets their habits take care of themselves has a weary life of endless friction with the children."

Don't you cry for it all the same?
I don't think it is such a comfort
To have only oneself to blame.'

So, like a dear, kind aunt, don't scold us, but help us to do better. Is Kitty constant to anything? you ask. Does she stick to any of the '*many* things so much nicer than lessons'? I am afraid that here, too, our little girl is 'unstable as water.' And the worst of it is, she is all agog to be at a thing, and then, when you think her settled to half an hour's pleasant play, off she is like any butterfly. She says her, 'How doth the little busy bee,' dutifully; but when I tell her she is not a bit like a busy bee, but rather like a foolish, flitting butterfly, I'm afraid she rather likes it, and makes up to the butterflies as if they were akin to her, and were having just the good time she would prefer. But you must come and see the child to understand how volatile she is.

" 'Oh, mother, *please* let me have a good doll's wash this afternoon; I'm quite unhappy about poor Peggy! I really think she *likes* to be dirty!'

"Great preparations follow in the way of little tub, and soap, and big apron; the little laundress sits down, greatly pleased with herself, to undress her dirty Peggy; but hardly is the second arm out of its sleeve, than, *presto!* a new idea; off goes Kitty to clean out her doll's house, deaf to all Nurse's remonstrances about 'nice hot water,' and 'poor dirty Peggy.'

"I'm afraid the child is no more constant to her loves than to her play; she is a loving little soul, as you know, and is always adoring somebody. Now it's her father, now Juno, now me, now Hugh; and the rain of warm kisses, the soft clasping arms, the nestling head, are delicious, whether to dog or man. But, alas! Kitty's blandishments are a whistle you must pay for; tomorrow it is somebody else's turn, and the bad part is that she has only room for one at a time. If we could get a little visit from you, now, Kitty would be in your pocket all day long; and we, even Peggy, would be left out in the cold. But do not flatter yourself it would last; I think none of Kitty's attachments has been known to last longer than two days.

"If the chief business of parents is to train *character* in their children, we have done nothing for Kitty; at six years old the child has no more power of application, no more habit of attention, is no more able to make herself do the thing she ought to do, indeed, has no more desire to do the right thing than she had at six months old. We are getting very unhappy about it. My husband feels strongly that parents should labour at character as the Hindoo gold-beater labours at his vase; that *character* is the one thing we are called upon to effect. And what have we done for Kitty? We have turned out a 'fine animal,' and are glad and thankful for that; but that is all; the child is as wayward, as unsteady, as a young colt. Do help us, dear aunt. Think our little girl's case over; if you can get at the source of the mischief, send us a few hints for our guidance, and we shall be yours gratefully evermore."

*   *   *   *   *

Now we pick up in the middle of the reply from the aunt, advising the mother what to do.

"And now for my poor little great-niece! Her mother piles up charges against her, but how interesting and amusing and like the free world of fairy-land it

> "The discipline of habit is at least a third part of the great whole which we call education."

would all be were it not for the *tendencies* which, in these days, we talk much about and watch little against. We bring up our children in the easiest, happy-go-lucky way, and all the time talk solemnly in big words about the momentous importance of every influence brought to bear upon them. But it is true; these naughty, winsome ways of Kitty's will end in her growing up like half the 'girls'— that is, young women—one meets. They talk glibly on many subjects; but test them, and they know nothing of any; they are ready to undertake anything, but they carry nothing through. This week, So-and-so is their most particular friend; next week, such another; even their amusements, their one real interest, fail and flag; but then, there is some useful thing to be learnt—how to set tiles or play the banjo! And, all the time, there is no denying, as you say, that this very fickleness has a charm, so long as the glamour of youth lasts, and the wayward girl has bright smiles and winning, graceful ways to disarm you with. But youth does not last; and the poor girl who began as a butterfly ends as a grub, tied to the earth by the duties she never learnt how to fulfil; that is, supposing she is a girl with a conscience; wanting that, she dances through life whatever befalls—children, husband, home, must take their chance. 'What a giddy old grandmother the Peterfields have!' remarked a pert young man of my acquaintance. But, indeed, the 'giddy old grandmother' is not an unknown quantity.

"Are you saying to yourself, a prosy old 'great-aunt' is as bad as a 'giddy old grandmother'? I really have prosed abominably, but Kitty has been on my mind all the time, and it is quite true, you must take her in hand.

"First, as to her lessons: you *must* help her to gain the power of attention; that should have been done long ago, but better late than never, and an aunt who has given her mind to these matters takes blame to herself for not having seen the want sooner. 'But,' I fancy you are saying, 'if the child has no faculty of attention, how can we give it to her? It's just a natural defect.' Not a bit of it! Attention is not a faculty at all, though I believe it is worth more than all the so-called faculties put together; this, at any rate, is true, that no talent, no genius, is worth much without the power of attention; and this is the power which makes men or women successful in life. (I talk like a book without scruple, because you know my light is borrowed; Professor Weissall is our luminary.)

"Attention is no more than this—the power of giving your mind to what you are about—the bigger the better so far as the mind goes, and great minds do great things; but have you never known a person with a great mind, 'real genius,' his friends say, who goes through life without accomplishing anything? It is just because he wants the power to 'turn on,' so to speak, the whole of his great mind; he is unable to bring the whole of his power to bear on the subject in hand. 'But Kitty?' Yes, Kitty must get this power of 'turning on.' She must be taught to give her mind to sums and reading, and even to dusters. Go slowly; a little to-day and a little more tomorrow. In the first place, her lessons must be made *interesting*. Do not let her scramble through a page of 'reading,' for instance, spelling every third word and then waiting to be told what it spells, but let every day bring the complete mastery of a few new words, as well as the keeping up of the old ones.

"But do not let the lesson last more than ten minutes, and insist, with brisk, bright determination, on the child's full concentrated attention of eye and mind for the whole ten minutes. Do not allow a moment's dawdling at lessons.

"I should not give her rows of figures to add yet; use dominoes or the domino cards prepared for the purpose, the point being to add or subtract the dots on the

"Do not let the lesson last more than ten minutes, and insist, with brisk, bright determination, on the child's full concentrated attention."

two halves in a twinkling. You will find that the three can work together at this as at the reading, and the children will find it as exciting and delightful as 'old soldier.' Kitty will be all alive here, and will take her share of work merrily; and this is a point gained. Do not, if you can help it, single the little maid out from the rest and throw her on her own responsibility. 'Tis 'a heavy and a weary weight' for the bravest of us, and the little back will get a trick of bending under life if you do not train her to carry it lightly, as an Eastern woman her pitcher.

"Then, vary the lessons; now head, and now hands; now tripping feet and tuneful tongue; but in every lesson let Kitty and the other two carry away the joyous sense of—

  " 'Something attempted, something done.'

"Allow of no droning wearily over the old stale work—which must be kept up all the time, it is true, but rather by way of an exciting game than as the lesson of the day, which should always be a distinct *step* that the children can recognise.

"You have no notion, until you try, how the 'now-or-never' feeling about a lesson quickens the attention of even the most volatile child; what you can drone through all day, you will; what *must* be done, is done. Then, there is a by-the-way gain besides that of quickened attention. I once heard a wise man say that, if he must choose between the two, he would rather his child should learn the meaning of 'must' than inherit a fortune. And here you will be able to bring moral force to bear on wayward Kitty. Every lesson must have its own time, and no other time in this world is there for it. The sense of the preciousness of time, of the irreparable loss when a ten minutes' lesson is thrown away, must be brought home.

"Let your own unaffected distress at the loss of 'golden minutes' be felt by the children, and also be visited upon them by the loss of some small childish pleasure which the day should have held. It is a sad thing to let a child dawdle through a day and be let off scot-free. You see, I am talking of the children, and not of Kitty alone, because it is so much easier to be good in company; and what is good for her will be good for the trio.

"But there are other charges; poor Kitty is neither steady in play nor steadfast in love! May not the *habit* of attending to her lessons help her to stick to her play? Then, encourage her. 'What! The doll's tea-party over! That's not the way grown-up ladies have tea; they sit and talk for a long time. See if you can make your tea-party last twenty minutes by my watch!' This failing of Kitty's is just a case where a little gentle ridicule might do a great deal of good. It is a weapon to be handled warily, for one child may resent, and another take pleasure in being laughed at; but managed with tact I do believe it's good for children and grown-ups to see the comic side of their doings.

"I think we err in not enough holding up certain virtues for our children's admiration. Put a premium of praise on every finished thing, if it be only a house of cards. Steadiness in work is a step on the way towards steadfastness in love. Here, too, the praise of constancy might very well go with good-humoured family 'chaff,' not about the new loves, which are lawful, whether of kitten or playmate, but about the discarded old loves. Let Kitty and all of them grow up to glory in their constancy to every friend.

"There, I am sending you a notable preachment instead of the few delicate hints I meant to offer; but never mount a woman on her hobby—who knows when she will get off again?"

See also Attention on page 50.

Notes

Some Practical Suggestions from "Inconstant Kitty"

1. Keep lessons interesting!
2. Keep lessons short; for younger children, no longer than ten minutes.
3. Insist with brisk, bright determination on your child's full attention.
4. Alternate the types of lessons to engage different parts of your child's brain and body.
5. Review material with a game instead of long droning lectures.
6. Assign a time-table in which lessons must be completed.
7. Praise any evidence of sustained attention on your child's part; for example, work he finished around the house.

Ability

In "Ability" (Vol. 5, pp. 89–97), Charlotte wrote a living story to help us understand how to correct the bad habit of forgetfulness. The story, given here in its entirety, is written as if the mother were talking with the family doctor about her concerns. A summary of the main points is given at the end.

"Be *sure* you call at Mrs Milner's, Fred, for the address of her laundress."

"All right, mother!" And Fred was half-way down the path before his mother had time to add a second injunction. A second? Nay, a seventh, for this was already the sixth time of asking; and Mrs Bruce's half-troubled expression showed she placed little faith in her son's "All right."

"I don't know what to do with Fred, doctor; I am not in the least sure he will do my message. Indeed, to speak honestly, I am sure he will not. This is a trifling matter; but when the same thing happens twenty times a day—when his rule is to forget everything he is desired to remember—it makes us anxious about the boy's future."

Dr Maclehose drummed meditatively on the table, and put his lips into form for a whistle. This remark of Mrs Bruce's was "nuts" to him. He had assisted, professionally, at the appearance of the nine young Bruces, and the family had no more esteemed friend and general confidant. For his part, he liked the Bruces. Who could help it? The parents, intelligent and genial, the young folk well looking, well grown, and open-hearted, they were just the family to make friends. All the same, the doctor found in the Bruces occasion to mount his pet hobby:— "My Utopia is the land where the family doctor has leave to play schoolmaster to the parents. To think of a fine brood like the young Bruces running to waste in half-a-dozen different ways through the invincible ignorance of father and mother! Nice people, too!"

For seventeen years, Dr Maclehose had been deep in the family counsels, yet never till now had he seen the way to put in his oar anent any question of the bringing up of the children. Wherefore he drummed on the table, and pondered:—"Fair and softly, my good fellow; fair and softly! Make a mess of it now, and it's your last chance; hit the nail on the head, and, who knows?"

"Does the same sort of thing go on about his school work?"

"Precisely; he is always in arrears. He has forgotten to take a book, or to write

"Habit begins as a cobweb, and ends as a cable."

an exercise, or learn a lesson; in fact, his school life is a record of forgets and penalties."

"Worse than that Dean of Canterbury, whose wife *would* make him keep account of his expenditure; and thus stood the entries for one week:—'Gloves, 5s.; Forgets, £4, 15s.' His writing was none too legible, so his wife, looking over his shoulder, cried, 'Faggots! Faggots! What in the world! Have you been buying wood?' 'No, my dear; those are *forgets*:'—his wife gave it up."

"A capital story; but what is amusing in a Dean won't help a boy to get through the world, and we are both uneasy about Fred."

"He is one of the 'School Eleven,' isn't he?"

"Oh yes, and is wild about it: and there, I grant you, he never forgets. It's, 'Mother, get cook to give us an early dinner: we must be on the field by two!' 'Don't forget to have my flannels clean for Friday, will you, mumsy?' he knows when to coax. 'Subscription is due on Thursday, mother!' and this, every day till he gets the money."

"I congratulate you, my dear friend; there's nothing seriously amiss with the boy's brain."

"Good heavens, doctor! Whoever thought there was? You take my breath away!"

"Well, well, I didn't mean to frighten you, but, don't you see, it comes to this: either it's a case of chronic disease, open only to medical treatment, if to any; or it is just a case of defective education, a piece of mischief bred of allowance which his parents cannot too soon set themselves to cure."

Mrs Bruce was the least in the world nettled at this serious view of the case. It was one thing for *her* to write down hard things of her eldest boy, the pride of her heart, but a different matter for another to take her *au sérieux*.

"But, my dear doctor, are you not taking a common fault of youth too seriously? It's tiresome that he should forget so, but give him a year or two, and he will grow out of it, you'll see. Time will steady him. It's just the volatility of youth, and for my part I don't like to see a boy with a man's head on his shoulders." The doctor resumed his drumming on the table. He had put his foot in it already, and confounded his own foolhardiness.

"Well, I daresay you are right in allowing something on the score of youthful volatility; but we old doctors, whose business it is to study the close connection between mind and matter, see our way to only one conclusion, that any failing of mind or body, left to itself, can do no other than strengthen."

"Have another cup of tea, doctor? I am not sure I understand. I know nothing about science. You mean that Fred will become more forgetful and less dependable the older he gets?"

"I don't know that I should have ventured to put it so baldly, but that's about the fact. But, of course, circumstances may give him a bent in the other direction, and Fred may develop into such a careful old sobersides that his mother will be ashamed of him."

"Don't laugh at me, doctor; you make the whole thing too serious for a laughing matter." To which there was no answer, and there was silence in the room for the space of fully three minutes, while the two pondered.

"You say," in an imperious tone, "that 'a fault left to itself must strengthen.' What are we to do? His father and I wish, at any rate, to do our duty." Her ruffled maternal plumage notwithstanding, Mrs Bruce was in earnest, all her wits on

Notes

Amour propre *means "sense of one's dignity or worth; self-esteem."*

"He must have the *habit* of paying attention, so that he will naturally take heed to what he is told, whether he cares about the matter or not."

the alert. "Come, I've scored one!" thought the doctor; and then, with respectful gravity, which should soothe any woman's *amour propre,*—

"You ask a question not quite easy to answer. But allow me, first, to try and make the principle plain to you: that done, the question of what to do settles itself. Fred never forgets his cricket or other pleasure engagements? No? And why not? Because his interest is excited; therefore his whole attention is fixed on the fact to be remembered. Now, as a matter of fact, what you have regarded with full attention, it is next to impossible to forget. First, get Fred to fix his attention on the matter in hand, and you may be sure he won't forget it."

"That may be very true; but how can I make a message to Mrs Milner as interesting to him as the affairs of his club?"

"Ah! There you have me. Had you begun with Fred at a year old the thing would have settled itself. The *habit* would have been formed."

To the rescue, Mrs Bruce's woman's wit:—"I see; he must have the *habit* of paying attention, so that he will naturally take heed to what he is told, whether he cares about the matter or not."

"My dear madam, you've hit it; all except the word 'naturally.' At present Fred is in a delightful state of nature in this and a few other respects. But the educational use of *habit* is to correct nature. If parents would only see this fact, the world would become a huge reformatory, and the next generation, or, at any rate, the third, would dwell in the kingdom of heaven as a regular thing, and not by fits and starts, and here and there, which is the best that happens to us."

"I'm not sure I see what you mean; but," said this persistent woman, "to return to this habit of attention which is to reform my Fred—do try and tell me what to do. You gentlemen are so fond of going off into general principles, while we poor women can grasp no more than a practical hint or two to go on with. My boy would be cut up to know how little his fast friend, 'the doctor,' thinks of him!"

" 'Poor women,' truly! and already you have thrown me with two staggering buffets. My theories have no practical outcome, and I think little of Fred, who has been my choice chum ever since he left off draperies! It remains for the vanquished to 'behave pretty.' Pray, ma'am, what would you like me to say next?"

"To 'habit,' doctor, to 'habit'; and don't talk nonsense while the precious time is going. We'll suppose that Fred is just twelve months old today. Now, if you please, tell me how I'm to make him *begin* to pay attention. And, by the way, why in the world didn't you talk to me about it when the child really was young?"

"I don't remember that you asked me; and who would be pert enough to think of schooling a young mother? Not I, at any rate. Don't I know that every mother of a first child is infallible, and knows more about children than all the old doctors in creation? But, supposing you had asked me, I should have said—Get him each day to occupy himself a little longer with one plaything than he did the day before. He plucks a daisy, gurgles over it with glee, and then in an instant it drops from the nerveless grasp. Then you take it up, and with the sweet coaxings you mothers know how to employ, get him to examine it, in his infant fashion, for a minute, two minutes, three whole minutes at a time."

"I see; fix his thoughts on one thing at a time, and for as long as you can, whether on what he sees or what he hears. You think if you go on with that sort of thing with a child from his infancy he gets accustomed to pay attention?"

"Not a doubt of it; and you may rely on it that what is called *ability*—a different thing from genius, mind you, or even talent—ability is simply the power of fixing the attention steadily on the matter in hand, and success in life turns upon this cultivated power far more than on any natural faculty. Lay a case before a successful barrister, an able man of business, notice how he absorbs all you say; tell your tale as ill as you like, he keeps the thread, straightens the tangle, and by the time you have finished, has the whole matter spread out in order under his mind's eye. Now comes in talent, or genius, or what you will, to deal with the facts he has taken in. But attention is the attribute of the trained intellect, without which genius makes shots in the dark."

"But, don't you think attention itself is a natural faculty, or talent, or whatever we should call it?"

"Not a bit of it; it is entirely the result of training. A man may be born with some faculty or talent for figures, or drawing, or music, but attention is a different matter; it is simply the power of bending such powers as one has to the work in hand; it is a key to success within the reach of every one, but the skill to turn it comes of training. Circumstances may compel a man to train himself, but he does so at the cost of great effort, and the chances are ten to one against his making the effort. For the child, on the other hand, who has been trained by his parents to fix his thoughts, all is plain sailing. He will succeed, not a doubt of it."

"But I thought school-work, Latin and mathematics, and that sort of thing, should give this kind of intellectual training?"

"They should; but it's the merest chance whether the right spring is touched, and from what you say of Fred's school-work, I should say it has not been touched in his case. It is incredible how much solid learning a boy will contrive to let slip by him instead of into him! No; I'm afraid you must tackle the difficulty yourself. It would be a thousand pities to let a fine fellow like Fred run to waste."

"What can I do?"

"Well, we must begin where we are; Fred *can* attend, and therefore remember: and he remembers what interests him. Now, to return to your question. How are you to make a message to Mrs Milner as interesting to him as the affairs of his cricket club? There is no interest in the thing itself; you must put interest into it from without. There are a hundred ways of doing this: try one, and when that is used up, turn to another. Only, with a boy of Fred's age, you cannot form the habit of attention as you could with a child. You can only aid and abet; give the impulse; the training he must do for himself."

"Make it a little plainer, doctor; I have not yet reduced your remarks to the practical level of something I can do."

"No? Well, Fred must train himself, and you must feed him with motives. Run over with him what we have been saying about attention. Let him know how the land lies; that you cannot help him, but that if he wants to make a man of himself he must *make* himself attend and remember. Tell him it will be a stand-up fight, for this habit is contrary to nature. He will like that; it is boy nature to show fight, and the bigger and blacker you make the other side, the more will he like to pitch in. When I was a boy I had to fight this very battle for myself, and I'll tell you what I did. I stuck up a card every week, divided down the middle. One side was for 'Remembers'; the other side for 'Forgets.' I took myself to task every night—the very effort was a help—and put a stroke for every 'Remember' and 'Forget' of the day. *I* scored for every 'Remember,' and 't'other fellow' for every 'Forget.' You don't know how exciting it got. If by Thursday I had thirty-three 'Remembers' and he thirty-six 'Forgets,' it behoved me to look alive; it was

> "Fred must train himself, and you must feed him with motives."

Notes

See also Attention on page 50.

not only that 'Forget' might win the game, which was up on Saturday night, but unless 'Remember' scored ten in advance, the game was 'drawn'—hardly a remove from lost."

"That's delightful! But I wish, doctor, you would speak to Fred yourself. A word from you would go a long way."

"I'll look out for a chance, but an outsider cannot do much; everything rests with the boy himself, and his parents."

Some Practical Suggestions from "Ability"

1. Get your child's whole attention fixed on the fact to be remembered.
2. Extend a baby's attention span by giving him one object to look at and enticing a little more attention (1–3 minutes more) when baby thinks he's done.
3. With an older child, you cannot form the habit of attention as you could with a child. You can only aid and abet, give the impulse and encouragement. The training he must do for himself.
4. Talk with an older child about the problem. Encourage him to develop the habit in order to make a man of himself.
5. The older child might keep a record during the week of "Forgets" and "Remembers." He could keep score each night. He must win by ten points or it's a tie.

"Every habit has its beginning. The beginning is the *idea* which comes with a stir and takes possession of us."

Chapter 12
Dealing with Malicious, Mean Behavior

Along with these specific suggestions directed toward the habit of malicious, mean behavior, take into consideration the general principles in chapter 9, "Breaking a Bad Habit."

1. Treat meanness as a bad habit that needs to be replaced with kindness, and devote several weeks to the task.

"A child has an odious custom, so constant, that it is his quality, will be his *character*, if you let him alone; he is spiteful, he is sly, he is sullen. No one is to blame for it; it was born in him. What are you to do with such inveterate habit of nature? Just this; treat it as a bad *habit*, and set up the opposite good habit. Henry is more than mischievous; he is a malicious little boy. There are always tears in the nursery, because, with 'pinches, nips, and bobs,' he is making some child wretched. Even his pets are not safe; he has done his canary to death by poking at it with a stick through the bars of its cage; howls from his dog, screeches from his cat, betray him in some vicious trick. He makes fearful faces at his timid little sister; sets traps with string for the housemaid with her water-cans to fall over; there is no end to the malicious tricks, beyond the mere savagery of untrained boyhood, which come to his mother's ear. What is to be done? 'Oh, he will grow out of it!' say the more hopeful who pin their faith to time. But many an experienced mother will say, 'You can't cure him; what is in will out, and he will be a pest to society all his life.' Yet the child may be cured in a month if the mother will set herself to the task with both hands and of set purpose; at any rate, the cure may be well begun, and that is half done" (Vol. 2, pp. 85, 86).

2. Eliminate the practice of meanness for several weeks by keeping your child happily occupied under your watchful, approving eye.

"Let the month of treatment be a deliciously happy month to him, he living all the time in the sunshine of his mother's smile. Let him not be left to himself to meditate or carry out ugly pranks. Let him feel himself always under a watchful, loving, and *approving* eye. Keep him happily occupied, well amused. All this, to break the old custom which is assuredly broken when a certain length of time goes by without its repetition" (Vol. 2, p. 86).

3. During those weeks, build the new habit of kindness by giving him ample opportunity to help and please others.

"But one habit drives out another. Lay new lines in the old place. Open

"Treat it as a bad *habit*, and set up the opposite good habit."

See also Kindness on page 31.

Notes

avenues of kindness for him. Let him enjoy, daily, hourly, the pleasure of pleasing. Get him into the way of making little plots for the pleasure of the rest—a plaything of his contriving, a dish of strawberries of his gathering, shadow rabbits to amuse the baby; take him on kind errands to poor neighbours, carrying and giving of his own. For a whole month the child's whole heart is flowing out in deeds and schemes and thoughts of lovingkindness, and the ingenuity which spent itself in malicious tricks becomes an acquisition to his family when his devices are benevolent" (Vol. 2, pp. 86, 87).

4. Realize that it will take energy and effort on your part, but think of it as nursing your child through a serious illness.

"Yes; but where is his mother to get time in these encroaching days to put Henry under special treatment? She has other children and other duties, and simply cannot give herself up for a month or a week to one child. If the boy were ill, in danger, would she find time for him then? Would not other duties go to the wall, and leave her little son, for the time, her chief object in life?" (Vol. 2, p. 87).

"One habit drives out another. Lay new lines in the old place."

Chapter 13
Dealing with Temper Tantrums

Along with these specific suggestions directed toward the habit of temper tantrums, take into consideration the general principles in chapter 9, "Breaking a Bad Habit."

The Philosopher At Home

In "The Philosopher At Home" (Vol. 5, pp. 3–23), Charlotte wrote a living story to help us understand how to correct the bad habit of throwing a temper tantrum. The story, given here in its entirety, follows a father as he considers and directs the retraining of his son, who is prone to pitch fits of temper. A summary of the main points is given at the end.

"He has *such* a temper, ma'am!"

And there, hot, flurried, and generally at her wits' end, stood the poor nurse at the door of her mistress's room. The terrific bellowing which filled the house was enough to account for the girl's distress. Mrs Belmont looked worried. She went up wearily to what she well knew was a weary task. A quarter of an hour ago life had looked very bright—the sun shining, sparrows chirping, lilac and laburnum making a gay show in the suburban gardens about; she thought of her three nestlings in the nursery, and her heart was like a singing-bird giving out chirps of thanks and praise. But that was all changed. The outside world was as bright as ever, but she was under a cloud. She knew too well how those screams from the nursery would spoil her day.

There the boy lay, beating the ground with fists and feet; emitting one prodigious roar after another, features convulsed, eyes protruding, in the unrestrained rage of a wild creature, so transfigured by passion that even his mother doubted if the noble countenance and lovely smile of her son had any existence beyond her fond imagination. He eyed his mother askance through his tumbled, yellow hair, but her presence seemed only to aggravate the demon in possession. The screams became more violent; the beating of the ground more than ever like a maniac's rage.

"Get up, Guy."

Renewed screams; more violent action of the limbs!

"Did you hear me, Guy?" in tones of enforced calmness.

The uproar subsided a little; but when Mrs Belmont laid her hand on his shoulder to raise him, the boy sprang to his feet, ran into her head-foremost, like a young bull, kicked her, beat her with his fists, tore her dress with his teeth, and would no doubt have ended by overthrowing his delicate mother, but that Mr

"Above all, 'watch unto prayer' and teach your child dependence upon divine aid in this warfare of the spirit; but, also, the absolute necessity for his own efforts."

Belmont, no longer able to endure the disturbance, came up in time to disengage the raging child and carry him off to his mother's room. Once in, the key was turned upon him, and Guy was left to "subside at his leisure," said his father.

Breakfast was not a cheerful meal, either upstairs or down. Nurse was put out; snapped up little Flo, shook baby for being tiresome, until she had them both in tears. In the dining-room, Mr Belmont read the *Times* with a frown which last night's debate did not warrant; sharp words were at his tongue's end, but, in turning the paper, he caught sight of his wife's pale face and untasted breakfast. He said nothing, but she knew and suffered under his thoughts fully as much as if they had been uttered. Meantime, two closed doors and the wide space between the rooms hardly served to dull the ear-torturing sounds that came from the prisoner.

All at once there was a lull, a sudden and complete cessation of sound. Was the child in a fit?

"Excuse me a minute, Edward;" and Mrs Belmont flew upstairs, followed shortly by her husband. What was her surprise to see Guy with composed features contemplating himself in the glass! He held in his hand a proof of his own photograph which had just come from the photographers. The boy had been greatly interested in the process; and here was the picture arrived, and Guy was solemnly comparing it with that image of himself which the looking-glass presented.

Nothing more was said on the subject; Mr Belmont went to the City, and his wife went about her household affairs with a lighter heart than she had expected to carry that day. Guy was released, and allowed to return to the nursery for his breakfast, which his mother found him eating in much content and with the sweetest face in the world; there was no more trace of passion than a June day bears when the sun comes out after a thunderstorm. Guy was, indeed, delightful; attentive and obedient to Harriet, full of charming play to amuse the two little ones, and very docile and sweet with his mother, saying from time to time the quaintest things. You would have thought he had been trying to make up for the morning's fracas, had he not looked quite unconscious of wrong-doing.

This sort of thing had gone on since the child's infancy. Now, a frantic outburst of passion, to be so instantly followed by a sweet April-day face and a sunshiny temper that the resolutions his parents made about punishing or endeavouring to reform him passed away like hoar-frost before the child's genial mood.

A sunshiny day followed this stormy morning; the next day passed in peace and gladness, but, the next, some hair astray, some crumpled rose-leaf under him, brought on another of Guy's furious outbursts. Once again the same dreary routine was gone through; and, once again, the tempestuous morning was forgotten in the sunshine of the child's day.

Not by the father, though: at last, Mr Belmont was roused to give his full attention to the mischief which had been going on under his eyes for nearly the five years of Guy's short life. It dawned upon him—other people had seen it for years—that his wife's nervous headaches and general want of tone might well be due to this constantly recurring distress. He was a man of reading and intelligence, in touch with the scientific thought of the day, and especially interested in what may be called the physical basis of character—the interaction which is ever taking place between the material brain and the immaterial thought and feeling of which it is the organ. He had even made little observations and experiments, declared to be valuable by his friend and ally, Dr Weissall, the head physician of the county hospital.

For a whole month he spread crumbs on the window-sill every morning at five minutes to eight; the birds gathered as punctually, and by eight o'clock the "table" was cleared and not a crumb remained. So far, the experiment was a great delight to the children, Guy and Flo, who were all agog to know how the birds knew the time.

After a month of free breakfasts: "You shall see now whether or no the birds come because they see the crumbs." The prospect was delightful, but, alas! this stage of the experiment was very much otherwise to the pitiful childish hearts.

"Oh, father, *please* let us put out crumbs for the poor little birds, they are so hungry!" a prayer seconded by Mrs Belmont, met with very ready acceptance. The best of us have our moments of weakness.

"Very interesting;" said the two savants; "nothing could show more clearly the readiness with which a habit is formed in even the less intelligent of the creatures."

"Yes, and more than that, it shows the automatic nature of the action once the habit is formed. Observe, the birds came punctually and regularly when there were no longer crumbs for them. They did not come, look for their breakfast, and take sudden flight when it was not there, but they settled as before, stayed as long as before, and then flew off without any sign of disappointment. That is, they came, as we set one foot before another in walking, just out of habit, without any looking for crumbs, or conscious intention of any sort—a mere automatic or machine-like action with which conscious thought has nothing to do."

Of another little experiment Mr Belmont was especially proud, because it brought down, as it were, two quarries at a stroke; touched heredity and automatic action in one little series of observations. Rover, the family dog, appeared in the first place as a miserable puppy saved from drowning. He was of no breed to speak of, but care and good living agreed with him. He developed a handsome shaggy white coat, a quiet, well-featured face, and betrayed his low origin only by one inveterate habit; carts he took no notice of, but never a carriage, small or great, appeared in sight but he ran yelping at the heels of the horses in an intolerable way, contriving at the same time to dodge the whip like any street Arab. Oddly enough, it came out through the milkman that Rover came of a mother who met with her death through this very peccadillo.

Here was an opportunity. The point was, to prove not only that the barking was automatic, but that the most inveterate habit, even an inherited habit, is open to cure.

Mr Belmont devoted himself to the experiment: he gave orders that, for a month, Rover should go out with no one but himself. Two pairs of ears were on the alert for wheels; two, distinguished between carriage and cart. Now Rover was the master of an accomplishment of which he and the family were proud: he could carry a newspaper in his mouth. Wheels in the distance, then, "Hi! Rover!" and Rover trotted along, the proud bearer of the *Times*. This went on daily for a month, until at last the association between wheels and newspaper was established, and a distant rumble would bring him up—a demand in his eyes. Rover was cured. By-and-by the paper was unnecessary, and "To heel! good dog!" was enough when an ominous falling of the jaw threatened a return of the old

"The man who knows the power of habit has a key wherewith to regulate his own life."

Notes

habit.

It is extraordinary how wide is the gap between theory and practice in most of our lives. "The man who knows the power of habit has a key wherewith to regulate his own life and the lives of his household, down to that of the cat sitting at his hearth." (*Applause.*) Thus, Mr Belmont at a scientific gathering. But only this morning did it dawn upon him that, with this key between his fingers, he was letting his wife's health, his child's life, be ruined by a habit fatal alike to present peace, and to the hope of manly self-control in the future. Poor man! he had a bad half-hour that morning on his way Citywards. He was not given to introspection, but, when it was forced upon him, he dealt honestly.

"I must see Weissall to-night, and talk the whole thing out with him."

*   *   *   *   *   *

"Ah, so; the dear Guy! And how long is it, do you say, since the boy has thus out-broken?"

"All his life, for anything I know—certainly it began in his infancy."

"And do you think, my good friend"—here the Doctor laid a hand on his friend's arm, and peered at him with twinkling eyes and gravely set mouth— "do you think it possible that he has—er—*inherited* this little weakness? A grandfather, perhaps?"

"You mean me, I know; yes, it's a fact. And I got it from my father, and he, from his. We're not a good stock. I know I'm an irascible fellow, and it has stood in my way all through life."

"Fair and softly, my dear fellow! go not so fast. I cannot let you say bad things of my best friend. But this I allow; there are thorns, bristles all over; and they come out at a touch. How much better for you and for Science had the father cured all that!"

"As I must for Guy! Yes, and how much happier for wife, children, and servants; how much pleasanter for friends. Well, Guy is the question now. What do you advise?"

The two sat far into the night discussing a problem on the solution of which depended the future of a noble boy, the happiness of a family. No wonder they found the subject so profoundly interesting that 'two' by the church clock startled them into a hasty separation. Both Mrs Belmont and Mrs Weissall resented this dereliction on the part of their several lords; but these ladies would have been meeker than Sarah herself had they known that, not science, not politics, but the bringing up of the children, was the engrossing topic.

Breakfast-time three days later. Scene, the dining room.
NURSE *in presence of* MASTER *and* MISTRESS.

"You have been a faithful servant and good friend, both to us and the children, Harriet, but we blame you a little for Guy's passionate outbreaks. Do not be offended, we blame ourselves more. Your share of blame is that you have worshipped him from his babyhood, and have allowed him to have his own way in everything. Now, your part of the cure is, to do exactly as we desire. At present, I shall only ask you to remember that, Prevention is better than cure. The thing for all of us is to take precautions against even one more of these outbreaks.

"Meeker than Sarah herself" refers to 1 Peter 3:5 and 6.

"Prevention is better than cure."

"Keep your eye upon Guy; if you notice—no matter what the cause—flushed cheeks, pouting lips, flashing eye, frowning forehead, with two little upright lines between the eyebrows, limbs held stiffly, hands, perhaps, closed, head thrown slightly back; if you notice any or all of these signs, the boy is on the verge of an outbreak. Do not stop to ask questions, or soothe him, or make peace, or threaten. Change his thoughts. That is the one hope. Say quite naturally and pleasantly, as if you saw nothing, 'Your father wants you to garden with him,' or, 'for a game of dominoes'; or, 'Your mother wants you to help her in the store-room,' or, 'to tidy her work-box.' Be ruled by the time of the day, and how you know we are employed. And be quite sure we *do* want the boy."

"But, sir, please excuse me, is it any good to save him from breaking out when the passion is there in his heart?"

"Yes, Harriet, all the good in the world. Your master thinks that Guy's passions have become a habit, and that the way to cure him is to keep him a long time, a month or two, without a single outbreak; if we can manage that, the trouble will be over. As for the passion in his heart, that comes with the outer signs, and both will be cured together. Do, Harriet, like a good woman, help us in this matter, and your master and I will always be grateful to you!"

"I'm sure, ma'am," with a sob (Harriet was a soft-hearted woman, and was very much touched to be taken thus into the confidence of her master and mistress), "I'm sure I'll do my best, especially as I've had a hand in it; but I'm sure I never meant to, and, if I forget, I hope you'll kindly forgive me."

"No, Harriet, you must not forget any more than you'd forget to snatch a sharp knife from the baby. This is almost a matter of life and death."

"Very well, sir, I'll remember; and thank you for telling me."

*   *   *   *   *   *

Breakfast time was unlucky; the very morning after the above talk, Nurse had her opportunity. Flo, for some inscrutable reason, preferred to eat her porridge with her brother's spoon. Behold, quick as a flash, flushed cheeks, puckered brow, rigid frame!

"Master Guy, dear," in a quite easy, friendly tone (Harriet had mastered her lesson), "run down to your father; he wants you to help him in the garden."

Instantly the flash in the eye became a sparkle of delight, the rigid limbs were all active and eager; out of his chair, out of the room, downstairs, by his father's side, in less time than it takes to tell. And the face—joyous, sparkling, full of eager expectation—surely Nurse had been mistaken this time? But no; both parents knew how quickly Guy emerged from the shadow of a cloud, and they trusted Harriet's discretion.

"Well, boy, so you've come to help me garden? But I've not done breakfast. Have you finished yours?"

"No, father," with a dropping lip.

"Well, I'll tell you what. You run up and eat your porridge and come down as soon as you're ready; I shall make haste, too, and we shall get a good half-hour in the garden before I go out."

Up again went Guy with hasty, willing feet.

"Nurse" (breathless hurry and importance), "I must make haste with my porridge. Father wants me *directly* to help him in the garden."

"Character is the result not merely of the great ideas which are given to us, but of the habits which we labour to form *upon those ideas.*"

Notes

Nurse winked hard at the fact that the porridge was gobbled. The happy little boy trotted off to one of the greatest treats he knew, and that day passed without calamity.

* * * * * *

"I can see it will answer, and life will be another thing without Guy's passions; but do you think, Edward, it's *right* to give the child pleasures when he's naughty—in fact, to put a premium upon naughtiness, for it amounts to that?"

"You're not quite right there. The child does not know he is naughty; the emotions of 'naughtiness' are there; he is in a physical tumult, but wilfulness has not set in; he does not yet *mean* to be naughty, and all is gained if we avert the set of the will towards wrong-doing. He has not had time to recognise that he is naughty, and his thoughts are changed so suddenly that he is not in the least aware of what was going on in him before. The new thing comes to him as naturally and graciously as do all the joys of the childish day. The question of desert does not occur."

* * * * * *

For a week all went well. Nurse was on the alert, was quick to note the ruddy storm-signal in the fair little face; she never failed to despatch Guy instantly, and with a quiet unconscious manner, on some errand to father or mother; nay, she improved on her instructions; when father and mother were out of the way, she herself invented some pleasant errand to cook about the pudding for dinner; to get fresh water for Dickie, or to see if Rover had had his breakfast. Nurse was really clever in inventing expedients, in hitting instantly on something to be done novel and amusing enough to fill the child's fancy. A mistake in this direction would, experience told her, be fatal; propose what was stale, and not only would Guy decline to give up the immediate gratification of a passionate outbreak—for it *is* a gratification, that must be borne in mind—but he would begin to look suspiciously on the "something else" which so often came in the way of this gratification.

Security has its own risks. A morning came when Nurse was not on the alert. Baby was teething and fractious, Nurse was overdone, and the nursery was not a cheerful place. Guy, very sensitive to the moral atmosphere about him, got, in Nurse's phrase, out of sorts. He relieved himself by drumming on the table with a couple of ninepins, just as Nurse was getting baby off after a wakeful night.

"Stop that noise this minute, you naughty boy! Don't you see your poor little brother is going to sleep?" in a loud whisper. The noise was redoubled, and assisted by kicks on chair-rungs and table-legs. Sleep vanished and baby broke into a piteous wail. This was too much; the Nurse laid down the child, seized the young culprit, chair and all, carried him to the farthest corner, and, desiring him not to move till she gave him leave, set him down with a vigorous shaking. There were days when Guy would stand this style of treatment cheerfully, but this was not one. Before Harriet had even noted the danger signals, the storm had broken out. For half an hour the nursery was a scene of frantic uproar, baby assisting, and even little Flo. Half an hour is nothing to speak of; in pleasant chat, over an amusing book, the thirty minutes fly like five; but half an hour in struggle with

"We know that to form in his child right habits of thinking and behaving is a parent's chief duty, and that this can be done for every child definitely and within given limits of time."

a raging child is a day and a night in length. Mr and Mrs Belmont were out, so Harriet had it all to herself, and it was contrary to orders that she should attempt to place the child in confinement; solitude and locked doors involved risks that the parents would, rightly, allow no one but themselves to run. At last the tempest subsided, spent, apparently, by its own force.

A child cannot bear estrangement, disapproval; he must needs live in the light of a countenance smiling upon him. His passion over, Guy set himself laboriously to be good, keeping watch out of the corner of his eye to see how Nurse took it. She was too much vexed to respond in any way, even by a smile. But her heart was touched; and though, by-and-by when Mrs Belmont came in, she did say—"Master Guy has been in one of his worst tempers again, ma'am: screaming for better than half an hour"—yet she did not tell her tale with the *empressement* necessary to show what a very bad half-hour they had had. His mother looked with grave reproof at the delinquent, but she was not proof against his coaxing ways.

After dinner she remarked to her husband, "You will be sorry to hear that Guy has had one of his worst bouts again. Nurse said he screamed steadily for more than half an hour."

"What did you do?"

"I was out at the time doing some shopping. But when I came back, after letting him know how grieved I was, I did as you say, changed his thoughts and did my best to give him a happy day.'

"How did you let him know you were grieved?"

"I looked at him in a way he quite understood, and you should have seen the deliciously coaxing, half-ashamed look he shot up at me. What eyes he has!"

"Yes, the little monkey! and no doubt he measured their effect on his mother; you must allow me to say that my theory certainly is *not* to give him a happy day after an outbreak of this sort."

"Why, I thought your whole plan was to change his thoughts, to keep him so well occupied with pleasant things that he does not dwell on what agitated him."

"Yes, but did you not tell me the passion was over when you found him?"

"Quite over; he was as good as gold."

"Well, the thing we settled on was to *avert* a threatened outbreak by a pleasant change of thought; and to do so in order that, at last, the *habit* of these outbreaks may be broken. Don't you see, that is a very different thing from pampering him with a pleasant day when he has already pampered himself with the full indulgence of his passion?"

"Pampered himself! Why, you surely don't think those terrible scenes give the poor child any pleasure. I always thought he was a deal more to be pitied than we."

"Indeed I do. Pleasure is perhaps hardly the word; but that the display of temper is a form of self-indulgence, there is no doubt at all. You, my dear, are too amiable to know what a relief it is to us irritable people to have a good storm and clear the air."

"Nonsense, Edward! But what should I have done? What is the best course *after* the child has given way?"

"I think we must, as you once suggested, consider how we ourselves are governed. Estrangement, isolation are the immediate consequences of sin, even of what may seem a small sin of harshness or selfishness."

Empressement *means "cordial enthusiasm."*

"The display of temper is a form of self-indulgence."

Notes

"Oh, but don't you think that is our delusion? that God is loving us all the time, and it is *we* who estrange ourselves?'

"Without doubt; and we are aware of the love all the time, but, also, we are aware of a cloud between it and ourselves; we know we are out of favour. We know, too, that there is only one way back, through the fire. It is common to speak of repentance as a light thing, rather pleasant than otherwise; but it is searching and bitter: so much so, that the Christian soul dreads to sin, even the sin of coldness, from an almost cowardly dread of the anguish of repentance, purging fire though it be."

Mrs Belmont could not clear her throat to answer for a minute. She had never before had such a glimpse into her husband's soul. Here were deeper things in the spiritual life than any of which she yet knew.

"Well then, dear, about Guy; must he feel this estrangement, go through this fire?"

"I think so, in his small degree; but he must never doubt our love. He must see and feel that it is always there, though under a cloud of sorrow which he only can break through."

*   *   *   *   *   *

Guy's lapse prepared the way for further lapses. Not two days passed before he was again in a passion. The boy, his outbreak over, was ready at once to emerge into the sunshine. Not so his mother. His most bewitching arts met only with sad looks and silence.

He told his small scraps of nursery news, looking in vain for the customary answering smile and merry words. He sidled up to his mother, and stroked her cheek; that did not do, so he stroked her hand; then her gown; no answering touch, no smile, no word; nothing but sorrowful eyes when he ventured to raise his own. Poor little fellow! The iron was beginning to enter; he moved a step or two away from his mother, and raised to hers eyes full of piteous doubt and pleading. He saw love, which could not reach him, and sorrow, which he was just beginning to comprehend. But his mother could bear it no longer: she got up hastily and left the room. Then the little boy, keeping close to the wall, as if even that were something to interpose between him and this new sense of desolation, edged off to the farthest corner of the room, and sinking on the floor with a sad, new quietness, sobbed in his loneliness; Nurse had had her lesson, and although she too was crying for her boy, nobody went near him but Flo. A little arm was passed round his neck; a hot little cheek pressed against his curls:

"Don't cry, Guy!" two or three times, and when the sobs came all the thicker, there was nothing for it but that Flo must cry too; poor little outcasts!

At last bedtime came, and his mother; but her face had still that sad far-away look, and Guy could see she had been crying. How he longed to spring up and hug her and kiss her as he would have done yesterday. But somehow he dared not; and she never smiled nor spoke, and yet never before had Guy known how his mother loved him.

She sat in her accustomed chair by the little white bed, and beckoned the little boy in his nightgown to come and say his prayers. He knelt at his mother's knee as usual, and then she laid her hands upon his.

" 'Our Father'—oh, mother, mo—o—ther, mother!" and a torrent of tears

"He must never doubt our love."

drowned the rest, and Guy was again in his mother's arms, and she was raining kisses upon him, and crying with him.

Next morning his father received him with open arms.

"So my poor little boy had a bad day yesterday!"

Guy hung his head and said nothing.

"Would you like me to tell you how you may help ever having quite such another bad day?"

"Oh yes, please, father; I thought I couldn't help."

"Can you tell when the 'Cross-man' is coming?"

Guy hesitated. "Sometimes, I think. I get all hot."

"Well, the minute you find he's coming, even if you have begun to cry, say, 'Please excuse me, Nurse,' and run downstairs, and then four times round the paddock as fast as you can, without stopping to take breath!"

"What a good way! Shall I try it now?"

"Why, the 'Cross-man' isn't there now. But I'll tell you a secret: he always goes away if you begin to do something else as hard as you can; and if you can remember to run away from him round the garden, you'll find he won't run after you; at the very worst, he won't run after you more than *once* round!"

"Oh, father, I'll try! What fun! See if I don't beat him! Won't I just give Mr 'Cross-man' a race! He shall be quite out of breath before we get round the fourth time."

The vivid imagination of the boy personified the foe, and the father jumped with his humour. Guy was eager for the fray; the parents had found an ally in their boy; the final victory was surely within appreciable distance.

*　　*　　*　　*　　*　　*

"This is glorious, Edward; and it's as interesting as painting a picture or writing a book! What a capital device the race with 'Mr Cross-man' is! It's like 'Sintram.' He'll be so busy looking out for 'Cross-man' that he'll forget to be cross. The only danger I see is that of many false alarms. He'll try the race, in all good faith, when there is no foe in pursuit."

"That's very likely; but it will do no harm. He is getting the habit of running away from the evil, and may for that be the more ready to run when it's at his heels; this, of running away from temptation, is the right principle, and may be useful to him in a thousand ways."

"Indeed, it may be a safeguard to him through life. How did you get the idea?"

"Do you remember how Rover was cured of barking after carriages? There were two stages to the cure; the habit of barking was stopped, and a new habit was put in its place; I worked upon the recognised law of association of ideas, and got Rover to associate the rumble of wheels with a newspaper in his mouth. I tried at the time to explain how it was possible to act thus on the 'mind' of a dog."

"I recollect quite well; you said that the stuff—nervous tissue, you called it—of which the brain is made is shaped in the same sort of way—at least so I understood—by the thoughts that are in it, as the cover of a tart is shaped by the plums below. And then, when there's a place ready for them in the brain, the same sort of thoughts always come to fill it."

"I did not intend to say precisely that," said Mr Belmont, laughing, "especially the plum part. However, it will do. Pray go on with your metaphor. It is decided

The story referred to is "Sintram and His Companions" by Friedrich de la Motte Fouque, in which Sintram is pursued by temptation personified.

"He is getting the habit of running away from the evil."

that plums are not wholesome eating. You put in your thumb, and pick out a plum; and that the place may be filled, and well filled, you pop in a—a—figures fail me—a peach!"

"I see! I see! Guy's screaming fits are the unwholesome plum which we are picking out, and the running away from Cross-man the peach to be got in instead. (I don't see why it should be a peach though, unpractical man!) His brain is to grow to the shape of the peach, and behold, the place is filled. No more room for the plum."

"You have it; you have put, in a light way, a most interesting law, and I take much blame to myself that I never thought until now of applying it to Guy's case. But now I think we are making way; we have made provision for dislodging the old habit and setting a new one in its place."

"Don't you think the child will be a hero in a very small way, when he makes himself run away from his temper?"

"Not in a small way at all; the child will be a hero. But we cannot be heroes all the time. In sudden gusts of temptation, God grant him grace to play the hero, if only through hasty flight; but in what are called besetting sins, there is nothing safe but the contrary besetting good habit. And here is where parents have immense power over the future of the children."

"Don't think me superstitious and stupid; but somehow this scientific training, good as I see it is, seems to me to undervalue the help we get from above in times of difficulty and temptation."

"Let me say that it is you who undervalue the virtue, and limit the scope of the Divine action. Whose are the laws Science labours to reveal? Whose are the works, body or brain, or what you like, upon which these laws act?"

"How foolish of me! But one gets into a way of thinking that God cares only for what we call spiritual things. Let me ask you one more question. I do see that all this watchful training is necessary, and do not wish to be idle or cowardly about it. But don't you think Guy would grow out of these violent tempers naturally, as he gets older?"

"Well, he would not, as youth or man, fling himself on the ground and roar; but no doubt he would grow up touchy, fiery, open at any minute to a sudden storm of rage. The man who has too much self-respect for an open exhibition may, as you know well enough, poor wife, indulge in continual irritability, suffer himself to be annoyed by trifling matters. No, there is nothing for it but to look upon an irate habit as one to be displaced by a contrary habit. Who knows what cheerful days we may yet have, and whether in curing Guy I may not cure myself? The thing can be done; only one is so lazy about one's own habits. Suppose you take me in hand?"

"Oh, I couldn't! and yet it's your only fault."

"*Only* fault! well, we'll see. In the meantime there's another thing I wish we could do for Guy—stop him in the midst of an outbreak. Do you remember the morning we found him admiring himself in the glass?"

"Yes, with the photograph in his hand."

"That was it; perhaps the Cross-man race will answer even in the middle of a tempest. If not, we must try something else."

"It won't work."

"Why not?"

"Guy will have no more rages; how then can he be stopped in mid-tempest?"

"Look upon an irate habit as one to be displaced by a contrary habit."

"Most hopeful of women! But don't deceive yourself. Our work is only well begun, but that, let us hope, is half done."

*   *   *   *   *   *

His father was right. Opportunities to check him in mid-career occurred; and Guy answered to the rein. Mr Cross-man worked wonders. A record of outbreaks was kept; now a month intervened; two months; a year; two years; and at last his parents forgot their early troubles with their sweet-tempered, frank-natured boy.

See also Sweet, Even Temper on page 108 and Self-Control on page 105.

Some Practical Suggestions from "The Philosopher at Home"

1. Distract your child when you see the cloud beginning to form.
2. If your child pitches a fit, demonstrate broken fellowship until he shows true repentance.
3. Share the responsibility with your child by helping him to choose an alternate action to do when he feels a cloud coming on. (The story used the idea of running around the paddock four times to lose "Cross-man.")

"Mothers work wonders once they are convinced that wonders are demanded of them."

Chapter 14
Dealing with a Sullen, Moody Child

Along with these specific suggestions directed toward the habit of sullen moodiness, or sulking, take into consideration the general principles in chapter 9, "Breaking a Bad Habit."

Under a Cloud

In "Under a Cloud" (Vol. 5, pp. 33–40), Charlotte wrote a living story to help us understand how to correct the bad habit of moodiness and a sullen countenance in a young child. The story, given here in its entirety, is written as if the mother were recounting her experience to the reader. A summary of the main points is given at the end.

You wish me to tell you the story of my little girl? Well, to begin at the beginning. In looking back through the pages of my journal I find many scattered notices of Agnes, and I always write of her, I find, as to "poor Agnes." Now, I wonder why? The child is certainly neither unhealthy nor unhappy—at least, not with any reason; but again and again I find this sort of entry:—

"Agnes displeased with her porridge; says nothing, but looks black all day."

"Harry upset his sister's work-basket—by accident, I truly believe; but she can't get over it—speaks to no one, and looks as if under a cloud."

I need not go on; the fact is, the child is sensible of many injuries heaped upon her; I think there is no ground for the feeling, for she is really very sweet when she has not, as the children say, the black dog on her back.

It is quite plain to me, and to others also, I think that we have let this sort of thing go on too long without dealing with it. We must take the matter in hand. Please God, our little Agnes must not grow up in this sullen habit, for all our sakes, but chiefly for her own, poor child. I felt that in this matter I might be of more use than Edward, who simply does not understand a temper less sunny and open than his own. I pondered and pondered, and, at last, some light broke in upon me. I thought I should get hold of one principle at a time, work that out thoroughly, and then take up the next, and so on, until all the springs of sullenness were exhausted, and all supplies from without stopped. I was beginning to suspect that the laws of habit worked here as elsewhere, and that, if I could get our dear child to pass, say, six weeks without a "fallen countenance," she might lose this distressing failing for life.

I meant at first to take most of the trouble of this experiment upon myself; but I think men have clearer heads than we women—that is, they can see *both* sides of a question and are not carried away by the one side presented to them. So I said—

"Few things are more sad than to see a beautiful body, made for health, strength, and happiness—made in the image of God—injured and destroyed by bad habits."

Notes

Malaise *means "a sense of ill-being or lack of health."*

"Well, Edward, our little Agnes does not get over her sulky fits; in fact, they last longer, and are harder to get out of than ever!"

"Poor little girl! It is unhappy for her and for all of us. But don't you think it is a sort of childish *malaise* she will soon grow out of?"

"Now, have you not said, again and again, that a childish fault, left to itself, can do no other than strengthen?"

"True; I suppose the fact is I am slow to realise the fault. But you are right. From the point of view of *habit* we are pledged to deal with it. Have you made any plans?"

"Yes; I have been trying to work the thing out on Professor Weissall's lines. We must watch the rise of the sullen cloud, and change her thoughts before she has time to realise that the black fit is coming."

"You are right; if we can keep the child for only a week without this settling of the cloud, the mere habit would be somewhat broken."

We had not to wait for our opportunity. At breakfast next day—whether Harry's porridge looked more inviting than her own, or whether he should not have been helped first, or whether the child had a little pain of which she was hardly aware—suddenly, her eyes fell, brows dropped, lips pouted, the whole face became slightly paler than before, the figure limp, limbs lax, hands nerveless— and our gentle child was transformed, become entirely unlovable. So far, her feelings were in the emotional stage; her injury, whatever it was, had not yet taken shape in her thoughts; she could not have told you what was the matter, because she did not know; but very soon the thinking brain would come to the aid of the quick emotions, and then she would be sulky of fixed purpose. Her father saw the symptoms rise and knew what they would lead to, and, with the promptness which has often saved us, he cried out—

"Agnes, come here, and hold up your pinafore!" and Agnes trotted up to his side, her pinafore held up very much to receive the morning dole of crumbs for the birds; presently, she came back radiant with the joy of having given the birds a good breakfast, and we had no more sulky fits that day. This went on for a fortnight or so with fair but not perfect success. Whenever her father or I was present, we caught the emotion before the child was conscious of it, and succeeded in turning her thoughts into some pleasant channel. But poor nurse has had bad hours with Agnes; there would sit the child, pale and silent, for hours together, doing nothing because she liked to do it, but only because she must. And, once the fit had settled down, thick and steady as a London fog, neither her father nor I could help in the least. Oh, the inconceivable settled cloudiness and irresponsiveness of that child face!

Our tactics were at fault. No doubt they helped so far as they went. We managed to secure bright days that might otherwise have been cloudy when we happened to be present at the first rise of the sullen mood. But it seemed impossible to bring about so long an abstinence from sullen fits as would nullify the *habit*. We pictured to ourselves the dreary life that lay before our pretty little girl; the distrust of her sweetness, to which even one such sullen fit would give rise; worse, the isolation which accompanies this sort of temper, and the anguish of repentance to follow. And then, I know, madness is often bred of this strong sense of injured personality.

It is not a pleasant thing to look an evil in the face. Whether or no "a little knowledge is a dangerous," certainly, it is a trying thing. If we could only have

"Truly parents are happy people—to have God's children lent to them."

contented ourselves with, "Oh, she'll grow out of it by-and-by," we could have put up with even a daily cloud. But these forecasts of our little girl's future made the saving of the child at *any* cost our most anxious care.

"I'll tell you what, Helen; we must strike out a new line. In a general way, I do believe it's best to deal with a child's faults without making him aware that he has them. It fills the little beings with a ridiculous sense of importance to have anything belonging to *them*, even a fault. But in this case, I think, we shall have to strike home and deal with *the cause* at least as much as with *the effects*, and that, chiefly, because we have not effects entirely under our control."

"But, what if there is no cure? What if this odious temper were *hereditary*— our child's inheritance from those who should have brought her only good?"

"The question is not 'How has it come?' but 'How are we to deal with it?'— equally, you and I. Poor things! It's but a very half-and-half kind of matrimony if each is to pick out his or her own particular bundle of failings, and deal with it single-handed. This poor man finds the prospect too much for him! As a matter of fact, though, I believe that failings of mind, body, temper, and what not, are matters of inheritance, and that each parent's particular business in life is to pass his family forward freed from that particular vicious tendency which has been his own bane—or hers, if you prefer it."

"Well, do as you will; I can trust you. What it would be in these days of greater insight to be married to a man who would say, 'There, that boy may thank his mother' for this or the other failure! Of course, the thing is done now, but more often than not as a random guess."

"To return to Agnes. I think we shall have to show her to herself in this matter, to rake up the ugly feeling, however involuntary, and let her see how hateful it is. Yes, I do not wonder you shrink from this. So do I. It will destroy the child's unconsciousness."

"Oh, Edward, how I dread to poke into the little wounded heart, and bring up worse things to startle her!"

"I am sorry for you, but I think it must be done; and don't you think you are the person to do it? While they have a mother I don't think I could presume to pry too much into the secrets of the children's hearts."

"I'll try; but if I get into a mess you must help me through."

The opportunity came soon enough. It was pears this time. Harry would never have known whether he had the biggest or the least. But we had told Nurse to be especially careful in this matter. "Each of the children must have the biggest or best as often as one another, but there must be no fuss, no taking turns, about such trifles. Therefore, very rightly, you gave Harry the bigger and Agnes the smaller pear."

Agnes's pear was not touched; there the child sat, without word or sob, but all gathered into herself, like a sea-anemone whose tentacles have been touched. The stillness, whiteness, and brooding sullenness of the face, the limp figure and desolate attitude, would have made me take the little girl in my arms if I had not too often failed to reach her in that way. This went on all day, all of us suffering; and in the evening, when I went to hear the children's prayers before bed, I meant to have it out.

We were both frozen up with sadness, and the weary child was ready to creep into her mother's arms again. But I must not let her yet.

"So my poor Agnes has had a very sad day?"

"No other part of the world's work is of such supreme difficulty, delicacy and importance, as that of parents in the right bringing up of their children."

Notes

"Yes, mother," with a sob.

"And do you know we have all had a very sad day—father, mother, your little brother, Nurse—every one of us has felt as if a black curtain had been hung up to shut out the sunshine?"

The child was sympathetic, and shivered at the sight of the black curtain and the warm sunshine shut out.

"And do you know who has put us all out in the dark and the cold? Our little girl drew the curtain, because she would not speak to any of us, or be kind to any of us, or love any of us all the day long; so we could not get into the sunshine, and have been shivering and sad in the cold."

"Mother, mother!" with gasping sobs; "*not* you and father?"

"Ah! I thought my little girl would be sorry. Now let us try to find out how it all happened. Is it possible that Agnes noticed that her brother's pear was larger than her own?"

"Oh, mother, how could I?" The poor little face was hidden in her mother's breast, and the outbreak of sobs that followed was very painful. I feared it might mean actual illness for the sensitive child. I think it was the right thing to do; but I had barely courage enough to leave the results in more loving hands.

"Never mind; don't cry any more, darling, and we will ask 'Our Father' to forgive and forget all about it. Mother knows that her dear little Agnes will try not to love herself best any more. And then the black curtain will never fall, and we shall never again be a whole long day standing sadly out in the cold. Good-night from mother, and another good-night from father."

The treatment seems to answer. On the slightest return of the old sullen symptoms we show our little girl what they mean. The grief that follows is so painful that I'm afraid we could not go on with it for the sake of the child's health; but, happily, we very rarely see a sulky face now; and when we do we turn and look upon our child, and the look melts her into gentleness and penitence.

Some Practical Suggestions from "Under a Cloud"

1. Try to distract your child's thoughts when you see a cloud beginning to form, while the child is still experiencing an emotional response without conscious reasoning.
2. Explain to your child how sulking and sullenness ruins the day for everyone around whom he loves.
3. Remind your child with a sorrowful look when he begins to relapse into sullenness.
4. Pray with your child for help to think of others instead of self.

See also Sweet, Even Temper on page 108.

Dorothy Elmore's Achievement

In "Dorothy Elmore's Achievement" (Vol. 5, pp. 41–67), Charlotte wrote a living story in five chapters to help us understand how to correct the bad habit of sulking in an older child. The story, given here in its entirety, is written as if the mother were recounting her experience to the reader. A summary of the main points is given at the end.

"I have been brought to look upon habit as the means whereby the parent may make almost anything he chooses of his child."

Chapter 1

I know of no happier moment for parents than that when their eldest daughter returns from school to take her place finally by her mother's side. It was two years that very day since we had seen Dorothy, when her father set out for Lausanne to bring her home; and how the children and I got through the few days of his absence, I don't know. The last touches had been put many times over to her rooms—not the plain little room she had left, but a dainty bower for our young maiden, a little sitting-room opening into a pure nest of a bedroom. Our eyes met, her father's and mine, and moistened as we conjured up I don't know what visions of pure young life to be lived there, of the virginal prayers to be offered at the little prayer table, the gaiety of heart that should, from this nook, bubble over the house; and, who knows, by-and-by, the dreams of young love which should come to glorify the two little rooms.

Two or three times already had the children put fresh flowers into everything that would hold a flower. Pretty frocks and sweet faces, bright hair and bright eyes had been ready this long time to meet sister Dorothy.

At last, a telegram from Dover—"Home by five"—and our restlessness subsided into a hush of expectation.

Wheels sounded on the gravel, and we flew to the hall door and stood in two files, children and maids, Rover and Floss, waiting to welcome the child of the house. Then, a lovely face, glad to tears, looking out of a nest of furs; then, a light leap, almost before the carriage drew up, and I had her in my arms, my Dorothy, the child of my heart! The order of the day was "high tea," to which every one, down to baby May, sat up. We two, her father and I, gave her up to the children, only exchanging notes by the species of telegraphy married folk understand.

"Indubitably lovely!" said her father's eyes. "And what grace—what an elegant girl she is!" answered mine. "And do but see what tact she shows with the little ones—" "And notice the way she has with us, as if her heart were brimming with reverence and affection." Thus, we two with our eyes. For a week or more we could not settle down. As it was the Christmas holidays, we had not Miss Grimshaw to keep us in order, and so it happened that wherever Dorothy ran—no, she went with a quick noiseless step, but never ran—about the house to find out the old dear nooks, we all followed, a troop of children with their mother in the rear; their father too, if he happened to be in. Truly we were a ridiculous family, and did our best to turn the child's head. Every much has its more-so. Dorothy's two special partisans were Elsie, our girl of fifteen years, fast treading in her sister's steps, and Herbert, our eldest son, soon to go to college. Elsie would come to my room and discourse by the hour, her text being ever, "Dorothy says." And as for Herbs, it was pleasant to see his budding manhood express itself in all sorts of little attentions to his lovely sister.

For lovely she was; there could not be two opinions on that point. A lily maid, tall and graceful, without a trace of awkwardness or self-consciousness; the exquisite complexion of the Elmores (they are a Devonshire family), warm, lovely rose on creamy white, no hint of brunette colouring; a smile which meant spring and love and other good things; and deep blue eyes reflecting the light of her smile—this was Dorothy.

Never, not even during the raptures of early married life, have I known a month of such joyous exhilaration as that which followed Dorothy's return, and I think her father would own as much.

"The habits of the child are, as it were, so many little hammers beating out by slow degrees the character of the man."

Notes

What a month it was! There was the pleasant earthly joy of going to town to get frocks for Dorothy; then, the bewilderment of not being able to find out what suited her best.

"Anything becomes her!" exclaims Mdme. la Modiste; "that figure, that complexion, may wear anything."

And then, how pleasant it was to enter a room where all eyes were bent upon us in kindliness—our dear old friends hurrying forward to make much of the child. The deference and gentleness of her manner to these, and the warmth with which she was received by her compeers, both maidens and men; her grace in the dance; her simplicity in conversation; the perfection of her manner, which was not manner at all but her own nature, in every situation—all these added to our delight. After all, she liked best to be at home, and was more amiable and lovely with father and mother, brothers and sisters, than with the most fascinating strangers. Our good child! We had grown a little shy of speaking to her about the best things, but we knew she said her prayers: how else this outflow of sweet maiden life upon us all?

I can imagine these ramblings of mine falling into the hands of a young pair whose life is in each other: "Oh, only the outpourings of a doting mother;" and they toss the pages aside. But never believe, young people, that yours are the only ecstatic moments, yours the only experiences worth recording; wait and see.

Chapter 2

These happy days had lasted for a month or more, when, one bright day in February, I remember it well, a little cloud arose. This is how it was: Dorothy had promised Elsie that she would drive her in the pony-carriage to Banford to choose a doll for May's birthday. Now, it happened that I wanted the little carriage to take to my "Mothers" at Ditchling the clothing I had bought in London with their club money. My errand could not be deferred; it must be done that day or a week later. But I did not see why the children's commission would not do as well to-morrow; and so I said, in good faith, as I was stepping into the carriage, hardly noticing the silence with which my remark was received.

I came home tired, after a long afternoon, looking forward to the welcome of the girls. The two seniors were sitting in the firelight, bright enough just then to show me Dorothy, limp and pale, in a low chair, and Elsie watching her with a perplexed and anxious expression. Dorothy did look up to say, "Are you tired, mother?" but only her eyes looked, there was nothing behind them.

"*You* look tired and cold enough, my dear; what has been the matter?"

"Oh, I'm very well, thank you; but I am tired, I think I'll go to bed." And she held up a cold cheek for the mother's kiss for which she offered no return.

Elsie and I gazed at one another in consternation; our fairy princess, our idol—was it indeed so?—what had come to her?

"What is the matter with Dorothy? Has she a headache?"

"Oh, mother, I don't know," said the poor child, on the verge of tears. "She has been like this ever since you went, saying 'Yes,' and 'No,' and 'No, thank you,' quite kindly, but never saying a word of herself. Has any one been grieving our Dorothy, or is she going to be ill? Oh, mother, mother!"

"Nay, child, don't cry. Dorothy is overdone; you know she has been out twice this week, and three times last, and late hours don't suit her. We must take better care of her, that's all."

"Do not let the endless succession of small things crowd great ideals out of sight and out of mind."

Elsie was comforted, but not so her mother. I believed every word I had said to the child; but all the time there was a stir in my heart like the rustling of a snake in the grass. But I put it from me.

It was with a hidden fear that I came down to breakfast. Dorothy was in the room already, doing the little duties of the breakfast table. But she was pale and still; her hands moved, her figure hung, in the limp way I had noticed the night before. Her check, a cold "Good-morning, mother," and a smile on her lips that brought no light to her eyes, was all the morning salutation I got. Breakfast was an uncomfortable, constrained meal. The children wondered what was the matter, and nobody knew. Her father got on best with Dorothy, for he knew nothing of the evening's history, so he petted her as usual, making all the more of her for her pale looks.

For a whole week this went on, and never once was I allowed to meet Dorothy eye to eye. The children were hardly better served, for they, too, had noticed something amiss; only her father could win any of the old friendliness, because he treated her as the Dorothy who had come home to us, only a little done up.

"We must have the doctor for that child, wife. Don't you see she is beginning to lose flesh, and how the roses she brought home are fading! She has no appetite and no spirits. But, why, you surely don't think our dainty moth has singed her wings already? There's nobody here, unless it's young Gardiner, and she would never waste herself on a gawky lad like that!"

This was a new idea, and I stopped a moment to consider, for I knew of at least half-a-dozen young men who had been attentive to Dorothy, all to be preferred to this hobbledehoy young Gardiner. But, no! I could trace the change from the moment of my return from Ditchling. But I jumped at the notion of the doctor; it would, at any rate, take her out of herself, and—we should see.

The doctor came; said she wanted tone; advised, not physic, but fresh air, exercise, and early hours. So we all laid ourselves out to obey his directions that day, but with no success to speak of.

But the next was one of those glorious February days when every twig is holding itself stiffly in the pride of coming leafage, and the snowdrops in the garden beds lift dainty heads out of the brown earth. The joy of the spring did it. We found her in the breakfast-room, snowdrops at her throat, rosy, beaming, joyous; a greeting, sweet and tender, for each; and never had we known her talk so sparkling, her air so full of dainty freshness. There was no relapse after this sudden cure. Our good friend Dr Evans called again, to find her in such flourishing health that ten minutes' raillery of "my poor patient" was the only attention he thought necessary. But, "H'm! Mighty sudden cure!" as he was going out, showed that he, too, found something odd in this sudden change.

In a day or two we had forgotten all about our bad week. All went well for awhile. At the end of five weeks, however, we were again pulled up—another attack of sudden indisposition, so outsiders thought. What did I think? Well, my thoughts were not enviable.

"Father, I wish you would call at Walker's and choose me some flowers for this evening." It was the evening of the Brisbanes' dance, and I had half an idea that Arthur Brisbane had made some impression on Dorothy. *His* state of mind was evident enough. But, without thinking twice, I interrupted with—

"Don't you think what we have in the 'house' will do, dear? Nothing could make up better than stephanotis and maidenhair."

"There is a sort of artistic pleasure in putting the fine touches to character."

Dorothy made no answer, and her father, thinking all was right, went off at once; he was already rather late. We thought no more of the matter for a minute or two, when, at the same moment, Elsie and I found our eyes fixed upon Dorothy. The former symptoms followed—days of pallor and indisposition, which were, at the same time, days of estrangement from us all. Again we had in Dr Evans, "just to look at her," and this time I noticed—not without a foolish mother's resentment—that his greeting was other than cordial. "Well, young lady, and what's gone amiss this time?" he said, knitting his bushy brows, and gazing steadily at her out of the eyes which could be keen as well as kind. Dorothy flushed and fidgeted under his gaze, but gave only the cold unsatisfactory replies we had been favoured with. The prescription was as before; but again the recovery was sudden, and without apparent cause.

Chapter 3

To make a long story short, this sort of thing went on, at longer or shorter intervals, through all that winter and summer and winter again. My husband, in the simplicity of his nature, could see nothing but—

"The child is out of sorts; we must take her abroad for a month or two; she wants change of air and scene."

The children were quicker-eyed; children are always quick to resent unevenness of temper in those about them. A single angry outbreak, harsh word, and you may lay yourself out to please them for months before they will believe in you again. George was the first to let the cat out of the bag.

"Dorothy is in a sulky fit again, mother; I wish she wouldn't!"

Elsie, who has her father's quick temper, was in the room.

"You naughty, ungrateful little boy, you! How can you say such a thing of Dorothy? Didn't she sit all yesterday morning making sails for your boat?"

"Yes," said George, a little mollified; "but why need she be sulky to-day? We all liked her yesterday, and I'm sure I want to, to-day!"

Now that the mask was fallen and even the children could see what was amiss, I felt that the task before me must not be put off. I had had great misgivings since the first exhibition of Dorothy's sullen temper; now I saw what must be done, and braced myself for a heavy task. But I could not act alone; I must take my husband into my confidence, and that was the worst of it.

"George, how do you account for Dorothy's fits of wretchedness?"

"Why, my dear, haven't I told you? The child is out of sorts, and must have change. We'll have a little trip up the Rhine, and perhaps into Switzerland, as soon as the weather is fit. It will be worth something to see her face light up at some things I mean to show her!"

"I doubt if there is anything the matter with her health; remember how perfectly well and happy she is between these fits of depression."

"What is it, then? You don't think she's in love, do you?"

"Not a bit of it; her heart is untouched, and her dearest loves are home loves."

My husband blew his nose, with a "Bless the little girl! I could find it in my heart to wish it might always be so with her. But what is your notion? I can see you have got to the bottom of the little mystery. Trust you women for seeing through a stone wall!"

"Each attack of what we have called 'poorliness' has been a fit of sullenness, lasting sometimes for days, sometimes for more than a week, and passing off as

"Habit is to life what rails are to transport cars."

suddenly as it came."

My dear husband's face clouded with serious displeasure; never before had it worn such an expression for me. I had a sense of separation from him, as if we two, who had so long been one, were two once more.

"This is an extraordinary charge for a mother to bring against her child. How have you come to this conclusion?"

Already was my husband become my judge. He did not see that I was ill, agitated, still standing, and hardly able to keep my feet. And there was worse to come: how was I to go through with it?

"What causes for resentment can Dorothy conceivably have?' he repeated, in the same cold judicial tone.

"It is possible to feel resentment, it is possible to nurse resentment, to let it hang as a heavy cloud-curtain between you and all you love the best, without any adequate cause, without any cause, that you can see yourself when the fit is over!"

My voice sounded strange and distant in my own ears: I held by the back of a chair to steady myself, but I was not fainting; I was acutely alive to all that was passing in my husband's mind. He looked at me curiously, inquisitively, but not as if I belonged to him and were part and parcel of his life.

"You seem to be curiously familiar with a state of feeling which I should have judged to be the last a Christian lady would know anything about."

"Oh, husband, don't you see you are hurting me? I am not going through this anguish for nothing. I *do* know what it is. And if Dorothy, my poor child, suffers, it is all my fault! There is nothing bad in her but what she has got from me."

George was moved; he put his arm round me in time to save me. But I was not surprised, a few days later, to find my first grey hairs. If that hour were to be repeated, I think I could not bear it.

"Poor wife! I see; it is to yourself you have been savagely cruel, and not to our little girl. Forgive me, dear, that I did not understand at once; but we men are slow and dull. I suppose you are putting yourself (and me too) to all this pain because there is something to be gained by it. You see some way out of the difficulty, if there is one!"

"Don't say 'if there is one.' How could I go through this pain if I did not think some way of helping our daughter would come out of it?"

"Ah! appearances were against you, but I knew you loved the child all the time. Clumsy wretch that I am, how could I doubt it? But, to my mind, there are two difficulties: First, I cannot believe that you ever cherished a thought of resentment; and next, who could associate such a feeling with our child's angelic countenance? Believe me, you are suffering under a morbid fancy; it is you, and not Dorothy, who need entire change of scene and thought."

How should I convince him? And how again run the risk of his even momentary aversion? But if Dorothy were to be saved, the thing must be done. And, oh, how could he for a moment suppose that I should deal unlovingly with my firstborn?

"Be patient with me, George. I want to tell you everything from the beginning. Do you remember when you wooed me in the shady paths of our old rectory garden, how I tried hard to show you that I was not the loved and lovely home-daughter you pictured? I told you how I was cross about this and that; how little things put me out for days, so that I was under a cloud, and really *couldn't* speak to, or care about anybody; how, not I, but (forgive the word) my plain sister

"Habit is inevitable. If we fail to ease life by laying down habits of right thinking and right acting, habits of wrong thinking and wrong acting fix themselves of their own accord."

Esther, was the beloved child of the house, adored by the children, by my parents, by all the folk of the village, who must in one way or other have dealings with the parson's daughters. Do you recollect any of this?"

"Yes; but what of it? I have never for a moment rued my choice, nor wished that it had fallen on our good Esther, kindest of friends to us and ours."

"And you, dear heart, put all I said down to generosity and humility; every effort I made to show you the truth was put down to the count of some beautiful virtue, until at last I gave it up; you *would* only think the more of me, and think the less kindly of my dear home people, because, indeed, they didn't 'appreciate' me. How I hated the word. I'm not sure I was sorry to give up the effort to show you myself as I was. The fact is, your love made me all it believed me to be, and I thought the old things had passed away."

"Well, and wasn't I right? Have we had a single cloud upon our married life?"

"Ah, dear man, little you know what the first two years of married life were to me. If you read your newspaper, I resented it; if you spent half an hour in your smoking den, or an hour with a friend, if you admired another woman, I resented each and all, kept sulky silence for days, even for weeks. And you, all the time, thought no evil, but were sorry for your poor 'little wife,' made much of her, and loved her all the more, the more sullen and resentful she became. She was 'out of sorts,' you said, and planned a little foreign tour, as you are now doing for Dorothy. I do believe you loved me out of it at last. The time came when I felt myself hunted down by these sullen rages. I ran away, took immense walks, read voraciously, but could not help myself till our first child came; God's gift, our little Dorothy. Her baby fingers healed me as not even your love could do. But, oh, George, don't you see?"

"My poor Mary! Yes, I see; your healing was bought at the little child's expense, and the plague you felt within you was passed on to her. This, I see, is your idea; but I still believe it is a morbid fancy, and I still think my little trip will cure both mother and daughter."

"You say well, mother and daughter. The proverb should run, not, 'a burnt child dreads the fire,' but 'a burnt child will soonest catch fire!' I feel that all my old misery will come back upon me if I am to see the same thing repeated in Dorothy."

George sat musing for a minute or two, but my fear of him was gone; his face was full of tenderness for both of us.

"Do you know, Mary, I doubt if I'm right to treat this effort of yours with a high hand, and prescribe for evils I don't understand. Should you mind very much our calling our old friend, Dr Evans, into council? I believe, after all, it will turn out to be an affair for him rather than for me."

This was worse than all. Were the miseries of this day to know no end? Should we, my Dorothy and her mother, end our days in a madhouse? I looked at my husband, and he understood.

"Nonsense, wife, not that! Now you really are absurd, and must allow me the relief of laughing at you. There, I feel better now, but I understand; a few years ago a doctor was never consulted about this kind of thing unless it was supposed to denote insanity. But we have changed all that, and you're as mad as a hatter to get the notion. You've no idea how interesting it is to hear Evans talk of the mutual relations between thought and brain, and on the other hand, between thought and character. Homely an air as he has, he is up to all that's going on.

"There is nothing which a mother cannot bring her child up to."

You know he went through a course of study at Leipsic, where they know more than we about the brain and its behaviour, and then, he runs across every year to keep himself abreast with the times. It isn't every country town that is blessed with such a man."

I thought I was being let down gently to the everyday level, and answered as we answer remarks about the weather, until George said—

"Well, when shall we send for Evans? The sooner we get more light on this matter, the better for all of us."

"Very well, send for him to-morrow; tell him all I have told you, and, if you like, I shall be here to answer further questions."

Chapter 4

"Mrs. Elmore is quite right; this is no morbid fancy of hers. I have observed your pretty Miss Dorothy, and had my own speculations. Now, the whole thing lies in a nutshell."

"Can you deal with our trouble, doctor?" I cried out.

"Deal with it, my dear madam? Of course I can. I am not a pupil of Weissall's for nothing. Your Dorothy is a good girl, and will yield herself to treatment. As to that, you don't want me. The doctor is only useful on the principle that lookers-on see most of the game. Once understand the thing, and it is with you the cure must lie."

"Please explain; you will find me very obedient."

"I'm not so sure of that; you know the whole of my mental property has not been gathered in Midlington. You ladies look very meek; but directly one begins to air one's theories—which are not theories, by the way, but fixed principles of belief and conduct—you scent all manner of heterodoxy, and because a valuable line of scientific thought and discovery is new to you, you take up arms, with the notion that it flies in the face of the Bible. When, as a matter of fact, every new advance in science is a further revelation, growing out, naturally, from that we already have."

"Try me, doctor; your 'doxy shall be my 'doxy if you will only take us in hand, and I shall be ready enough to believe that your science is by revelation."

"Well, here goes. In for a penny, in for a pound. In the first place, I want to do away with the sense of moral responsibility, both for yourself and Dorothy, which is wearing you out. Or, rather, I want to circumscribe its area and intensify its force. Dorothy has, perhaps, and conceivably her mother has also, inherited her peculiar temperament; but you are not immediately responsible for that. She, again, has fostered this inherited trait, but neither is she immediately responsible for the fact."

"How do you mean, doctor? That we can't help it, and must take our nature as we find it? But that is worse than ever. No; I cannot believe it. Certainly my husband has done a great deal to cure me."

"No doubt he has. And how he has done it—without intention, I dare say—I hope by-and-by to show you. Perhaps you now and then remark, What creatures of habit we are!"

"And what of that? No one can help being struck now and then with the fact; especially, no mother."

"Well, and what does this force of habit amount to? and how do you account for it?"

'Doxy *is short for* orthodoxy *and means "foundational beliefs."*

"Anything may be accomplished by training, that is, the cultivation of persistent habits."

Notes

"Why, I suppose it amounts to this, that you can do almost anything once you get into the way of it. Why, I don't know; I suppose it's the natural constitution of the mind."

"The 'natural constitution of the mind' is a conversational counter with whose value I am not acquainted. That you can get into the way of doing almost anything, is simple fact; but you must add, of thinking anything, of feeling anything, before you begin to limit the force of habit."

"I think I begin to see what you mean. We, my child and I, are not so much to blame now for our sullen and resentful feelings, because we have got the habit of them. But surely habits may be cured?"

"Ah, once we begin to see that, we are to blame for them. We must ask, How are we to set about the cure? What's to be *done*? What hopeless idiots we are, the best of us, not to see that the very existence of an evil is a demand for its cure, and that, in the moral world, there's a dock for every nettle!"

"And then, surely, the sins of the fathers visited upon the children, is a bitter law. How could Dorothy help what she inherited?"

"Dorothy could not help it, but you could; and what have you two excellent parents been about to defer until the child is budding into womanhood this cure which should have been achieved in her infancy? Surely, seventeen years ago at least, you must have seen indications of the failing which must needs be shown up now, to the poor girl's discredit."

I grew hot all over under this home thrust, while George looked half dubious, half repentant, not being quite sure where his offence lay.

"It is doubly my fault, doctor; I see it all now. When Dorothy was a child I *would* not face the fact. It was too awful to think my child would be as I still was. So we had many little fictions that both nurse and mother saw through: the child was poorly, was getting her second teeth, was overdone. The same thing, only more so, went on during her schoolroom life. Dorothy was delicate, wanted stamina, must have a tonic. And this, though we had a governess who tried to convince me that it was temper and not delicacy that ailed my little girl. The worst of deceiving yourself is that you get to believe the lie. I saw much less of the schoolroom, than of the nursery party, and firmly believed in Dorothy's frequent attacks of indisposition."

"But, supposing you had faced the truth, what would you have done?"

"There is my excuse; I had no idea that anything could be done."

"Now, please, don't write me down a pagan if I try to show you what might have been done, and may yet be done."

"Doctor Evans!"

"Oh, yes, 'tis a fact; you good women are convinced that the setting of a broken limb is a work for human skill, but that the cure of a fault of disposition is for Providence alone to effect, and you say your prayers and do nothing, looking down from great heights upon us who believe that skill and knowledge come in here too, and are meant to do so in the divine scheme of things. It's startling when you come to think of it, that every pair of parents has so largely the *making* of their child!"

"But what of *inherited* failings—such cases as this of ours? "

"Precisely a case in point. Don't you see, such a case is just a problem set before parents with a, 'See, how will you work out this so as to pass your family on free from taint?' "

"It rests with parents and teachers to lay down lines of habit on which the life of the child may run henceforth with little jolting or miscarriage, and may advance in the right direction with the minimum of effort."

"That's a noble thought of yours, Evans. It gives every parent a share in working out the salvation of the world, even to thousands of generations.— Come, Mary, we're on our promotion! To pass on our children free from the blemishes they get from us is a thing worth living for."

"Indeed it is. But don't think me narrow-minded, doctor, nor that I should presume to think hard things of you men of science, if I confess that I still think the ills of the flesh fall within the province of man, but the evils of the spirit within the province of God."

"I'm not sure but that I'm of your mind; where we differ is as to the boundary-line between flesh and spirit. Now, every fault of disposition and temper, though it may have begun in error of the spirit in ourselves or in some ancestor, by the time it becomes a fault of character is a *failing of the flesh*, and is to be dealt with as such—that is, by appropriate treatment. Observe, I am not speaking of occasional and sudden temptations and falls, or of as sudden impulses towards good, and the reaching of heights undreamed of before. These things are of the spiritual world, and are to be spiritually discerned. But the failing or the virtue which has become habitual to us is flesh of our flesh, and must be treated on that basis whether it is to be uprooted or fostered."

"I confess I don't follow: this line of argument should make the work of redemption gratuitous. According to this theory, every parent can save his child, and every man can save himself."

"No, my dear; there you're wrong. I agree with Evans. It is we who lose the efficacy of the great Redemption by failing to see what it *has* accomplished. That we have still to engage in a spiritual warfare, enabled by spiritual aids, Dr Evans allows. His point is, as I understand it, why embarrass ourselves with these less material ills of the flesh which are open to treatment on the same lines, barring the drugs, as a broken limb or a disordered stomach. Don't you see how it works? We fall, and fret, and repent, and fall again; and are so over-busy with our own internal affairs, that we have no time to get that knowledge of God which is the life of the living soul?"

"All this is beyond me. I confess it is neither the creed nor the practice in which I was brought up. Meantime, how is it to affect Dorothy? That is the practical question."

Dr Evans threw a smiling "I told you so" glance at my husband, which was a little annoying; however, he went on:—

"To be sure; that is the point. Poor Dorothy is just now the occasional victim of a troop of sullen, resentful thoughts and feelings, which wear her out, shut out the sunshine, and are as a curtain between her and all she loves. Does she want these thoughts? No; she hates and deplores them on her knees, we need not doubt; resolves against them; goes through much spiritual conflict. She is a good girl, and we may be sure of all this. Now we must bring physical science to her aid. How those thoughts began we need not ask, but there they are; they go patter, patter, to and fro, to and fro, in the nervous tissue of the brain until—here is the curious point of contact between the material and the immaterial, we see by results that there is such point of contact, but how or why it is so we have not even a guess to offer—until the nervous tissue is modified under the continued traffic in the same order of thoughts. Now, these thoughts become automatic; they come of themselves, and spread and flow as a river makes and enlarges its bed. Such habit of thought is set up, and must go on indefinitely, in spite

"Every day, every hour, the parents are either passively or actively forming those habits in their children upon which, more than upon anything else, future character and conduct depend."

Notes

of struggles, unless—and here is the word of hope—a contrary habit is set up, diverting the thoughts into some quite new channel. Keep the thoughts running briskly in the new channel, and, behold, the old connections are broken, whilst a new growth of brain substance is perpetually taking place. The old thoughts return, and there is no place for them, and Dorothy has time to make herself think of other things before they can establish again the old links. There is, shortly, the philosophy of ordering our thoughts—the first duty of us all."

"That is deeply interesting, and should help us. Thank you very much; I had no idea that our *thoughts* were part and parcel, as it were, of any substance. But I am not sure yet how this is to apply to Dorothy. It seems to me that it will be very difficult for her, poor child, to bring all this to bear on herself. It will be like being put into trigonometry before you are out of subtraction."

"You are right, Mrs Elmore, it will be a difficult piece of work, to which she will have to give herself up for two or three months. If I am not mistaken in my estimate of her, by that time we shall have a cure. But if you had done the work in her childhood, a month or two would have effected it, and the child herself would have been unconscious of effort."

"How sorry I am. Do tell me what I should have done."

"The tendency was there, we will allow; but you should never have allowed the *habit* of this sort of feeling to be set up. You should have been on the watch for the outward signs—the same then as now, some degree of pallor, with general limpness of attitude, and more or less dropping of the lips and eyes. The moment one such sign appeared, you should have been at hand to seize the child out of the cloud she was entering, and to let her bask for an hour or two in love and light, forcing her to meet you eye to eye, and to find love and gaiety in yours. Every sullen attack averted is so much against setting up the habit; and habit, as you know, is a chief factor in character."

"And can we do nothing for her now?"

"Certainly you can. Ignore the sullen humours; let gay life go on as if she was not there, only drawing her into it now and then by an appeal for her opinion, or for her laugh at a joke. Above all, when good manners compel her to look up, let her meet unclouded eyes, full of pleasure in her; for, believe, whatever cause of offence she gives to you, she is far more deeply offensive to herself. And you should do this all the more because, poor girl, the brunt of the battle will fall upon her."

"I see you are right; all along, her sullenness has given away before her father's delight in her, and indeed it is in this way that my husband has so far cured me. I suppose you would say he had broken the habit. But won't you see her and talk to her? I know you can help her most."

"Well, to tell you the truth, I was going to ask you if I might; her sensitive nature must be gently handled; and, just because she has no such love for me as for her parents, I run less risk of wounding her. Besides, I have a secret to tell which should help her in the management of herself."

"Thank you, Evans; we are more grateful than I can say. Will you strike while the iron's hot? Shall we go away and send her to you, letting her suppose it is a mere medical call?"

Chapter 5
"Good-morning, Miss Dorothy; do you know I think it's quite time this state

"Every sullen attack averted is so much against setting up the habit; and habit, as you know, is a chief factor in character."

of things should come to an end. We are both tired of the humbug of treating you for want of health when you are quite strong and well."

Dorothy looked up with flushed face (I had it all later from both Dr Evans and Dorothy herself), and eyes half relieved, half doubtful, but not resentful, and stood quietly waiting.

"All the same, I think you are in a bad way, and are in great need of help. Will you bear with me while I tell you what is the matter, and how you may be cured?"

Dorothy was past speaking, and gave a silent assent.

"Don't be frightened, poor child; I don't speak to hurt you, but to help. A considerable part of a life which should be all innocent gaiety of heart, is spent in gloom and miserable isolation. Some one fails to dot his i's, and you resent it, not in words or manner, being too well brought up; but the light within you is darkened by a flight of black thoughts. 'He (or she) shouldn't have done it! It's too bad! They don't care how they hurt me! I should never have done so to her!'—and so on without end. Presently you find yourself swathed in a sort of invisible shroud; you cannot reach out a living hand to anybody, nor speak in living tones, nor meet your dear ones eye to eye with a living and loving glance. There you sit, like a dead man at the feast. By this time you have forgotten the first offence, and would give the world to get out of this death-in-life. You cry, you say your prayers, beg to be forgiven and restored, but your eyes are fixed upon yourself as a hateful person, and you are still wrapped in the cloud; until, suddenly (no doubt in answer to your prayers), a hug from little May, the first primrose of the year, a lark, filling the world with his gladness, and, presto! the key is turned, the enchanted princess liberated, glad as the lark, sweet as the flower, and gay as the bright child!"

No answer: Dorothy's arms were on the table, and her face hidden upon them. At last she said in a choked voice—"Please go on, doctor!"

"All this may be helped" (she looked up), "may, within two or three months, be completely cured, become a horrid memory and nothing more!" Dorothy raised streaming eyes, where the light of hope was struggling with fear and shame.

"This is very trying for you, dear child! But I must get on with my task, and when I have done, it's my belief you'll forget the pain for joy. In the first place, you are not a very wicked girl because these ugly thoughts master you; I don't say, mind you, that you will be without offence once you get the key between your fingers; but as it is, you need not sit in judgment on yourself any more."

Then Dr Evans went on to make clear to Dorothy what he had already made clear to us of the interaction of thought and brain; how that Thought, Brain & Co. were such close allies that nobody could tell which of the two did what: that they even ran a business of their own, independently of *Ego*, who was supposed to be the active head of the firm, and so on.

Dorothy listened with absorbed intentness, as if every word were saving; but the light of hope died slowly out.

"I think I see what you mean; these black thoughts come and rampage even against the desire of the *Ego*, I, myself: but, oh doctor, don't you see, that's all the worse for me?"

"Stop a bit, stop a bit, my dear young lady, I have not done yet. *Ego* sees things are going wrong and asserts himself; sets up new thoughts in a new course, and stops the old traffic; and in course of time, and a very short time too, the old nerve connections are broken, and the old way under tillage; no more opening for

"We entertain the idea which gives birth to the act and the act repeated again and again becomes the habit."

See also Sweet, Even Temper on page 108.

"Better than he that taketh a city" refers to Proverbs 16:32 and describes a person who can rule his spirit.

"The man who can make himself do what he wills has the world before him, and it rests with parents to give their children this self-compelling power as a mere matter of habit."

traffic there. Have you got it?"

"I think so. I'm to think of something else, and soon there will be no room in the brain for the ugly thoughts which distress me. But that's just the thing I can't do!"

"But that is exactly the only thing you have power to do! Have you any idea what the will is, and what are its functions?"

"I don't know much about it. I suppose your will should make you able to do the right thing when you feel you can't! You should say, 'I *will*,' and go and do it. But you don't know how weak I am. It makes no difference to me to say, I will!"

"Well, now, to own up honestly, I don't think it ever made much difference to anybody outside of the story-books. All the same, Will is a mighty fellow in his own way, but he goes with a sling and a stone, and not with the sword of Goliath. He attacks the giant with what seems a child's plaything, and the giant is slain. This is how it works. When ill thoughts *begin* to molest you, turn away your mind with a vigorous turn, and *think of something else*. I don't mean think good forgiving thoughts, perhaps you are not ready for that yet; but think of something interesting and pleasant; the new dress you must plan, the friend you like best, the book you are reading; best of all, fill heart and mind suddenly with some capital plan for giving pleasure to some poor body whose days are dull. The more exciting the thing you think of, the safer you are. Never mind about fighting the evil thought. This is the one thing you have to do; for this is, perhaps, the sole power the will has. It enables you to change your thoughts; to turn yourself round from gloomy thoughts to cheerful ones. Then you will find that your prayers will be answered, for you will know what to ask for, and will not turn your back on the answer when it comes. There, child, I have told you the best secret I know—given to me by a man I revere—and have put into your hands the key of self-government and a happy life. Now you know how to be better than he that taketh a city."

"Thank you a thousand times for your precious secret. You have lifted my feet out of the slough. I *will* change my thoughts (may I say that?). You shall find that your key does not rust for want of use. I trust I may be helped never to enter that cloud again."

It is five years since Dorothy had that talk in the library with Dr Evans (he died within the year, to our exceeding regret). What battles she fought we never heard; never again was the subject alluded to. For two years she was our joyous home daughter; for three, she has been Arthur Brisbane's happy wife; and her little sunbeam of an Elsie—no fear that she will ever enter the cloud in which mother and grandmother were so nearly lost.

Some Practical Suggestions from "Dorothy Elmore's Achievement"

1. Don't let your child's sullenness ruin life for those around him. Continue to enjoy the day and casually invite him to do the same.

2. Reassure your child of your love with looks of pleasure, not reproach.

3. Teach your child to replace his sullen thoughts with good ones. Teach an older child to distract himself mentally.

Laying Down the Rails Checklist

Charlotte encouraged parents to be intentional about developing habits in their children's lives. She more than once mentioned the idea of having a record of habits that you want to cultivate in each child, and keeping track of his or her progress. Birthdays make good milestones for regular evaluations and plans. "Obedience in the first year, and all the virtues of the good life as the years go on; every year with its own definite work to show in the training of character. Is Edward a selfish child when his fifth birthday comes? The fact is noted in his parents' year-book, with the resolve that by his sixth birthday he shall, please God, be a generous child" (Vol. 2, p. 65).

This checklist is given to help you be intentional about laying down the rails of the habits in this book. There is also space for you to evaluate your own progress, since many of Charlotte's comments are directed toward the parent more than the child. Suggestions that would apply only to a parent, not to a child, have X's in the children's boxes, leaving only the parent's box open. All the other suggestions can apply to both parents and children.

Feel free to duplicate this checklist as many times as you need. I hope it will be a trusty tool as you lay down the rails.

Habits	*Me*					
Decency and Propriety Habits						
Cleanliness (p. 28)						
Own room is aired.						
Own room smells sweet and fresh.						
Keeps own room (and the rest of the house) clean and fresh.						
Airs out clothing and bedding that will be used again before washing.						
Isn't afraid to get dirty; cleans self up.						
Washes hands for family meals.						
Grooms self adequately, including fingernails and hair.						
Attends to self in bath or shower.						
Courtesy (p. 30)						
Demonstrates courtesy consistently, even to familiar people.						
Gives and returns courteous gestures.						
Exhibits courtesy on the telephone and in person.						
Courteous to child/parent.						
Kindness (p. 31)						
Thinks the best of other people.						

Doesn't assume others will laugh at a kindness shown.						
Defends and protects other people's good character.						
Responds kindly to those with tiresome tempers.						
Responds kindly when injured by another.						
Eager to make others happy by showing kindness.						
Rejects selfish messages from outside influences.						
Manners (p. 34)						
Practices good manners in various situations.						
Shows good manners in body language and action, as well as words.						
Respects the older; protects the younger.						
Modesty and Purity (p. 35)						
Keeps self covered.						
Respects own private parts.						
Does not joke or tease about private parts.						
Displays modesty and purity as a matter of obedience.						
Displays modesty and purity as a matter of honor.						
Encourages older child in purity.		X	X	X	X	X
Prays daily for child to remain pure.		X	X	X	X	X
Chooses words carefully when discussing purity.						
Keeps life full of healthy interests and activities.						
Is motivated by Scripture and heroic examples of purity.						
Neatness (p. 38)						
Has pleasant and suitable surroundings in good taste.						
Arranges own things nicely.						
Does not have vulgar toys, pictures, or books in poor taste.						
Displays well-chosen works of art.						
Order (p. 39)						
Keeps own room orderly.						
Takes care of nice things.						

Does not allow emotion to prevent orderliness.						
Has adequate space for storage of own things.						
Understands that simplicity makes orderliness easier.						
Regularity (p. 41)						
Has a regular bedtime.						
Eats at regular intervals throughout the day.						
Has a regular schedule, or routine, for a typical day.						
Understands that a schedule is flexible.						
Candor (p. 43)						
Is free from prejudice or malice.						
Treats others' opinions fairly.						
Communicates honestly and sincerely in a straightforward manner.						
Courage (p. 44)						
Perseveres in spite of danger, fear, or difficulty.						
Diligence (p. 44)						
Exhibits steady, earnest, and energetic effort.						
Generosity (p. 45)						
Gives liberally.						
Gentleness (p. 45)						
Is mild in manner and disposition.						
Is not harsh, stern, or violent.						
Meekness (p. 46)						
Endures injury without resentment.						
Patience (p. 46)						
Bears pain or trials calmly.						
Does not complain.						
Is not hasty or impetuous.						
Is steadfast despite opposition, difficulty, or adversity.						
Temperance (p. 47)						
Shows moderation in action, thought, and feeling.						
Exhibits restraint.						
Thrift (p. 47)						
Carefully manages money and possessions.						

Mental Habits						
Attention (p. 50)						
Gives attention top priority.						
Makes appropriate mental associations.						
Doesn't let associative thoughts take control.						
Gives attention during homeschool lessons.						
Looks at an object longer than naturally inclined to.						
Plays "What Did You See?" well.						
Puts aside a lesson when dawdling, changes pace, then returns to complete it.						
Varies the day's lessons.						
Has a natural desire for knowledge.						
Completes short lessons within given timetable.						
Is motivated by natural consequences that come from dawdling or giving attention.						
Values conduct and character over cleverness.						
Understands lack of attention is a bad habit, not an inability.						
Knows how to fix own thoughts on the matter at hand.						
Avoids things that might encourage inattentiveness.						
Is careful not to require too much work or too difficult of work.		X	X	X	X	X
Narrates after a single reading.						
Completes homework within given timetable.						
Completes everyday activities promptly.						
Is not constantly bored.						
Uses good books and minimal oral teaching in lessons.		X	X	X	X	X
Exhibits a lifelong habit of study and learning.						
Imagining (p. 61)						
Alternates lessons and activities between physical, intellectual, imagination, and reasoning skills.						
Does not read excessive nonsense books.						
Reads good story books.						

Imagination is captured by history and geography.					
Illustrates stories and poems.					
Meditation (p. 63)					
Mentally explores "What if?" scenarios.					
Practices both Biblical and intellectual meditation.					
Memorizing (p. 65)					
Regularly reviews material committed to memory.					
Memorizes Scripture or poetry.					
Memorizes noble poetry, not twaddle.					
Mental Effort (p. 67)					
Does daily mental work.					
Is alert during lessons.					
Has quick comprehension and rapid answers.					
Provides pleasing lessons.	X	X	X	X	X
Views steady work as honorable.					
Takes satisfaction in exerting mental effort.					
Does not read books that require no mental effort.					
Narrates what is read or heard.					
Expects mental work from both boys and girls.	X	X	X	X	X
Balances work with leisure.					
Observation (p. 70)					
Can describe a landscape in detail.					
Is building a mental "picture gallery" for future enjoyment.					
Is laying the groundwork for science lessons by observing nature.					
Provides lots of varied opportunities and encouragement to observe.	X	X	X	X	X
Has progressed beyond natural perceptions to methodical observation and accurate recall.					
Sees how words are spelled while reading.					
Perfect Execution (p. 74)					
Forms all handwork carefully.					
Does not excuse faulty work because of age.	X	X	X	X	X
Does not assign a task that cannot be perfectly done.	X	X	X	X	X

Prefers a little work done well rather than a lot of work done sloppily.						
Evaluates own work, pointing out imperfections, and perseveres to correct them.						
Celebrates any handwork well done.						
Accomplishes something perfectly in every writing lesson.						
Keeps writing lessons short: five or ten minutes.						
Values careful work before practice.						
Has mastered medium-size letters before moving on to smaller handwriting.						
Reading for Instruction (p. 77)						
Is cultivating this habit as a 6- to 12-year old.						
Reads aloud to older child only occasionally.		X	X	X	X	X
Evaluates comprehension by narrating.						
Carefully selects lesson books to present knowledge as attractive and delightful.		X	X	X	X	X
Does not confuse a love for reading with reading for instruction.						
Remembering (p. 81)						
Has many opportunities to learn.						
Can recall a memory at will.						
Does not cram for tests.						
Fixes full attention on what is to be remembered.						
Links each lesson to the previous one.						
Finds various kinds of links between subjects of lessons.						
Thinking (p. 84)						
Traces cause and effect.						
Traces comparison and contrast.						
Traces premise and conclusion.						
Practices logical thinking.						
Seeks to determine "Why?" instead of always asking others for the answer.						
Forms an opinion only after careful thought.						
Accuracy (p. 87)						
Works arithmetic equations correctly.						

Does not make errors in statements or messages.						
Conforms to the standard in daily affairs.						
Concentration (p. 87)						
Actively engages on the given problem.						
Reflection (p. 88)						
Ruminates on what is received.						
Thoroughness (p. 88)						
Seeks to learn more about a subject.						
Researches any doubtful points until satisfied with own level of knowledge on the subject.						
Moral Habits						
Integrity (p. 92)						
Prioritizes work.						
Finishes a project before beginning another one.						
Uses time wisely every day.						
Returns borrowed property promptly and in good repair.						
Understands how lapses in integrity affect character.						
Obedience (p. 96)						
Makes obedience top priority.						
Views willfulness as disobedience.						
Understands that parents are on assignment from God to teach children to obey.						
Desires to obey.						
Expects obedience.		X	X	X	X	X
Uses a quiet but firm tone of voice when telling a child to do something.		X	X	X	X	X
Insists on prompt, cheerful, and lasting obedience every time.		X	X	X	X	X
Doesn't give a command unless intends to see it carried out completely.		X	X	X	X	X
Does not pester the child with excessive commands.		X	X	X	X	X
Yields occasionally in matters that are not crucial.		X	X	X	X	X
Teaches obedience by the time the child is one year old.		X	X	X	X	X
Views obedience as training for future accomplishments.						
Responds to conscience within reason.						

Gives reasons for commands only when appropriate.		X	X	X	X	X
Gives set time to prepare for changes in activity.		X	X	X	X	X
Understands how discipline brings freedom.						
Views obedience as delightful and dignified.						
Chooses to obey all authorities in life.						
Personal Initiative (p. 101)						
Has plenty of free time.						
Is available to guide and inform as needed.		X	X	X	X	X
Doesn't try to control every moment of every day.		X	X	X	X	X
Invents own games and occupations within set boundaries.						
Doesn't rely on others to amuse.						
Adds personal touches to work within set boundaries.						
Reverence (p. 103)						
Respects others.						
Recognizes and rejects self-assertive attitudes in the world.						
Respects historical events and people.						
Shows respect for child as unique person.		X	X	X	X	X
Uses educational methods that respect the child as a person.		X	X	X	X	X
Self-Control (p. 105)						
Shows by word and example that self-control brings joy.		X	X	X	X	X
Desires to strengthen child's will in order to make it strong enough to do what is right.		X	X	X	X	X
Understands how obedience is a stepping-stone to self-control.						
Feels a sense of conquest when exhibits self-control.						
Cooperates in efforts to develop self-control.						
Applauds others' efforts toward self-control.						
Can change thoughts in order to change actions.						
Is introducing and reinforcing self-control principles little by little.		X	X	X	X	X

Sweet, Even Temper (p. 108)						
Doesn't excuse sour disposition because of family heredity or age.						
Can read child's thoughts on face.		X	X	X	X	X
Redirects sullen thoughts along good lines.						
Truthfulness (p. 110)						
States facts carefully and exactly, without omissions or exaggerations.						
Scrupulously requires exact truth.		X	X	X	X	X
Gathers and states facts carefully.						
Does not deliberately intend to deceive.						
Accurate in both small and important matters.						
Does not excuse lying for humor's sake.						
Views deceit as a radical character defect that must be corrected.						
Puts forth the effort to learn truthfulness now to avoid future problems.						
Does not qualify statements with "I think" or "perhaps."						
Thinks carefully and makes sure before speaking.						
Does not constantly correct another person's comments.						
Does not use exaggerations to manipulate.						
Carefully sifts what is heard or read so as not to spread rumors.						
Does not use excessive language for common situations.						
Does not generalize.						
Emphasizes simplicity, sincerity, and fidelity.						
Usefulness (p. 117)						
Carries out good intentions to actions.						
Is useful in our family.						
Understands that love is shown by acts of service.						
Continues to show love through useful service even if uncomfortable with hugs and kisses.						
Understands how usefulness now prepares for future callings.						

Physical Habits						
Alertness to Seize Opportunities (p. 122)						
Watches for opportunities to help and takes the initiative to do so.						
Watches for opportunities to learn.						
Is cultivating this habit early in child's life.		X	X	X	X	X
Fortitude (p. 123)						
Understands how physical fortitude can develop mental fortitude.						
Bears discomfort courageously.						
Concentrates on other things rather than the discomfort.						
Is not obsessed with physical sensations.						
Thinks of others instead of self and own comfort.						
Does not use physical ailments as an excuse.						
Does not turn child's thoughts toward physical ailment.		X	X	X	X	X
Does not intentionally inflict hardness on child.		X	X	X	X	X
Helps child redirect thoughts away from physical discomfort.		X	X	X	X	X
Watches for any physical danger or harm and deals with it calmly.		X	X	X	X	X
Concentrates on own duties and others' rights.						
Has a servant's heart.						
Models serving by actions.						
Uses stirring stories and examples to motivate toward fortitude.						
Health (p. 127)						
Has nutritious family meals.						
Uses family meals to learn good eating habits.						
Doesn't allow self unhealthy indulgences in eating.						
Doesn't allow self unhealthy indulgences in duty.						
Takes responsibility for own good health.						
Understands that poor health habits now will result in a failing body later.						
Managing One's Own Body (p. 129)						
Engages in physical exercise daily.						

Exercises attention, balance, and strength abilities.						
Understands how physical exercise supports moral training.						
Understands the similarity between training muscles and training in habits.						
Music (p. 133)						
Is surrounded with good music.						
Sings in tune.						
Is learning more about musical tones and intervals.						
Outdoor Life (p. 135)						
Understands how regular time outdoors affects attitudes and health.						
Finds nature study a delight.						
Marvels over and cares for God's creation.						
Quick Perception of Senses (p. 137)						
Uses all senses to observe objects.						
Supplements nature study with daily sensory gymnastics.						
Can examine an object and tell discoveries using only one sense.						
Plays "What Can You Remember?" well.						
Cultivates senses by getting to know nature.						
Randomly asks child for detail of shared situation.		X	X	X	X	X
Continues to cultivate the habit of observation.						
Self-Control in Emergencies (p. 139)						
Understands that a person who keeps presence of mind can be of great service to others.						
Keeps a calm spirit no matter what happens.						
Encourages child to keep a calm spirit.		X	X	X	X	X
Demonstrates physical calmness as well as mental calmness.						
Self-Discipline in Habits (p. 142)						
Continues good habits when not supervised.						
Continues good habits no matter the season or location.						
Makes the transition from supervised habits to self-disciplined habits in small steps.		X	X	X	X	X

Continues good habits of action, body language, and words.						
Self-Restraint in Indulgences (p. 144)						
Provides child's basic needs and comforts.		X	X	X	X	X
Is industrious in free time.						
Gets enough rest.						
Is not fatigued from too many activities.						
Training the Ear and Voice (p. 145)						
Pronounces vowel sounds correctly.						
Does not leave off the final consonant in words.						
Enjoys the game of pronouncing a difficult word precisely after a single hearing.						
Reinforces this habit with oral foreign language study.						
<div align="center">**Religious Habits**</div>						
Regularity in Devotions (p. 148)						
Communicates the importance of daily devotions by word and example.		X	X	X	X	X
Has an established time and place for devotions.						
Has unhurried devotions when fully awake and alert.						
Supplements devotional time with carefully selected books.						
Has both spontaneous prayer and set times of prayer.						
Has plenty of direct contact with Scripture appropriate for age.						
Understands that devotions are helpful but do not earn favor with God.						
Incorporates praise in devotions.						
Sings reverently, offering best praise.						
Knows several hymns.						
Reverent Attitude (p. 153)						
Uses reverent actions to encourage reverent feelings.						
Demonstrates a worshipful demeanor during prayer times.						
Desires to show as much respect for God as the angels do.						
Does not view reverent actions or postures as tiresome.						

Sits quietly during church service, participating as able.						
Sunday-Keeping (p. 155)						
Keeps Sunday activities special—not rigid or dull, but quiet and glad.						
Understands how a change of pace on Sunday is helpful physically and mentally.						
Seeks communion with God and nature during Sunday activities.						
Emphasizes the pleasure of Sunday activities rather than restrictions.						
Makes Sundays pleasant in attitude and conversation.						
Has a special book or poetry for family to read aloud.		X	X	X	X	X
Leaves room to be aware of and contemplate on any thoughts God impresses on mind.						
Uses appropriate music to help make Sundays pleasant.						
Thanksgiving (p. 157)						
Thanks God for answered prayer.						
Has a thankful heart for all God's blessings throughout the day.						
Thought of God (p. 159)						
Thinks rightly about God in all that happens during the day.						
Answers child's questions about God by guiding into true, happy thinking about God.		X	X	X	X	X
Views God as a loving Father and sovereign King, not just Someone Who requires us to "be good."						
Practices the presence of God.						

Habits Index

A

Accuracy, 87, 112, 138
Alertness to Seize Opportunities, 117, 122, 123
Attention, 12, 50–60, 67, 68, 71, 82, 83, 87, 164, 182–192

B

Borrowed Property (Integrity), 92–96

C

Candor, 43
Cleanliness, 17, 28, 29
Concentration, 87, 88
Courage, 17, 43, 44, 123, 124, 141, 172, 173
Courtesy, 17, 19, 30, 31, 43

D, E

Dawdling, 58, 143, 181–192
Diligence, 43–45, 53, 55, 93

F

Finishing (Integrity), 92–96
Fortitude, 43, 123–127

G

Generosity, 43, 45
Gentleness, 43, 45, 46, 55

H

Health, 102, 124, 127–129, 135, 156

I, J

Imagining, 61–63
Integrity, 92–96

K

Kindness, 30, 31–34, 43

L

Lying, 91, 111–113, 115, 116, 171–180

M

Malicious, Mean Behavior, 193, 194
Managing One's Own Body, 129–131
Manners, 17, 34, 35
Meditation, 63–65
Meekness, 43, 46
Memorizing, 65–67
Mental Effort, 51, 67–70
Modesty and Purity, 35–38
Music, 133–135, 151, 152, 156

N

Neatness, 12, 17, 21, 38, 39, 43

O

Obedience, 12, 21–25, 36, 55, 96–101, 106, 118, 128
Observation, 70–74, 139
Order, 39–41
Outdoor Life, 135–137

P

Patience, 43, 46, 47
Perfect Execution, 74–77
Personal Initiative, 101–103
Praise (Regularity in Devotions), 148–152
Prayer (Regularity in Devotions), 148–152
Priorities (Integrity), 92–96
Purity (Modesty), 35–38

Q

Quick Perception of Senses, 137–139

R

Reading Aloud as a Family, 156, 163, 164
Reading for Instruction, 77–81
Reading the Bible (Regularity in Devotions), 148–152
Reflection, 88
Regularity, 41, 42
Regularity in Devotions, 148–152
Remembering, 81–84
Respect for Other People (Reverence), 43, 103–105
Reverence, 103–105
Reverent Attitude, 153–155

S

Self-Control, 105–108
Self-Control in Emergencies, 139–141
Self-Discipline in Habits, 142, 143
Self-Restraint in Indulgences, 144, 145
Sullen, Moody Child, 207–222
Sunday-Keeping, 155–157
Sweet, Even Temper, 108–110

T

Temper Tantrums, 195–205
Temperance, 43, 47
Thanksgiving, 157, 158
Thinking, 84–86
Thoroughness, 88, 89
Thought of God, 159–161
Thrift, 43, 47, 48
Training the Ear and Voice, 145, 146
Truthfulness, 110–116

U—Z

Use of Time (Integrity), 92–96
Usefulness, 117–119

Personal Help with Habits

We invite you to visit the SCM Community Forum where you may discuss habit training with other parents, ask questions, read practical suggestions for cultivating the habits mentioned in this book, and add your own ideas.

http://simplycharlottemason.com/scmforum/